Corporate Social Responsibility

Also by David E. Hawkins

Sun Tzu and the Project Battleground
(*with Shan Rajagopal*)

The Bending Moment

CORPORATE SOCIAL RESPONSIBILITY

BALANCING TOMORROW'S SUSTAINABILITY AND TODAY'S PROFITABILITY

David E. Hawkins

First published 2006 by
PALGRAVE MACMILLAN
Houndmills, Basingstoke, Hampshire RG21 6XS and
175 Fifth Avenue, New York, N.Y. 10010
Companies and representatives throughout the world

PALGRAVE MACMILLAN is the global academic imprint of the Palgrave
Macmillan division of St. Martin's Press, LLC and of Palgrave Macmillan Ltd.
Macmillan® is a registered trademark in the United States, United Kingdom
and other countries. Palgrave is a registered trademark in the European
Union and other countries.

ISBN-13: 978–0–230–00220–3
ISBN-10: 0–230–00220–X

This book is printed on paper suitable for recycling and made from fully
managed and sustained forest sources.

A catalogue record for this book is available from the British Library.

A catalog record for this book is available from the Library of Congress.

10   9   8   7   6   5   4   3   2   1
15   14   13   12   11   10   09   08   07   06

Printed and bound in China

Dedicated to my granddaughter Chloe and children
everywhere; we have to provide for them today
whilst protecting their heritage for tomorrow

Contents

Preface

There can be few in the business community who have not had to address some aspect of sustainability within the past few years. It has proved almost impossible in recent times to pick up any business publication or newspaper and not be faced with an article addressing some aspect of corporate social responsibility (or CSR). The focus of these initiatives has ranged across a wide and diverse landscape of social and ethical challenges, from tree-hugging to criminal exploitation. These in turn have led to regulatory and non-governmental organization (NGO) pressures raining down on corporate leaders, in addition to the changes that have emerged at both customer and shareholder levels towards an expectation of a more responsible approach to business.

There is no doubt that many of the actions of a few major corporations have shown the worst side of commercial exploitation, whether this has been in the form of social or environmental exploitation or through manipulation leading to major financial catastrophes that have harmed many at all levels of society. On the other hand, there has been a growth in support for NGOs that have set their sights on raising awareness and stopping exploitation of any natural resources, using any and all means to further their particular cause irrespective of the impacts on others in society, such as the business community.

The difficulty is that many of these individual crusades are in fact interlinked and, whilst in isolation each may present a very good and valid case, the overall impact tends to present business leaders with the problem of trying to satisfy every possible implication whilst being the central focus for all ills. These leaders are frequently being held up as failing in what is perhaps an impossible task given the diversity of demands and integrated nature of operating within an aware market place.

This predicament often creates an environment where, instead of appropriate strategies being developed, the focus is on urgent compliance, public relations projects and short-term protection. At the same time, the customer or consumer still requires product development and innovation provided at a competitive price, whilst the shareholder looks for dividends and security of investment from organizations which can also demonstrate they adhere to the vast number of legal and moral codes, which are continuously being added to.

The utopia that all seek is unlikely ever to be a reality, but that should not mean that we stop striving for that goal and raising standards and awareness in an effort to improve some, if not all aspects of the interaction of society's wide-ranging demands. We should all, however, recognize that every action has a reaction and much of what is strived for has consequences for others. Travelling around the world, it is not hard to appreciate the different standards, opportunities and challenges that others face. It is also very clear that we cannot solve all these problems overnight or develop a balance between society and nature that satisfies the many factions, cultures and interest groups. This view may seem cynical or even defeatist but perhaps reflects reality.

Researching into the many aspects of sustainability that are being pursued under the banner of CSR and the impacts of these on the business community, what becomes clear is that there is no common strategy that can be deployed. There is also a very clear distance between the future planning profiles of senior executives focusing on meeting the short-term demands of shareholders, which is certainly at odds with the medium-term focus of governments trying to do (or be seen to be doing) the right thing within a limited election time span and the reality of developing long-term sustainable investment plans that will be unlikely to give a return in less than 15–20 years.

It is perhaps easy to see where financial controls need immediate action and that environmental controls are necessary to protect an evaluation process. It is also reasonable that decisions which do affect the environment are taken through a robust process of debate, even if the practical outcome of these reviews is to move developments forward given the balance of current needs. Many will disagree with this since they are strongly committed to their particular cause and see any concession as a defeat. These highly focused groups should consider that they too have a responsibility to the community at large, and they should be working towards solutions, not conflict.

The truth, which seems to get lost in many of these debates, is that there has to be a balance that recognizes the right of others to develop. Much of what gets voiced is in fact not rhetoric but plain common sense, and for the business community to do 'what is right' there has to be a foundation of commercial benefit. The business community creates wealth from which others can benefit.

It is also worth considering that perhaps much of what is happening to raise the profile of sustainability is driven by commercial self-interest but that is not necessarily a bad thing. It perhaps does not really matter why organizations undertake CSR programmes: what is important is that they do. What is in conflict with the overall aims is when there is artificial compliance in order simply to meet shareholder aspirations and expectations. First, this is not an honest approach, and second, the investments to provide a smoke screen could just as easily be used productively. What stakeholders have to recognize is that if organizations are prepared to be open and constructive then they should be applauded and not harangued about speeding up the process. Even worse are those who try to stop companies going about their legitimate business to maintain a principle.

Investigating the many and varied views propounded around sustainability and CSR opened up the prospect of seeing that at its core is a practical benefit for all stakeholders. If CSR can be evaluated and developed within the overall business strategy then the prospect of meeting some of the long-term sustainability challenges may be more readily achieved. Where commercial benefit can be recognized, promoted and integrated with the ability to help developing regions then progress can be both valuable and productive. At the same time, if the stakeholders could collaborate to look at practical objectives and incentives then the foundation to move to a more sustainable future could be laid within the business strategy. The alternative is that we continue a 'them and us' conflict, within which governments find themselves caught between trying to balance the needs of industry and people.

The objective of this book is to consider the realities of CSR, not the rhetoric of the 'business for business' community, the NIMBYs (Not In My Back Yard) or the Bananas (Build Absolutely Nothing at All Near Anyone). We are all stakeholders and unless we focus on creating solutions the effort will be spent protecting traditional positions. CSR is not about compliance, though this has to be recognized; it is about adapting business approaches within a commercial framework that does not penalize competitiveness, and developing forward-looking strategies that underpin the business objectives and provide profitable platforms on which to reinforce the longer-term aims of the whole community.

Sustainability is important to us all. Applying common sense more widely across the range of stakeholders could do more than small groups trying to force opinions through. Recognizing that there has to be a balance between the demands of today and the impacts of tomorrow is the only way forward. For business leaders there needs to be a greater focus on the commercial contribution that effective strategies can provide, whilst the wider community must temper its demands on business that may well be in conflict with the principles they would like to see enforced.

The environment is clearly important to us all and future generations, but it is unrealistic to reverse the Industrial Revolution. At a personal level we wish to help those developing regions that have not yet attained the benefits of industrialized communities, assuming they want them. One must not forget, however, that their evolution is progressing and utopia will not come overnight.

The aim of this book, then, is to highlight some of the many factors that influence sustainability, but more importantly to raise awareness and ideally stimulate strategy makers to consider alternative approaches. It is certainly not intended to attack the business drivers but, on the contrary, to focus on where sustainable objectives can and should be adopted to provide profitable contributions.

Experience working in a number of what many would consider dirty industries such as oil, power generation and mining provides a background to areas where NGOs would like to close down commercial development but fail to recognize these are driven by the market place, of which they are a part. The exposure to corporate strategies also often highlights a narrow focus on many of the sustainable issues without considering the possibilities to combine profit and common sense. The aim is to promote ideas and discussion based on common sense, which is often not very common. This is not a crusade but a practical look at an arena that is progressively becoming more important to business leaders and managers.

DAVID E. HAWKINS

Acknowledgements

The author would like to acknowledge Neela Bettridge, Chris Hines, Alan Knight, Ralph M. Schonenbach and Linzie Forrester for their valuable input. I would also like to thank the many organizations, both public and private, who through their published papers, views and comments provided valuable background to my research and helped to shape my thinking. There are so many that to acknowledge them individually would be impractical and it would be erroneous to single out any specifically. The arena of sustainability is both complex and diverse and I hope through this book they will appreciate my intention to encourage continued openness and dialogue towards a common goal.

Finally, I would like to thank Stephen Rutt, Palgrave Macmillan's publishing director, for his continued confidence in me as an author and Keith Povey for his skilful editing.

List of abbreviations

ACIA	Arctic Climate Impact Assessment
ANSI	American National Standards Institute
BaFIN	Bundesanstalt für Finanzdienstleistungsaufsicht
BPOs	business process operations
BVR	boycott vulnerability ratio
CEO	Chief Executive Officer
CIA	Central Intelligence Agency
CSFs	critical success factors
CSR	corporate social responsibility
DJSI	Dow Jones Sustainability Index
ETI	Ethical Trading Initiative
FoTE	Friends of the Earth
FSC	Forest Stewardship Council
GHG	greenhouse gases
GM	genetically modified
GMI	Global Market Insite
GRI	Global Reporting Initiative
H&S	health and safety
HIV/AIDS	human immuno-deficiency virus/acquired immuno-deficiency syndrome
HKM	Hong Kong Monetary Authority
ICT	information and communication technology
IMF	International Monetary Fund
ISO	International Organization for Standardization
KPI	key performance indicator
LBG	London Benchmarking Group
LHWD	Lesotho Highland Water Development
NASA	National Aeronautics and Space Administration
NGO	non-governmental organization
NIC	National Intelligence Council
NPD	new product development
OCC	Office of the Comptroller of Currency
OFR	operating and financial review

PC	personal computer
PR	public relations
R&D	research and development
ROI	return on investment
SARS	Severe Acute Respiratory Syndrome
SD	sustainable development
SMEs	small and medium enterprises
SOX	Sarbanes-Oxley Act
TI	Transparency International
UNEP	United National Environment Programme
WNC	waste-neutral concept

Foreword

As someone who has delivered many speeches on corporate social development and sustainable development I always regret that I will never see the day when a consumer product – a bar of chocolate, a leather football or garden bench made from tropical timber – walks up to the podium and delivers a speech about its life. One extreme story could be a life of environmental destruction, sweatshops and consumer harm, while the other could be a story of biodiversity conservation, fair trade and consumer well-being. It all depends on the CSR policy of the various links in the supply chain that made that product.

How the CEOs in the supply chain of despair would cringe with embarrassment as the garden bench described the harvesting of logs that destroyed the forest. Imagine the pride of the same CEO if the story was one of rainforest conservation.

Businesses have choices and CSR is about making a judgement as to what is the right choice. A failing business helps no one and the benefits of a business thriving through the exploitation of nature or people are short-lived. Sustainable development is sustainable business. This book should stimulate the debate.

The challenges will only become more complex. We live in a world where most of the population still live in poverty. Ending poverty is a genuine and important goal but we are already living in a world using too much stuff. We only have one planet, but if everyone in the world had the same lifestyle as we do in the UK we would need three planets. The ultimate challenge for CSR is to produce stuff that consumers want and make great profits but in a way that does not make the poor even poorer and enjoy the resources of one planet, not three, four or however many it will take when India, China and Africa come to enjoy our western lifestyle.

CSR or SD – it does not matter what you call them – they are both the same thing. They are good business, good citizenship and common sense.

ALAN KNIGHT
Head of Corporate Accountability for SABMiller, and
Co-chair of UK's Government's Roundtable on Sustainable Consumption

CHAPTER 1

Conflicts of sustainability

The major challenge for any writer in addressing the wide-ranging spectre of sustainability is that there is so much written and so many interest groups that one can only try to capture the essence of the issues involved. The trigger came from a discussion that centred on the subject of sustainability and CSR. In the business community it is perhaps the view of many that corporate social responsibility (CSR) is the primary focus and that sustainability belongs on the next level down. This may seem a little trite but it highlights one of the potential conflicts that sits at the core of business strategy. More importantly it demonstrates the potential diversity of opinion.

On the one hand, CSR has become somewhat of a millstone for the business community, creating a whole new raft of pressures in what is an increasingly complex trading environment. On the other hand, the concept of sustainability, which was once a sensible idea to conserve resources, has become a buzzword for every NGO trying to generate support. Typically one reads of sustainable housing programmes and such like that, unless they truly are built from wholly renewable resources, cannot be considered sustainable in the strictest sense, when forest land is being converted to housing.

Sustainable originally meant 'capable of being borne or endured', but in more recent times it became 'capable of being upheld or defended'. Environmentalists clearly drive towards the former view whilst business tends towards the second, and governments vacillate between the two. If one starts from this position of conflict then progress is frequently going to stall whilst the various stakeholders challenge each other's perspective. In the main the protagonists for the environment will tend to vilify the business community and developers will push their agenda based on short-term needs.

We are, of course, all part of a community and whilst it is easy to accept that the drivers for the business world are focused on the impacts on their commercial dealings it must also be accepted that interaction with the wider social community is part of the trading environment. It should also be clear that the community provides both the customers and the resources to fulfil business objectives. As such this community, whether local or global, is influenced by the benefits gleaned from the trading world, and so it shares a degree of responsibility for how business performs and contributes.

In essence the three major groups in the market place are, first, the organizations that provide the trading, manufacturing and service operations; this group includes those that seek to invest and benefit from successful business operations. Then there are the customer and consumer communities that they serve. The third group is the governments that represent the people and provide the framework within which all exist and operate. It does not take a rocket scientist to appreciate that as individuals we sit in at least two of the groups and influence the third. It is therefore unrealistic to consider that sustainability can be fragmented and boxed into a single concept such as CSR for business.

The business world has no mandate if it does not have customers and those customers significantly influence the performance of the businesses that serve them. There is a simple model that reflects the drivers for a customer, which are price, delivery and quality. These three elements create the constituents for any trading process and it is not difficult to see that as the customer defines the requirements then these will have knockon effects in many of the areas that the customer may consider subject to pressures on the wider sustainable environment. The more global we become, the more diverse the impacts and consideration that must be addressed.

The process of manufacturing and delivering to customer demands causes organizations to constantly expand their business profiles and operations. As demand grows then so do the impacts of these demands on other communities. Thus customers have a responsibility to look carefully at their needs and not simply expect others to do the right thing. Businesses have an obligation to survive and prosper, and so the more competitive the market the more potential there is to reach out and affect the lives of others. Employees look to their leaders to maintain demand and through this to spread wealth into the community. Clearly many of these same employees and customers are also shareholders and they expect good returns for their investment, which increases the pressure on business leaders to exploit opportunities. This integrated relationship then means that expectations and aspirations are frequently in conflict.

The spectre of sustainable development is extremely complex, as outlined in Figure 1.1. Again we see these same three groups interacting behind and across this spectrum of issues. The business leaders have relatively short-term horizons within which to deliver performance to their shareholders (this group frequently includes pension funds), and through

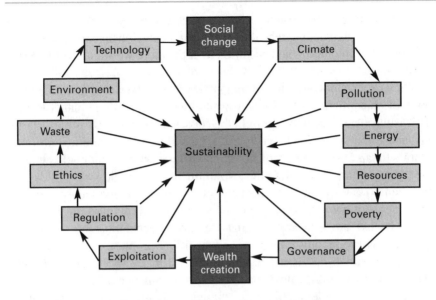

Figure 1.1 The conflicts and complexity of sustainability

these investments to provide the capital for further development and growth. Wealth creation is a fundamental factor of business and trade without which the wider community would be unable to develop its own aspirations, either individually or as a group.

Governments operate within relatively brief time spans during which their mandate is to establish the regulatory frameworks and to provide services to the community. At the same time they are the vehicles through which social change is driven. It is of course largely the wealth creation process that provides the ability to contribute to those regions that are less advanced and need support. At the same time they need to look at the long-term impacts, which may involve programmes where delivery of benefits will not be seen in the lifespan of either government or business leaders. This creates another conflict in terms of taking sustainability into the strategic business.

The environment is perhaps the most obvious concern that faces all sectors of the community, whether it be global warming or the impacts of natural disasters, which have always been part of the picture. It is often these that highlight the disparities across the world and raise the question of exploitation and perhaps guilt. One must also consider the impacts of manmade disasters, which are in some ways inevitable if the thirst for growth and demand is maintained. Clearly some may come from negligence and corner cutting but some result from the fallibility of humankind. We must also acknowledge that some environmental change is a result of progressive exploitation and pollution. But the more we want, the more risk we create.

There is a proposition that to bring everyone in the world up to the same level of consumption we would need the resources of three planet Earths. This is frequently used to highlight the causes of NGOs but it is both alarming and often so abstract that it has little value. First, there are no other worlds to tap into; second, consumption will never abate but could be recycled more efficiently; third, the evolution of the developing worlds will take centuries to reach a similar level of consumption and technology will bring new options. The short-term anomaly is that those who say we should constrain use are also arguing that we should accelerate the developing regions' evolution, thus creating a self-fulfilling prophecy.

There is much discussion about waste and many would agree that the industrialized world creates amazing levels of waste in all its forms. What perhaps gets much less attention is that waste is just a commodity that we have not yet found a use for; yet suggest that we develop power from waste and the NIMBYs will be hard on the heels of the planners and developers. Technology can provide some solutions, but there has to be compromise in order to exploit the potential.

Globalization has added another factor to the sustainability arena and that is social change. Integration of cultures and communities brings about an increasing diversity, which in turn offers a wide variety of perspectives on what is important. The obvious business leaders frequently do not drive exploitation; sometimes this results from communities that see this as a natural evolution, with their expectations and needs over-riding what others may consider unacceptable standards.

In all of this one has to consider and rationalize sustainability at both an individual and group level. On the one hand we may well nurture ideals and objectives, but we must reflect these as part of one or more groups with which we interact. How we see the world often conflicts with those organizations we work with or for. This is also a consideration for organizations that seek to attract the best brains, but which may be seen as not having an appropriate sustainable profile.

Pollution is a major consideration resulting from industrial exploitation. In recent years this has produced significant conflicts and challenges for the community. Beyond the obvious events such as Chernobyl and the Exxon Valdez there is a more serious underlying commercial phenomenon emerging, which is the trading of pollution. This has received notoriety in recent years in terms of Kyoto and CO_2 emissions but has been around for a lot longer; as national standards have been raised so business ventures have been transferred to less regulated countries. This simply moves the problem, and sows the seeds of future conflict.

Many today would consider the lack of ethical trading as even more of a pollutant. Globalization has opened up the world's markets but has brought with it more open exposure to bribery and corruption. In some developing regions these practices have more of a detrimental impact than the prospect of industrial exploitation. In other parts of the world the culture of facilitation payments has been a practice for centuries and perhaps ignores the rights of a country to manage its own standards. The conflicts these business processes create add to the confusions within the sustainable agenda.

The advances in technology have contributed to (and perhaps offer solutions in) the wide range of sustainable arenas. Many innovations created for good have ultimately been condemned in a negative way. Cheap power from nuclear plants is both clean and reliable, providing the waste and containment is controlled. The proliferation of the personal computer (PC) has both opened global markets and (due to the speed of its development) created redundancy and a new waste product.

Behind all industrial evolution is the vista of energy from steam to nuclear power which drives the wealth creation processes. It also is the major contributor to pollution in many ways. Again we see that by trying to raise the living standards around the world we will generate additional pressure and pollution.

The response to much of this conflict is for governments to introduce more and more regulation. There is certainly a need to ensure that unscrupulous business ventures are controlled. Perhaps, however, the biggest winners are the lawyers and accountants that support the major companies to manage these rules. The losers are the smaller companies and the communities that become pawns in a much bigger game. Incentives rather than penalties might change the balance between compliance and commitment.

CSR has in the main been focused towards corporate governance and, when we see examples from Enron and WorldCom, there is clearly a need to protect the wider community. The changes that have started to be introduced have significantly increased the responsibilities of business leaders. This in turn has led to greater interest in the development of risk management strategies, which may be more tuned to protectionism than commitment.

Perhaps the major concern for the business community has been the issue of brand management and more importantly, brand protection. Global manufacture and trading brings many opportunities but also creates the potential to expose organizations to public criticism. This is then reflected by the investment market and short-term sales, which in turn results in losses and reductions in demand which ultimately may cost jobs. Consider this cycle in the case of Nike where, amongst those that suffered as a result of protests, were the workers who were being exploited.

The balance in this complex world of sustainability rests in the hands of the stakeholders and, more importantly, in the value concepts that they employ or deploy. Frequently these stakeholders can be both beneficiaries and critics at the same time. In the case of those working in government, they may also be the regulators and legislators.

Sustainable development as a concept now seeks to look further into the future before committing to business or investment strategies. This is perhaps reflected within a few organizations and is sometimes made a selling point. In the main, however, it is still the basic trading principles that drive development in response to customer demand.

What is now starting to come into the business language is the concept of eco-efficiency. The conservation of resources, materials, energy and reductions in waste, together with recycling, have a positive impact on the bottom line. Re-engineering business processes and working more with the value chain offers the opportunity to improve both performance and cost whilst contributing to a wider sustainability programme. This does, however, require the resolution of internal and external business conflicts and traditional approaches.

The increase in the utilization of concepts such as outsourcing and off-shoring has brought with it the opportunity to address some aspects within the environmental and sustainability portfolio, but at the same time has created conflicts for those whose employment has been transferred. It also raises the potential for exploitation and impacts the communities at both ends of the transfer.

Where the future will lead is a subject occupying the minds of several economists, politicians, business leaders and environmentalists. The predictions are many and varied and generally fail to provide a stable profile against which to plan. As a result the debates continue and the conflict rolls on unabated with the result that more effort gets expended on debate than is focused on considered actions in many cases.

Many outside the business community would tend to take a very harsh view of the right to make a profit, ignoring of course the fact that this wealth feeds back into the community and into development projects. As a result of these crystallized positions the focus of CSR will inevitably concentrate on the visible profit rather than the longer-term implications.

This in turn presents the opportunity for those outside the business to criticize rather than consult. CSR should be part of the corporate business plan and it should be linked to the profit profile, which will help to create the ethos at every level of the operation.

Change does not come quickly or easily in any established business and the integration of sustainable ideals and objectives will be harder than most. Innovation is always difficult but where this requires an alternative business approach it will be doubly difficult. It will bring conflicts in the value chain, from the developer through every stage of manufacture or delivery to the customer and consumer. This change process will have to be far more holistic and draw into the process all stakeholders.

As the sustainability agenda moves forward there is a need to establish robust measurements and reporting that counters the current rhetoric. Most importantly those that promote the potential of a sustainable approach need to provide evidence of the value created. At the same time there are programmes such as FTSE4Good, that support organizations which issue sustainability reports but they should not become graded measurements since many organizations are at different levels and progress will be paced differently. Rigid rules will simply create even more conflict or mistrust and even induce some to focus on presenting the right image as opposed to creating the ethos of sustainability.

It is easy to see how current investment and taxation strategies may well have been established to underpin social responsibility, but in many ways they have had a negative effect. The conflict between business drivers and those of the regulations frequently means avoidance and compliance as opposed to commitment. Governments themselves have sought political solutions such as emissions trading and compromise rather than address the core issues. Incentives to help the business community would perhaps have more effect than penalties, which can be factored into the commercial package.

There is clearly a need to look towards alternative business models for, whilst most organizations can manage internal efficiency, the wider implications necessitate addressing the boundaries between organizations. Developing business strategies and operating processes that incorporate a sustainable profile will provide an alternative to exporting or transferring negative issues. These alternatives require innovative thinking.

The need for the business community to succeed and for the wider community to recognize the need is a crucial part of reducing the existing conflicts and moving towards a proactive approach. The issues involved in the wider sustainable arena provide a constant platform for conflict that detracts from addressing the real issues. There has to be competitive balance between the drivers for the business sector and the aspirations of the community and special interest groups.

Collaboration rather than conflict will do more to build a long-term strategic approach, which does not preclude the ability of organizations to benefit from implementing a truly sustainable programme. Each sector of the community has a value profile that covers a wide spectrum. Each is valid providing it does not try to impose its views on others except by exercising personal choice to influence market demand. The reality is that as long as the conflicts continue then the real issues will probably not be resolved. Creating sustainable value requires the balancing of demands across a range of stakeholders. More importantly, it requires forward-looking leadership that can adopt the common-sense elements of exploiting sustainable issues. At the same time there is a need for innovation at every level and supported by all three primary pillars of the community, business, social and government.

Sustainability and the more localized impacts and issues of CSR create a recipe for conflict in every aspect of the trading cycle. The more conflict is allowed to ferment, the less likelihood there is of actually focusing efforts on the profit and value creation process. The more wealth that is created throughout the value chain, the greater the opportunity to spread it through to those areas that need support.

Effective business operations are more efficient and exploitation of materials, resources and regions has limited benefit in the longer term. Increasing output or reducing costs has a direct benefit to the bottom line. In developing business plans the wide variety of issues covered by the sustainability umbrella needs to be embedded in the strategic approach. The concept of sustainability should be promoted not from a defensive position but proactively, to exploit the benefits both internally within organizations and in the market place at large.

Building a strategy must recognize the business environment and the landscape of the community. The implications of globalization are a consistent factor to most business operations and this brings both opportunity and risk. The network of stakeholders contributes pressures and influences on the strategy that must be addressed, but if sustainability is to be a real concern and focus then they too need to validate their individual agendas. The conflicts that currently exist are largely generated by individuals and groups, which in themselves have contradicting drivers and demands. Balancing these will be a crucial part of eventually being able to deliver real progress.

In the meantime the challenge for the business world should be focusing on how they can create wealth or value benefits from alternative approaches which, in parallel, will contribute proactively and responsibly to the wider agenda and to real sustainable outcomes. It is unrealistic to assume that commercial stakeholders will support significant reductions of investment returns unless there is an alternative value being generated. It should not, however, be assumed that adopting a sustainability-based approach will simply be a drain on business values. When savings, production and process improvements can be balanced against market demands whilst incorporating longer-term sustainable objectives, then business can turn current conflicts to profitable outcomes.

CHAPTER 2

Global business (local impact)

Globalization is now a factor in every business, either directly or indirectly, and impacts every community; clearly demand growth must also be affecting the broad spectrum of sustainability issues. It offers both challenge and opportunity but is still feared by many, as the more open markets become the greater the pressure on traditional comfort zones. In every aspect of dealing across national boundaries and, more importantly, integration of developing regions into the business process, there are social and economic impacts to be encountered. Many of these have caused high-profile media exposure for a number of international business names.

It also has to be recognized that the global community is changing, as seen in Figure 2.1. Some predictions suggest that in the next two decades the influence of the Asian business machine will radically increase. New global players are emerging, such as China and India, together with others. The major impacts will significantly change the geopolitical profile. At the same time the world economy will continue to grow, perhaps by as much as 80 per cent by 2020, but it is also suggested that average per capita income will be 50 per cent higher. The global business community will progressively become much less westernized, and thus the implications for creating a western brand of sustainability seems less likely.

One should accept but not condone the reality that unscrupulous business leaders will drive some exploitation. It should also be appreciated that most in the business community do not set out simply to exploit local developing regions but it must also be accepted that these regions are at differing stages of development. They are also not likely to be able to absorb the changes that many think they should. Some of those outside the business world may see any interaction as exploitation and should perhaps consider that if there were no demand for resources or competitive advantage from local manufacture then there would be no development. Taking the debate further, without the wealth creation process there would be no help for these developing regions.

There have always been since the earliest records traders who have been

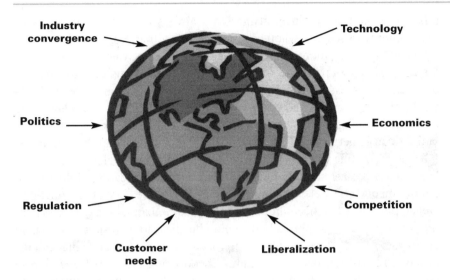

Figure 2.1   The impacts of globalization

the links between those that have resources and those that desire them. In this process there have been many horror stories going back over the centuries. There have also been many examples of how the trading interface has helped to create new wealth and development. It may not be popular to suggest that there are differing standards and stages of development, and that these differing plateaus create the essence of trading and the osmosis of knowledge transfer. The current access to information is a benefit in terms of bringing major issues to public notice but it also creates the perception that we can level the social standing of every region we see. Those that have spent time operating in the developing world will understand the dilemmas that exist. This includes many of the non-government organizations (NGOs).

The Bali Roundtable on developing countries, which took place in 2002, was a gathering of a number of government and international agencies which recognized that business is the primary driver of economic development. This was a precursor of the World Summit for Sustainability. It identified that the process of globalization and the active involvement of business was critical in alleviating poverty and achieving sustainable development. In many ways it also highlighted the progress that was being made towards changing roles, responsibilities, relationships, expectations and demands. There was certainly a concept that business was starting to recognize the benefits of working with the wider community. One might suggest this was a little naive since business has always understood the value of integrating with society, whether resources, customers or investors.

What is perhaps more interesting and constructive from these and similar discussion groups is the recognition that helping business to improve products, services, processes and relationships with society helps build wealth. Businesses, for their part, are perhaps appreciating more and more that practical support for their economic, environmental and social contributions can underpin wealth creation whilst reducing negative impacts.

Growing public interest in business operations in developing countries has brought issues such as human rights, labour standards, child labour, environmental impacts, corruption and fair trade into the limelight. Developing best practice can be more proactive than taking a more negative or even punitive approach to forcing business to be responsible. There clearly also needs to be a realistic approach which understands that change cannot and will not occur overnight. Encouraging business leadership to make the effort would be more productive than continuously battling against the easy target despite the efforts they make.

It is a complex task to factor sustainable economic, environmental and social objectives into business decision-making. At the same time, the developing countries are rightly looking to grow and so perhaps are themselves damaging the long-term sustainable infrastructure. There must also be consideration given to the pressures on business to meet CSR agendas in respect to developing regions when in many cases there is a local culture of corruption and exploitation.

Creating the environment for business to operate responsibly is part of changing local approaches. In the developing regions there is clearly a need to clean up the local culture and attract international players who can build critical mass towards a more responsible business culture. These unsustainable business cultures are themselves now creeping into the wider global trading environment and as such there is an emerging competitive challenge for those that would prefer a more structured CSR approach. There is clearly a need to create a partnership across these multiple factions in order to ensure that short-term focus on either side of the commercial divide does not negate the longer-term real needs and aspirations.

The impacts of global trading clearly have direct impacts on the local community and many would suggest that the business community is responsible for poverty. This shows a complete lack of understanding of the evolution of communities and societies. It also suggests that we can measure poverty against a common benchmark. However, it is true that how these business operations, whether local or external traders, deliver their results can seriously impact or aid the continuation of poverty. The impacts are easy to see in terms of resource use, waste and pollution, as well as employment exploitation and long-term exclusion through a lack of education.

What is perhaps less obvious is the economic pressures from cash flow and market dominance that prohibits true competition. For example, six international companies control 70 per cent of the world's agricultural commodities. Exports from the developing world are increasing dramatically, whilst inward investment is much less pronounced. Market demand places increasing pressures on producers such as the flowers being picked in Uganda the same day as the orders arrive, or in the garment trade, where most of the lead time is used up before the order hits the production floor.

Better working conditions and productive planning increase productivity and quality; this we have come to understand. It is also interesting to consider that poverty may provide low short-term costs but it increases absenteeism through ill health. A low educational base limits future growth options and raises the cost of training and recruiting.

A sustainable approach can thus increase productivity, quality and investment return. At the same time, clearly there are risks associated with failing to look beyond the immediate cost analysis. Beyond this there is the aspect of stakeholder pressure on investment and demand.

The trend in these type of dissertations is to focus on the smaller developing countries but the reality of course is that there are several big players which have a significant impact on the global social and business community. India has a growing population that is struggling to feed itself, whilst at the same time it has a growing industrial base. The gap between the top 8–10 per cent of society and the rest is ever widening. China, on the other hand, has a highly focused national investment profile, which includes socialistic programmes and yet allows more and more free market development.

The impact of this is that development in China is unsustainable according to UN reports. Its dramatic economic growth, together with major programmes on dams linked with drought, is placing increasing pressure on its neighbours in Thailand, Cambodia and Vietnam. Thus economic developments and progress often have a much wider reach and impact, not only in terms of influencing natural resources such as water but more widely in terms of infrastructure development. It is often suggested that future global conflicts will not be military, traditionally in search of economic benefit, but based on economics and the threat of economic terrorism.

Many, of course, still see globalization as a threat, particularly those that see their jobs going overseas. So the drive to improve competitiveness by looking to lower cost centres also bounces back on the traditional community. It is clearly not possible in today's market place to preclude overseas integration in some form. Thus blind protest is not realistic but what is more meaningful are the market pressures that these developments and process changes can create. The strategic considerations for the business leaders should be more directed to balancing the cost benefits with the wider stakeholder reactions.

Given the many different issues that the global markets bring forward and the challenges that can emerge from looking to develop competitive advantage through global trading, the subject of sustainability should be high on the agenda of business leaders, yet, in a study by IBM in 2004 involving over 400 senior executives, environmental and socio-economic factors were not seen as having an impact on their business. The principal driver was revenue growth against a background of global competition, continued uncertainty from issues such as 9/11 or Severe Acute Respiratory Syndrome (SARS), and changing market needs that are creating a complex market place.

Additional factors under consideration are the tried and tested issues of cost reduction, asset use and risk management. It is surprising, therefore, that the implications of sustainability factors are not high on Chief Executive Officer (CEO) profiles. Clearly the drive for global sourcing, off-shoring and outsourcing to support cost reduction involves potential direct risk but is also likely to reflect risk and reputation. This lack of focus may well reflect the belief that investors and customers are focused on cost and value, which is then driving growth potential. This would support the premise that to achieve wider adoption of sustainable approaches there has to be a change in the demand value concept.

As suggested earlier most CEOs saw China as a major focus for growth opportunities and a major market influence even for those that had no direct presence or strategy to harness China's growth. China's impact on supply and demand is enormous and growing. It can dramatically influence markets and many economists suggest corporate growth (certainly in Asia) will be dictated by China's ability to grow. In many areas, including manufacturing, China now represents the key trigger for economic development. This in turn must, surely influence smaller economies and accelerate the competitive challenges, bringing greater pressure to bear on long-term sustainability agendas.

Alongside, growth responsiveness is also seen as a major factor for business strategy. The dynamic changes that markets face provide a landscape that is only partially stable at any one time. As organizations seek to survive and grow, so their resource and supply network will also come under pressure. The implications for community investment are clear in that most will have to depend on their contributing value or fall by the wayside. Many organizations created value by being global and providing a conduit for customers to developing countries; with a more global economy this advantage has gone, resulting in the need to build new propositions.

Many will recognize that the skills necessary to ride these waves of change and still maintain a focus on corporate responsibility are not embedded in the majority of traditionally established organizations. They must also appreciate the dilemma that failing to manage the soft issues may ultimately cause a market backlash.

This relatively low profile given to sustainability issues is quite surprising but perhaps reflects the short-term focus on growth driven by the investment market. Unfortunately it also helps to create the catalyst for NGOs to promote the concept that business leaders have little or no concern for the communities that they serve or exploit. Experience would suggest that in the main this is not true, but integrating the longer-term aspects of sustainability into the global business agenda means balancing a very complex programme of issues and pressures.

Such pressures and concerns are frequently brought to the surface in order to temper the commerce-only focus of the business community. We have all seen the exposure that can come from exploiting the low-cost developing community. The sweatshop saga has been one that has been regularly thrown up as a direct result of globalization. Not only does the corporate world devastate traditional communities by moving production, but it also then adopts employment approaches that verge on slave labour. Child labour in Pakistan making footballs for the World Cup that carry the Coca-Cola and Adidas logos presents a nightmare picture for corporate public relations (PR) managers. It perhaps has less of a real impact on share values. It must also be remembered that in poor economies the local pressures of survival may be greater than wanting to foster a more equitable labour market.

Such cases of abuse and exploitation are frequently arising from across the globe, whether it is Wal-Mart and Timberland finding themselves implicated in labour issues in China, or toy manufactures such as Mattel in Mexico. We should make the point these are examples and should not be considered the only high-profile companies caught like rabbits in car headlights. Often they did not even realize the risks they were taking.

Even when organizations try to improve conditions in these sweatshops it is no easy task. Many, such as Reebok, Mattel, Nike and Adidas, have made special provisions within contracts to ensure that there is effective implementation of changes in working conditions, sanitary arrangements and health care. The challenge lies between the drivers of the consumer market, investor return and the cost profile negotiated at a local level. It must also be said that factory owners are not always as inscrutable as protesters would suggest, and it is the majors that are guilty of exploiting these markets.

What eventually does start to emerge when evaluating reports on sweatshops and labour abuse is that once changes and improvements have been put in place, so production and performance increases. The cost of improvement is often recouped over a short period and, when balanced also against the cost of training, the medium-term return is positive. Looking further into the future, a well-maintained workforce provides a platform for developing new products and services.

I have personal experience in India of seeing young boys working heavy machinery which led to their being sent home, only to return when inspectors had left. The real sufferers were the families that lost income and they probably felt little gratitude towards the western standards that had been unrealistically imposed on them. It is easy to assume that our way is right and to ignore the implications for the local economy; again there has to be a balance between good value and local exploitation.

In a global context clearly sourcing is a major area of concern for the majority of low-cost developing economies. Integration of manufacture often has by its very nature to focus on long-term investment and knowledge transfer, and in such cases there is clearly much more exchanging of ideas over a period of training, process validation and product delivery. Where there is more volatility is in the product, material or component supply where long-term contracting is less necessary. The implication is that to focus only on the short-term need and traditional price, quality and delivery tends to push the supply relationship to very competitive terms with little or no consideration for the future. It is in these situations that major players can find themselves exposed or implicated in exploitation claims and public pressure.

On the other hand, the growth in revenues for organizations such as Traidcraft and Fairtrade suggests that the consumer market is becoming more aware. At the same time China, which has influenced the world market through consumption for a number of years and will in the next decade become a global driver of markets, has declared its intention to focus on sustainable development. Whether this is politically driven or not the recognition of the impacts from a growing consumer society should be a warning to others.

Fairtrade has become widely appreciated as a sign of good practice and a sound approach to helping producers expand their markets and reap the benefits of better price levels. The focus is to fight poverty through trade and in recent years their impact on areas such as coffee sales has clearly started to influence the strategies of the majors, including Nestlé. Guaranteed pricing that is established to provide local investment has led to higher production and an increasing share of the market. The Fairtrade logo now has global recognition but remains vulnerable to healthy economies where anecdotal information would suggest that purchasing Fairtrade is fed by the feel-good factor and perhaps a little guilt. It has not yet established such a robust profile that the major players will embrace the Fairtrade principles and thus it is still only a model example of what can be achieved.

These principles, however, in the global market can provide a foundation for thinking across a wide range of organizations. As we have already said, the improved relationships with producers and manufacturers and investment in better working conditions can enhance production, yield, quality and consistency. There is clearly an issue that responsible sustainable approaches help to underpin brands and reputation. Building integrated relationships helps to establish a more effective risk management profile. The more investment is focused towards a mutually responsible approach, the more opportunity there is to exploit shareholder influence and future investment value.

The Fairtrade model, although limited in reach and scope, does show the way forward in terms of building ethical and fair trading chains that link the producer to the consumer, where each stage in the delivery process is equally transparent and mutually balanced. It has built a reputation that now sells its products at a premium because of the validation of the ethical approach and perhaps the feel-good factor that stimulates a degree of guilt at the consumer level. This is clearly not always popular with the major players but does show that at a basic level we do prefer a balanced approach.

When considering the sustainability agenda it is worth considering the fundamentals of globalization strategies, which in turn set the landscape for CSR challenges. These six dimensions, as shown in Figure 2.2, are both interactive and to some extent interdependent, creating a kaleidoscope of challenges for maintaining a balance in the sustainability matrix, which some may call a minefield.

The financial implications and economic influences clearly set the agenda for the global trading landscape but, in relation to the sustainable challenges, these introduce a wide range of factors. The growing influence of global players such as China and India are already changing the profile of trading patterns. As this influence increases, the Asian influence on business structures will also change. These growing markets, both pulling and

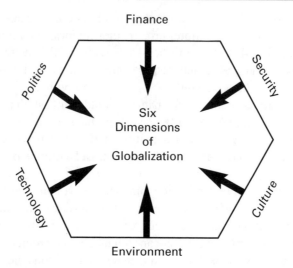

Figure 2.2 Dimensions of globalization

pushing demand, bring with them alternative business cultures. Regulation is also increasing to contain the shifts in business process operations (BPOs), such financial backroom operations, to ensure that, whilst benefiting from the obvious economic advantages, the reporting requirements are maintained. Within the financial aspects of global trading one must also consider the ethical trading implications and the control of corruption.

The political agendas across the globe are very diverse and frequently unstable, which creates a volatile climate in which to build and develop business operations. This, most will say, is not new but now one should perhaps be considering the desires of governments to exert their influence and exploit opportunities for development and economic growth. These aspirations may in themselves infringe our attitudes to sustainable development and as such create an alternative competitive pressure for short-term gain. The new political battleground is one of economic influence, which may be used to force through political agendas. These in turn will certainly impact the current major political power centres and over time there will clearly be new majors at the high table. The implications will probably bring positive and negative influences to the sustainability agenda. Wanting political power may induce some countries to adopt a more positive approach, whilst others may use the exploitation of natural resources to build influence.

Security is perhaps the single most visible influence on the global market. The growth in networked terrorism will continue to influence much of the business environment and thus the implications for developing sustainable programmes. Longer-term strategies and investments will be partially balanced against the local and logistical chain of security, the implication being that short-term projections will be more likely than long-term knowledge transfer programmes. This consideration of security also influences government support programmes that will dovetail with business investments focused on helping to bring sustainability to the developing countries. The implications and influence of aid-trade-debt must be tailored to build sustainability into the profile of deployment, which may also include (in some countries) developing approaches that circumvent the traditionally corrupt infrastructures so as to deliver programmes that are structured to ensure that benefits are not siphoned off or diluted before they reach the genuinely needy.

Technology at every level is a major factor in the globalization arena. As Tom Peters suggests in his book, *Liberation Management*, 'Globalisation and information technology are bringing about the most dramatic transformation in the history of business.'[1] At the highest level the explosion in capability and reach of communications technology has opened up the global market. As technology pervades the less developed markets it will inevitably lead to increasing the demand on energy and resources. The gap between the 'haves' and the 'have-nots' will certainly increase pressures on the market to balance sustainability against demand.

The progressive growth in populations in Asia over the next decade will change the balance of cultural influences. The global market place will become less western and the growth in the transient Islamic population will change the profile of the sustainable community. These business cultures will tend to become less formal and thus possibly less susceptible to the traits and pressures currently being held up as benchmarks. Business approaches that may be currently viewed by western NGOs as being exploitative are frequently viewed differently by other cultures. Issues such as HIV/AIDS greatly impact the natural resource-based economies and the investment profiles of the business community. The more resources we need, the greater the likelihood of local responsibility for community and health care.

The environment has been the main focus of sustainable development, and with current rates of consumption, waste and pollution the more we integrate globalization the greater the pressure on each of these aspects. Deforestation through to genetically modified (GM) crops creates a wide range of issues and challenges between the tree-huggers and the business community. It is inevitable that if we raise the living standards and opportunities to embrace an expanding population in the developing world, the drains on the resource pool ahead of its ability to replenish itself and pollution will both increase. If we do not address the aspect of waste then some suggest we will simply clog up the business arteries.

What should be clear to us all is that globalization is a factor in all our lives at every level; even those in the developing worlds that have not yet heard of globalization are being affected. Those regions that want to use their competitive advantage of resources (whether material or human) in order to exploit the opportunities of joining the global commercial market provide a challenge to those who would criticize the business community for participating.

The global market place is a complex environment within which the business community has to constantly strive for growth and competitiveness. The issues of sustainability impact on most (if not all) decisions made. The challenge going forward is to integrate sustainability into strategic thinking and operational activities. What must also be appreciated is that the global market place is diverse and demanding, and thus meeting every aspiration of every pressure group is not practical. The reality is that finding the appropriate balance is the best we can hope for, recognizing that others across the developing regions have their short-term development needs and have an equal right to share in the growth. It should also be recognized that each country has its own path and is at a different stage of evolution.

It was suggested a few years ago that western business and consumer demand was exploiting Chinese sweatshops. It is equally likely that the exploitation was more internally driven to secure a position in the market place. Soon, given growth patterns and demographic forecasts, China's internal consumer demand will be creating exploitation elsewhere. China supports sustainable development at the political level.

This observation is not to suggest that we disregard the obvious impacts of sustainability and just leave the world to find its own levels; it is simply to reflect the evolutionary nature of things. What we should be looking to do is ensure that we raise awareness in the business communities that sustainability can be profitably integrated, and share this knowledge with the emerging new commercial powers around the world.

CHAPTER 3

Strategic conflict

If sustainability is to be truly addressed by the community then it has to become embedded in the business culture and a clear focus within the strategic development plans of organizations. It cannot simply be consigned to the annual report and satisfying the superficial needs of the investment market's assessments. Business-driven sustainability has to be reflective of the wider community as well as the traditional commercial drivers. Yet clearly the three overlapping sectors of the community shown here in Figure 3.1 each have their own drivers, which need to be balanced or blended in order to establish effective strategies, and work in collaboration to deliver.

These drivers do, however, start from totally different perspectives that must be understood within the wider profiling of activities and pressures. The average tenure of most CEOs is currently in the region of 2–4 years,

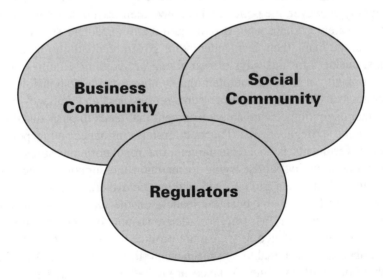

Figure 3.1   The overlapping communities

and within that span they will be expected continuously to deliver acceptable results to investors and shareholders. In fact their performance is crucial to generating wealth for the community at large. This short-term focus must be clearly reflected in the strategic investments under their governance and, whilst there may be some desire to take a longer-term perspective, the pressures are high. It must also be recognized that these strategies are being developed and implemented in a global environment where perhaps competitors have a different perspective of ethical trading and governance.

The community, on the other hand tends to look at sustainability from a personal or family impact first and then take a much longer view. The more remote the direct connection or constraint on their local position, the stronger the view on what others should be doing. It is this lack of balance, looking at the future wider arena, that to a large extent constrains the ability of business leaders to adopt what many would see as a more responsible approach. The social community is both the customer and the critic of the business community. If there is no compromise at the customer or consumer level then the business decision-maker's options are limited. The question of exploiting local social communities to support market competitiveness often brings values not previously seen. This creates a dynamic pull on the business strategy since competition will certainly exploit opportunities that are left open.

The third element driving the sustainable agenda is regulators and governments. Their challenge is to support the creation of wealth and balance this against the long-term impacts that over-exploitation can create. Frequently, however, the policy makers have their own time frames and for many these are perhaps only driving politically expedient solutions. The impact in the main, then, is a tendency for governments to introduce regulations, business to find ways of complying or avoiding penalties and for the community at large to complain that neither is being responsible.

Strategically the short-term pressures on business and demand-focused consumer aspirations create an environment that tends to push sustainability down the strategic agenda. The medium-term influence and responsibility of governments is to create targets and regulatory pressures on the business community, whilst trying to maintain the support of their local community. Without a global level playing field there is little chance of being able to focus many business leaders on the realities of reaching a return on investment as true long-term sustainable programmes are completely out of balance. If we cannot provide the impetus to understand and embed the sustainable approach then these three inter-dependent communities will continue to dance around each other but never really tackle the issues.

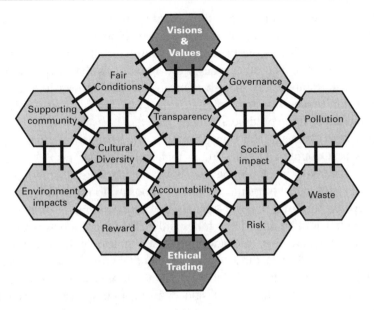

Figure 3.2 Interconnecting sustainable issues

This situation is reflected in research undertaken by the United Nations Environment Programme (UNEP) which suggests that communication of CSR issues is separated from the mainstream business communications processes, thus creating the illusion that the issues are not connected and further diluting the strategic focus. Sustainability touches every aspect of the business strategy as outlined in Figure 3.2; they are interconnected and thus it is crucial that organizations seek to identify the opportunities and risks that this entails.

The crisis that has created a backlash in the market place as regards corporate governance has perhaps over-shadowed the wider implications of sustainability. This is not to diminish the impact and importance that the Enron and WorldCom situations created but, whilst serious, they are not likely to have a major environmental impact. Certainly their investors would perhaps be less charitable (and who can blame them?), but we should not assume that sustainability is only about robust financial management.

The business leaders of today face increasing challenges from all sides and are between a rock and hard spot in terms of meeting everyone's aspirations. Some may suggest that these are problems for others and their role is to make money. This attempt to pull the blanket over one's head is flawed and shows that in many cases these responsible business leaders can benefit from sustainable approaches.

On one side pressure is not only external to the organization; it also comes up through the ranks, and poor consideration can also affect recruiting possibilities. This clearly builds on the external pressures for high-profile companies. The other side of the equation is that corporate values and approaches are a key factor in current investment profiling. If organizations don't meet investor aspirations then financial support for development and expansion could be affected.

To a large extent greater transparency is what needs to be put in place, but this is a double-edged sword in that if you are going to be open to scrutiny then you must be able to show a clean slate. Communications capability now puts companies at risk of exposure to pressure groups who can quickly turn minor over-sights into major issues. Companies are progressively joining up to Dow Jones and FTSE programmes to report and demonstrate where they are adopting sustainable approaches but many more are not and even those that do are perhaps even more vulnerable. Declare you are doing well and find small problems, and you may get worse treatment than those that said and did nothing within sustainable boundaries.

We hear lots of talk about corporate responsibility but what do we really expect it to be? It is generally assumed to be the ways we behave outside the regulatory controls. However, bear in mind that in the global trading environment there is a considerable disparity so which law companies are contravening can be difficult to assess. It is frequently these paradoxes that get exploited by those that see only short-term investment as the goal. Shifting operations to exploit low-cost labour, transferring pollution to other countries or even building firebreaks in the facilitation chains can all be legitimate actions. Multi-nationals can switch between friendly or more tolerant regimes, and all within the local legislation.

Responsibility is about commitment not compliance, and it is the challenge of this that becomes a dilemma for many business leaders. It would be easy to take a moral stance on this issue of responsibility but in the main this will drive organizations more towards compliance and short-term targets. What have to be evaluated are the commercial benefits of working differently, such as developing a cost-benefit analysis that supports an approach which improves customers acceptance, improves performance, reduces costs and in parallel helps contribute to the wider aspirations of society. We should also remember that for a business to be sustainable it has to have long-term growth prospects, which should be founded on customer expectations.

In the same envelope business leaders also have to consider the risks and rewards that come from operating in areas that attract high-profile criticism. When Shell decided to dump Brent Spar it learnt a big lesson from the public protests that hurt its European business. Exxon suffered because of its stance on global warming. There is a raft of websites focused on 'bad' companies only too ready to attack the commercial drivers in favour of local campaigns.

The potential to benefit from a sustainable approach is frequently not considered by organizations that adopt the traditional structured thinking. Eco-efficiency tries to focus on the cost savings that complement sustainable objectives. Moving a manufacturing plant may have cost benefits but could damage customer confidence. Similarly the service industry has seen the 'call centre challenge' being faced in many different ways. Some organizations are exploiting the idea of not off-shoring. Exploiting low-cost workers may deliver limited product savings, but could they deliver higher productivity given some investment in community, health, working conditions and tools?

Many organizations such as the Body Shop have made sustainability a key corporate value and as such are building their future with commitment to the community they serve. These values have to come from the top and the organizations need to be encouraged to be creative and innovative in order to deliver value to their stakeholders. Perhaps the biggest challenge will be to ensure that incentives also become contributors to these programmes rather than a potential constraint on compliance.

There are of course governmental programmes which are aimed at providing guidelines and measurements to promote the effective communications of strategies and performances. The United Nations Global Compact has now developed a package of guides called 'Communications on Progress' to support its initiatives, which expect participants to keep their stakeholders informed of progress on sustainable reporting. The EU is trying to establish a directive on annual accounts. The Global Reporting Initiative (GRI) has introduced their 'Boundaries Protocol' to help organizations define boundaries, significance, control and influence.

Governments have introduced sustainable development organizations with the objective not only of promoting actions in the business community but also monitoring their community's progress by measuring key aspects. These groupings are operating all over the world but as yet have not found a common set of measurements. The implications for this discontinuity are that business has to continuously adapt to meet local targets and restrictions. Clearly the Kyoto Agreement on carbon emissions set targets, but unfortunately not every country has signed up, and even within certain regions there is a degree of manipulation going on. It is alarming that governments do not begin to appreciate more fully that borders are artificial as the environment itself has no boundaries.

It would be easy for the business community to simply step back and play the field within these anomalies of government and regulators. There is, however, a greater driver and that is the customer; this is where government and business need to be jointly focused to educate the community at large. Even without this aspect it does not take a rocket scientist to understand that if you exploit resources or pollute the environment it is not sensible. Commitment at individual, corporate and national levels is needed to start the process.

Governments should be looking to create incentives for business leaders to invest in sustainable approaches, rather than simply penalizing failures. They should be setting parameters for the customer and educating them towards sustainable solutions. It should also be appreciated that sustainability and corporate responsibility are not just concerns for the multinationals: they affect, and should be a factor in, every business, large or small. Small and medium enterprises (SMEs) are a significant part of every economy and in most industrial nations are accepted as being the predominant employers and wealth generators collectively. They frequently operate in the global market place and are, to some extent, even more vulnerable to unfair competition than the majors.

A compliance strategy is a greater burden to SMEs than to major organizations particularly if these requirements are pushed down the food chain from major customers wishing to enhance their own sustainability compliance and reporting on a take-it-or-leave-it basis. However, since they are smaller, their managements are both closer to the action and more able to influence approaches in support of sustainability. Part of the responsible strategic business approach must be consideration of the impact of decisions on the supply chain, with the emphasis on working to find solutions rather than creating commercial red tape to compound that created by governments.

Strategic plans that feed down the business infrastructure therefore can also play a significant role in the overall sustainable profile. Sourcing strategies may carry implications for the community and for economic growth. Responsible purchasing has a great deal to offer and, whilst one would refrain from suggesting that traditional competitive drivers are not important, it should be a factor for consideration.

SMEs are more adaptable and more responsive and certainly would benefit from cost savings if these investments were not too high. These savings could have direct benefits to customers and the community at large. In a similar vein, when looking to take advantage of low cost producers, short-term exploitation opens the way to risks of supply security and market backlashes.

Again one sees opportunities for government and the business community to develop joint strategies, such that policies are growth generators and also contribute to the wider and longer-term aims of sustainability. Clearly governments can become victims of their policies and agendas. In the US, scientists and environmentalists have accused the White House administration of suppressing and distorting studies (both theirs and independent programmes) in order to avoid conflicts with policy programmes. These have included global warming, air quality and cancer. As one would expect these challenges have been denied, but there is reportedly strong evidence that government spin is clouding the picture.

One would not suggest that the US government is alone in these debates. There is a great demand for transparency at the business level but if we are to make informed decisions and develop effective strategies then there must be transparency across the communities involved. UK government advisers have suggested that the environment is a bigger threat than terrorism, the logic being that in general we can recover from an attack, but if we abuse the environment then we shall never recover. Again, in the UK the investment in alternative energy such as wind farms is lower than the investment in road development. Trying to maintain the balance creates more friction and the efforts are expended on the debate instead of looking towards integrated strategies.

For the leaders of the corporate world these mixed messages from government, pressures from the NGOs and the demands of the consumers provide little solace when trying to steer a course towards growth and wealth creation. Creating a responsible strategy (as in Figure 3.3) means integrating consideration for all pressures.

What we see is that the conflicts are clear but the issues of sustainability have added a new and complex dimension to the business leadership's strategic plans. Throughout the Industrial Revolution the creating of business ventures was very much a localized situation. The relationship between, say a mill owner, his employees and the wider community was clearly understood. It is true that in many cases exploitation was rife and the advent of trade unions brought some responsibility to the interdependence. In very few cases was there a moral foundation to these integrated communities; one can think of cases like the Cadbury family that bucked the trend but their approach was founded on religious grounds.

The community today is more diverse and certainly global, but the interdependence remains. Business needs resources and customers to create a market. It has to meet the constraints of regulations, which globally can be diverse and conflicting. It has to respond to the community wherever it operates, produces or sells. It has to do all this and meet the aspirations of

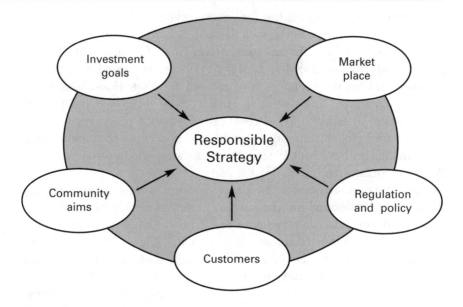

Figure 3.3   Integrating strategy

investors. Sustainability is now not simply about the long-term future of the business; it is about establishing responsiveness to the wider community.

Embedding sustainable principles at the heart of an organization will not change the world overnight. It is also unlikely that organizations will be able to address every aspect to the satisfaction of every pressure group or government. But much of the sustainability debate is not about turning the business community on its head, though perhaps some eco-terrorists would see this as their objective; it is about building into the core of business thinking the desire to look at each situation from a wider perspective.

Many of the risks that business faces in the global market can be turned to advantage by applying some common sense and taking the debate beyond short-term profit. When the corporate strategic trend was cost reduction the focus frequently shifted away from traditional common sense and addressed only the obvious cost issues. This frequently ignored performance, productivity and customer preference. As the trend shifts towards growth and expanding markets these issues should be addressed and, by considering the sustainable implications, can become both contributions to profitability and create customer recognition. Strategic intent and sustainable values can ride together in the business world, but the wider communities also have to play their part.

CHAPTER 4

Environmental change

The environment is a crucial part of all our lives and should be a concern in every aspect. The passion with which some champion their cause is probably a reflection of the worst exploitation. A change in the environment can result in all manner of implications, whether localized or global. Thus we should expect nothing less from our business leaders than that they commit to protecting the environment and conserving the ecological balance. Implementing effective environmental systems and safeguards is part of the business process. Clearly, however, this commitment frequently ranges from lip service to enthusiastic support but, in addition, on a global basis the appreciation for the bigger picture is often subdued by local pressures and understanding.

Companies should be expected to adapt to different business applications but maintain an overall sustainable profile. They should also be honest enough to report when there is a problem. Many however are reluctant to do this because they immediately become pilloried by the media and NGOs. Environmental standards have been established under ISO 1400, but again one finds a spectrum of adoption and application. Addressing the key issues such as pollution, energy consumption and waste are factors for every business to consider. These basics also have a clear opportunity to deliver value to the bottom line.

The threat of global warming has been with us for many years and yet there remains the debate as to whether this is caused by manmade influences or is simply part of the process of evolution. There are numerous reports of the Arctic ice cap melting rapidly; this has been confirmed after a 4-year study in the Arctic Climate Impact Assessment (ACIA) released in November 2004.[2] The results suggest the Arctic will warm by 4–7 degrees Celsius within the next 100 years. This will have a major global impact, including a contribution to rising sea levels.

Reports on the Greenland ice sheet by Reading University suggest an 8 degree Celsius warming in the next 350 years resulting in sea levels rising by up to 7 meters. Some may argue that these reports are so inconsistent that they are perhaps flawed but it might be more realistic to consider that, given the millions of years that have gone before, the variation in projections is negligible and the trend should be taken seriously.

In the twentieth century sea levels rose; during the 1990s this was happening at the rate of 0.25 centimetres per year. Shorelines across the world have eroded and some low islands have disappeared. The Arctic ice sheet is believed to be only 60 per cent as thick and covers 10 per cent less area now than it did a few decades ago. This reduction is causing habitat loss, and polar bears are losing weight through lack of hunting. Mountain glaciers have shrunk by up to 50 per cent. In the northern hemisphere spring is coming earlier and the growing season is lengthening, whereas in southern Africa the increase in droughts is thought to be due to climate change. Thus there is plenty of evidence to confirm the trend. What is perhaps harder to argue at this stage is the cause of this global warming. Is it manmade or simply due to evolution?

In our litigation-focused world assigning responsibility is a common trait amongst governments and commercial organizations. Historically the 'natural' disaster would have been put down to an act of God and this shelving of responsibility happens repeatedly even in this scientific age. One would hope that in deciding what is to be done today we would employ those most technically qualified to offer an opinion; however, even the technical experts have a tendency to disagree. There is general acceptance that global warming is occurring and the consensus seems to point to CO_2 emissions. There is disagreement as to whether the amount of extra heat generated by carbon emissions could account for this trend and perhaps in mathematical terms this could be extrapolated to provide a direct correlation.

Many theorists would suggest that global warming is a recurring process that can be tested against historical data which precede the ability to measure carbon emissions. An amusing and interesting approach was to trace global warming against wine production, which can at least be tracked in Europe. Some would suggest that what we are seeing is a 1,000-year cycle that can be validated against historical events and records. This idea is amply presented by Dr Alfred E. Brain in an article entitled 'Cycles of Global Warming as revealed by History', which is no longer available.

US scientists indicate that sea levels are rising and crop yields are falling, but despite the evidence for global warming Americans are still driving gas-guzzling cars. One doubts they will change dramatically. 'The risks are very large', is a sentiment echoed by US scientists, against a background that America is producing 36 per cent of warming emissions but has not signed up to Kyoto. US government experts may argue whether their pollution is the cause of warming but experts are agreed the real debate is around the extent of warming. This lack of commitment to the cause is diffusing the focus on the impact, which may be as a result of pressure to avoid the solution.

Some would suggest that global warming is nothing more than political hype and that historical weather patterns in many regions suggest that today's erratic weather is nothing new. These violent storms themselves are no less frequent but the number of people living in their path has increased, and of course telecommunications makes it graphically more available. There is much written about reducing ice in the Arctic but research suggests this situation was also present a few million years ago. So, long before we started burning fossil fuel, temperature changes were taking place. The impacts of the sun are still not fully understood but it could be that rising temperatures would induce increased cloud, which in turn may reduce global warming.

Evidence suggests that the ozone layer is fluctuating and most would say the weather is more erratic. The UN reported in 2003 that the ozone hole was the biggest ever; subsequent reports suggested some reduction but certainly there is a hole and the effects have yet to be fully understood. Work done by the UK's Open University suggests that acid rain is in fact slowing the progress of warming through the dilution of natural methane, which is a major greenhouse gas. Natural methane is produced in greater quantities than manmade product emissions but unfortunately acid rain kills off the forests which, as we know, help to control carbon dioxide.

Many suggest that global warming is more serious than terrorism and has been responsible for more deaths. More importantly, the effects are far-reaching and appear more permanent; they also affect the natural balance. The Gaia theory states that the Earth is a self-regulating system, which is a view that most people who have worked with the land have some sympathy towards. This balance between the species of flora and fauna is something that has been naturally evolving since time began and is only now being distorted by human intervention. By pollution or genetic restructuring we may be introducing evolutionary changes that will come back to bite us in the future.

Some have even tried to put a cost on global warming, and when one sees these numbers one does wonder how anyone ever made these calculations. What is certain is that the pollution we are creating must be having an effect, but as yet we as a race are not smart enough to fully understand the ramifications.

Is all this the fault of the business community, or the thirst of the community to have and to consume more, or a failure of government to legislate appropriately? The reality is that where we are today is a result of evolution and perhaps this is influencing the environment. To change the direction may or may not be possible but as previously outlined, it is a challenge for everyone; whilst we may impose regulation we must also maintain the rights and capability to create wealth.

Certainly the impact of pollution is adding to the challenge. It does not take a scientist to understand that if you dump chemicals into the environment and rapidly reduce the natural filters such as the rain forests you will create change. The impact of that change may take more scientific definition but we should not ignore the obvious. We also assume the right in the developed world to increase consumption but criticize the rights of business in developing countries to exploit their resources, either for domestic use or export.

When B&Q established their managed forestry purchasing initiative and, despite a very aggressive NGO campaign, it was the exporting governments that protested most because of the potential impact on the local economy. The World Conservation Union scientists are claiming that cloud forests are in danger of being wiped out due to climate change. These forests take moisture from the air and provide water for people in developing nations. They are also prey to logging, agriculture and construction, so in general terms what helps the developing economy today may be a major threat tomorrow.

The complexity of the environment and the impact of our actions should certainly be a factor in business strategies. The media flood us with reports on global warming but it is often difficult to be objective. Scientists are divided in terms of impacts and causes but most agree there is a change and the real debate is around the impacts and timing. Climate models predict increases in temperature, changes in rainfall and rises in sea levels over the next 100 years of perhaps 50 centimeters, which is a serious problem for low-lying countries such as Bangladesh.

There is much debate about the accuracy of these climate models but, as technology has improved, their predictability has increased exponentially. What is interesting is that whilst we focus on greenhouse gases (GHG) and beat ourselves up about the impacts of pollution, recent satellite research suggests that plant growth is increasing due to warming, which in turn means more CO_2 filtering. This CO_2 impact is frequently blamed on urbanization but some reports suggest that, contrary to generally accepted wisdom, no statistically significant impact of urbanization could be found in annual temperatures.

Climate change has a significant impact on global business since, as the established western world seeks to reduce its impacts on the environment,

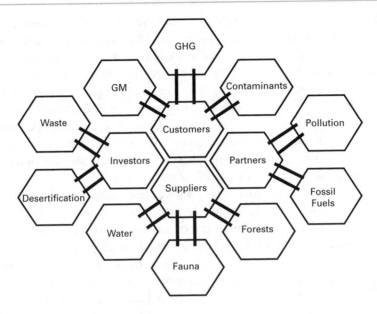

Figure 4.1 Environmental impacts

the emerging nations will increase their consumption and pollution impacts. In fact it might be suggested that the pressure on the west to commit to reducing impacts would have a major economic impact in terms of the global balance.

It would be quite easy to develop a conspiracy theory or to suggest that in view of the conflicting evidence one should do nothing. Doing nothing is for most not an option but getting the right balance is a challenge for the business community and one which should be encouraged. It does not take much to appreciate that we all need to be responsible and consider environmental impacts as in Figure 4.1, and that, whilst the theorist may fight and argue, much of what we contribute to the environment needs careful management.

GHG have been already discussed and clearly it makes good sense to avoid adding to a problem or developing approaches to reduce these emissions by a process of technology development and consumer education. It is perhaps more likely to succeed if there is a consistent approach, so Kyoto offers a platform; but if it becomes politically fudged then it will lose credibility.

The genetic modification debate is one that fires many on opposite extremes. There are those that say we are playing with the fundamental building blocks of life without understanding the long-term implications, while others would promote the idea that we can produce more food for those in the developing world. Many would argue that we have enough food; we just can't agree how to distribute it fairly. When the UK's Chief Scientist admits that genetic modification trials failed to recognize that butterflies can't read warning notices one does wonder if we are ready to play with these complex models. Clearly genetic modification is part of the intellectual evolution, but whether it can be seen as a natural evolution is another serious question. Since we can't yet all agree on climate change with sophisticated climate models what confidence can we have in the leading edge advances in genetic modification?

As the industrialized world advances we are capable of producing a wide variety of contaminants. Ignorance in the past has given us many examples of the natural balance being disturbed or even obliterated by failing to understand the impacts of manufacturing residues. In many ways the industrialized world solved the problem by transferring dirty factories overseas, which few can really consider appropriate action. Even the impacts of drugs, used to help people have in turn polluted the water table in some areas.

Waste in any form has a major impact on the environment and, as we continue to dump non-degradable products into the arena, we must realize that we are affecting the overall longer-term balance. In the same way, pollution (starting with GHG but reaching widely into the community) creates pressures on the environment, which may or may not lead to a degradation of the world we live in.

Fossil fuels are frequently blamed for the plight of climate change, and certainly it is easy to see how historically these have polluted and contaminated the environment. However, since these are here to stay and will be, in many ways, the practical solution for emerging countries then perhaps we should not be outlawing them but understanding how to manage them. Power plants in Asia are often built with pollution controls that are too expensive to operate, so whilst the ideas are there perhaps the impetus is not.

Desertification is an evolution that precedes the modern industrialized world but in recent years the pressure to produce more has encouraged farming communities to develop bigger fields with less sustainability. This process has become common practice in many parts of the world where the forests are making way for fields, but in the long term these will create unstable ground and become susceptible first to land slip and then to loss of fertile ground.

Forest stripping has been a highly volatile subject for many years and is perhaps one of the major conflicts between the developing world and the green industrialized communities. Forests create income for local communities but, as every schoolboy knows, trees are the lungs of the world. As the west demands more consumption and the local communities strive to raise their economic profile, the impact is obvious. Many in the forestry world would suggest that recycling paper is perhaps more damaging than properly managed forests. The process uses energy and chemicals to a greater extent than new pulp whilst at the same time the trees are helping the environment.

Water is the most crucial natural commodity that we are in danger of exploiting. As we damage the way that natural structures can retain and process water through deforestation, desertification and pollution we are heading towards water becoming an even more valuable commodity than it is already in some regions of the world.

Perhaps the element in all of this that gets the least attention is the impact we are having on the many species of wildlife across the globe. The depletion of tropical rain forests and species-rich habitats such as wetlands and coral reefs will continue to exacerbate the historical losses of many species.

Environmental issues will always be a subject for great debate and as we see more globalization the exploitation of the environment will probably become a differentiation factor for many customers and consumers. Thus not only will the business community be facing more and more regulation and legislation, but it will also have to take account of these factors in the business strategy.

Many organizations will claim the credit for helping to preserve the fauna whilst undertaking development projects. The truth is that we need to show the right face to the world in order to gain development approval. Thus if business only reacts to pressure then it is unlikely to gain the right to be treated as anything other than a pariah. Yet there are many organizations that integrate a responsible approach into the business culture and frequently exploit this as a differentiator in the market. In order to achieve this it is important that organizations educate their workforce to understand the balance between business and the community.

Frogs may not set many on fire with enthusiasm but the red-legged California frog was made famous by Mark Twain. It natural habitat was progressively destroyed, bringing it to endangered species status by 1996. AMEC found themselves faced with protecting the frogs at various sites, and according to reports they did a good job. One wonders if the CEO of AMEC is a frog-lover or whether a combination of practical concern and business responsibility created an opportunity to do the right thing and benefit the environment. Many might be cynical about the motives but perhaps what is important is that the company did it. What is even more important is that these episodes should be heralded and not decried in order to build these environmental values into the business ethos.

Environmental change is not simply an emotional or PR issue; it has a direct impact on business and understanding the risk may help to bring balance into the whole subject. First there are the direct impacts on the infrastructure such as floods, coastal erosion, wind and storm damage and subsidence, all of which clearly impact business performance. Resource usage change will affect power and water supply and demand, with less heating in the winter and cooling by summer.

Changes in the environment may also have ramifications for health in the work place from more winter-surviving germs and impacts from ultra violet rays as we enjoy more outdoor pursuits. Impacts on transport, power transmission and telecommunications are frequently the result of weather changes. In the longer term the impact on building designs and standards will surely flow from a significant change in the environment. In many countries the issues of renewable energy and sustainable construction are already part of the future regulations.

All of this will affect the insurance markets as they try to balance the impacts and potential risks to business. At the same time one can see that in many sectors litigation will increase as the predictability of the environ-mental impacts becomes more prominent. On the positive side, environ-mental change offers many the opportunity to exploit new markets such as increased leisure, changes in eating habits, new building technology, envi-ronmental technology and renewable energy.

Despite all of the impacts and opportunities that may be identified it would be foolish to over-state the significance of integrating these into the business agenda. Many if not all of these will affect organizations differ-ently and thus creating a one-size-fits-all approach is pointless. What is important is to ensure that organizations and business leaders incorporate into their overall strategic plans the need to recognize potential impacts. It is also crucial to understand the potential of any action that could contribute to the current situation.

The case for global warming may not yet be fully convincing but it is clear that the climate is changing. It makes no sense to ignore it or to simply put the responsibility on to the business community. Much of what has been done in the name of economic and industrial development may not be reversible. What clearly makes sense is that whilst some issues may be contained through natural or manmade intervention, every action has a reaction. Whilst some may not be clear-cut the majority need only a basic understanding to establish the merits and dangers of economic exploitation.

The predictions of global economic expansion over the coming decades suggest that we will see exponential growth in populations and thus an increase in the demand for resources and creation of waste and pollution. There can be any amount of regulation but until there is a global common approach, which must be extremely unlikely, then variations between countries and regions will provide the potential for exploitation. Making a difference must be developed at the consumer level and built into the ethos of the business community. Protecting the environment should be a business differentiator.

The key to embedding the environmental ethos into organizations will not come from external pressure, which would probably switch the focus to compliance. There is a need to explore and exploit the relationships between customers, investors and business partners and supply networks. The more responsible NGOs have recognized that business cannot trade on an environmentally bankrupt planet and that sustainability must come from successful business.

CHAPTER 5

Resources

As previously suggested, if everyone in the world were to enjoy the same level of consumption as currently enjoyed in the developed world then we would need the output of three planet Earths to support demand. This is probably true mathematically but only useful in terms of trying to make a point or to induce consumer guilt and reduce demand. The reality is that one would have to extrapolate the figures forward perhaps another millennium before that crisis would even come close and one would hope that many of the challenges we face today will have been solved by then. Not that we should simply ignore the situation until then; it's not only tomorrow's problem, it is the responsibility of today's community to make sure we provide the best possible base line going forward.

Estimates vary a little but the general view is that the world's population will exceed 7 billion by 2010; the majority of this growth will be in the developing countries. In the main one expects that urban growth will greatly exceed that in rural areas and, even where it is not, the migration to city life will produce mega-cities exceeding the 8 million mark. In the western world the age profile will continue towards an aging population that produces less but continues to consume at high levels boosted by financial strength. In the developing states the pressure will be on to grow the population and one should not expect any levelling off in the birth rate. The challenge will not be in creating the food to feed this growth but firing the political will alongside transportation and distribution. As a result one can still expect malnutrition and starvation to occur periodically. Further on the GM crop will ideally be able to fill gaps in production assuming we allow its deployment, which seems inevitable.

The World Wildlife Fund for Nature, amongst others, suggests we are using resources at a rate 20 per cent faster than the Earth can produce them, and that those resources are disproportionately being consumed. Certainly the Earth has limited capacity to produce certain resources such as fossil fuel. It not a question of how much oil is left but more a question of what do we use when it runs out. Nuclear fuel is viewed as being unacceptable but, in

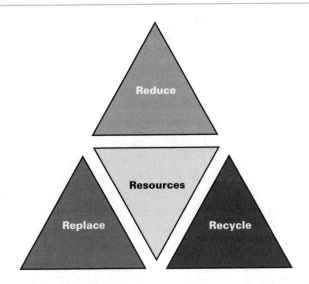

Figure 5.1   The 3 Rs

real terms, is perhaps the only current fuel source that is self-replacing. GM crops may enable us to increase harvests but as yet the jury is still out in terms of the potential long-term impacts. The big question is are we prepared to consider the simple challenge shown in Figure 5.1 to reduce, replace or recycle.

An expanding global economy will certainly increase the demand for raw materials, starting with oil, but in many areas the challenge will spread to support a growing consumer demand profile. Energy demand will probably grow by up to 50 per cent in the next couple of decades, which is almost double that of the previous two or three. But water is likely to be the scarcest resource available to the developing world and probably the major source of political friction. As water tends not to follow political boundary rules, controlling supply could influence local pressures. Despite the advances that every pundit promises for the future, poverty is still a problem today, and will certainly be a challenge for tomorrow as we consume more.

The environment also contributes to the reduction in our capacity to feed ourselves. As an example Lake Tanganyika the world's second deepest lake and Africa's second largest water body with over 350 species of fish is declining. Temperature increases are reducing the nutrient levels, which will lead to reduced fish stocks. Catches have fallen which is a major problem for those that depend on it for protein and the local economy.

On the other side of the consumption profile, increases in temperature are boosting the demand for air-conditioning where sales in Europe have increased by 10 per cent a year. Whilst these units use power to cool the inside of a house, they generate heat into the atmosphere which raises the temperature overall.

The deforestation of the rain forests to provide timber and clearing agricultural land adds a multiple demand on the resources of the planet. Satellite reports suggest that the rate of destruction of the Amazon forest is up by 40 per cent per year. It is also worth remembering that approximately a third of the world's surface is drying out and around 1,500 square miles become desert each year. This will clearly result in increased people movements. This situation was described by the UN as a creeping disaster caused through destructive agricultural approaches, water shortages, population growth and global warming. Some suggest that by 2025 two-thirds of Africa and Asia's arable land will have become desert.

For the business sector the logic is very simple, in that if you control resources the more rare the commodity the greater the price advantage. The principle has been applied to several materials that we now value as part of our global economic balance. Gold, as an example, is perhaps again replacing the instability of currency markets since the dissolution of the gold standard. This scarcity facet of the trading environment will not change but in fact we have more gold than we need for industrial purposes. A similar situation applies to diamonds. Thus when we focus on the resources we need perhaps there is often a distorted view of what's important.

As has been said already there is probably enough food to go round but we need to resolve the constraints that prevent it reaching the areas of need. There is the prospect of GM food being available to everyone but the question must be asked if this is in fact practical when industry and the developed world have little need for over-capacity. There have also been several reports which suggest that the assumed benefit of GM crops being more resilient to disease is perhaps not so certain. Even more worrying is the principal idea that GM crops can be protected against weed killers may not be true, and super-weeds are evolving.

For the business community the issue of resource consumption has a number of clear challenges. It does not take much to appreciate that if you can reduce the materials you use for any given product then you will reduce the cost profile. Maintaining competitive edge, then, has the potential to directly contribute to the drain on the raw materials pool. It needs to be recognized that global competition will act against this concept. China, for example, is now the third largest manufacturing base in the world, representing 12–14 per cent of the market.

The 'China price' is now the benchmark, but what should also be appreciated is that China is a net importer of the raw materials it exports. Russia, on the other hand, is a net exporter of energy and for the immediate future will be the energy provider for Europe. However, at the same time Russia has a declining demographic profile with an aging population so in time the energy-based economic model will need to be replaced. The economic growth in places such as China and India will create the need for perhaps double their current energy consumption by 2020.

Strangely minerals and natural resources in the main are dispersed in the developing world and global increases in consumption and demand could well be the spark that stimulates growth in these poorer economies. This could in time redress the balance between the haves and the have-nots, but in truth there can be few who have visited these countries who hold out much hope; not because they are not capable but because local rather than global exploitation will drain the resources without the complementary investment.

It is foolhardy to think that we can continue to consume resources at a greater pace than they can be created, and whilst it may be possible in 100 years to replant forests it certainly will take millions of years to replace oil fields or mineral deposits. There are those who say there is plenty to go round, and it is just a question of cost and political will. Clearly the more costly the raw materials the less chance there is that poorer communities will benefit from goods, but it could place them in unique trading positions. It is a question of balance.

Innovation in materials and applications could produce new, alternative approaches that are less damaging to the environment, at the same time reducing the drain on the resource pool. Biodegradable products and packaging should already be a must in the industrialized world, not only because alternatives are expensive and damaging but because organic raw products provide a more reliable supply chain, which is also sustainable. If it can be grown then there is a potentially renewable material supply.

In a similar vein the drive for more environmentally friendly products has in some parts become a market differentiator, particularly when one considers the value of being able to recycle waste effectively, which may be a cost factor for the business process. Frequently business decisions are made from a very narrow perspective. Regulatory pressures that provide no concessions for the responsible organization do not help this process because then there is no discrimination against those that simply exploit every aspect of the community.

Given the drain on raw materials and consumable resources it makes sense to consider optimizing the value of that material by recycling waste, scrap and unused products. The more we use the more we need to consider the implications of that consumption. Designing for recycling is perhaps the easiest step that organizations can take, and often this will involve simplification of the manufacturing processes. Reprocessing waste is perhaps the most simple of the contributions that any organization can make. It is particularly important that we look at chemicals used in production, which can be both costly and potential pollutants.

Amongst the key resources that should be considered is the question of human resources. In most of the developed world the population is either declining or stagnant but with an increasing age profile. In these regions the skills profile is also in decline, and so there are fewer and fewer people to provide for an increasingly aging population.

It may be considered exploitation to move production to low-cost labour centers, but it should also be considered that whilst cost was probably the initial driver we are looking at a significant demographic shift. In the longer term these developments help to raise the education and skills profile that is creating perhaps the world's scarcest resource: a sustainable effective workforce. Eventually the aging industrialized centres will have to depend on the developing labour economies in very much the same way as migrant populations are already taking over the lower levels of the employment ladder. Sustainability then starts to take on a different inflection, as it becomes no longer a question of exploitation but more one of interdependence. Certainly one should not expect to see this change happening overnight, but eventually the signs are obvious.

It should also be recognized that as part of the recovery of many of the materials and minerals resources required to fuel our industrial demands there is a dependence on the low-cost worker. This equation is one that is becoming more of a front-line issue for many organizations in the market place. Training and maintaining a highly-skilled workforce is a key factor in the economic development and investment of, for example, the mining industry. Historically the workforce in sub-Saharan Africa was considered expendable but, as we have seen, the ravages of HIV have created a need to preserve these investments.

This situation will become increasingly more apparent over the coming years across a spectrum that will include Africa, China, Russia and parts of Eurasia. Thus, having the mineral resources in the ground, as it were, is only part of the challenge; getting them out and to market may place considerably more strain on the business community. Farming and forestry offer similar challenges in many parts of the world since the continued pressure on labour costs is promoting either a migration towards urban employment or short-term exploitation, as is common in many of the rain forests.

Thus, considering a sustainable and balanced investment may involve not only the focus on the raw materials but also being able to recover training and investment through a sustainable workforce. At the same time exploiting those natural resources may require consideration for the environmental impact and a more integrated relationship with the local community.

The dilemma for the business leaders of tomorrow and for many today is that there is an ever-increasing demand. This may be viewed as being a short-term bonus but it should always be remembered that one man's price advantage is another's loss. More importantly, we must start to consider the rate of consumption and the impacts of that consumption.

The long-term perspective should consider the business process in terms of the potential benefits to the bottom line of seeking alternative materials and resources, including the value of reducing the resources needed to provide the product through innovative design improvements and adopting a greater focus on recycling to gain the maximum return from all materials. Each of these can in time make a contribution to the profit margin but at the same time reduce the global demand on resources.

The problem is that such investments will require support not only from stakeholders but also from the customer base. The investor and shareholder will always be looking for the best return, and although some will focus on long-term investments the majority will be looking for quick returns. It is this pressure that leads organizations to focus down on short-term cost and which explains why we see more and more volatility in the market place.

Only a limited number of investors are likely to support sustainable investments, which is disappointing when perhaps they should be sold on their long-term sustainable value. Thus in terms of building more focus into the operations it will be those short-term actions that reduce cost that will gain the most attention. Perhaps the strongest influence on business leaders and investors is the demand of the customers. When the customer takes a proactive view on the approaches that support a product then investors will follow the trend.

Sustainability does not have to be an additional cost and is nice to have, though it may provide a valuable competitive edge in some markets. If any business is looking for long-term value then a responsible approach to the environment and the workforce is a must. Investment in alternatives simply provides a risk management approach that could lead to market differentiation and increased competitiveness.

CHAPTER 6

Waste

In many respects waste is only a commodity which we have not yet learned how to exploit. If you travel to some of the developing countries you will see much greater industrial exploitation of waste. More importantly, when you consider the drain on resources for power then converting waste to energy must be a major consideration. On the other hand, running a business or community that is waste-neutral by strategically assessing design, use and buying patterns should also create a reduction in unused resources. The cost of waste does not make good business sense but many would rather look at short–term solutions.

It is reported that in the USA a meal on average travels 2,400 kilometers before it reaches the plate. This is a major waste of resources but a fact that is probably repeated around the world. It will also be recognized by many who have travelled to the USA that what is left on the plate at the end of the meal is significant.

The subject of waste in all its forms is perhaps the most frustrating of sustainability issues, since by its very nature waste represents no added value or benefit except to those who have established businesses processing rubbish. In any business efficiency drive the first port of call is to look for areas where processes, functions or materials are being wasted or not adding value. This may be as simple as improving utilization or as complex as re-engineering the whole business. We expect businesses to be efficient but perhaps from experience one would suggest that very few really are optimized. It is also important to consider that the customer drives much of what is required and, without collaboration, significant change is unlikely.

What also is seldom viewed constructively is the fact that consumer societies dump valuable products as waste simply to replace them with the next new model. In the USA, for example, it is reported that one million telephones are scrapped each week and one would suspect an even higher number of personal computers, both of which items could be reprocessed and sent overseas.

The growth in the use of PCs has in itself created a major waste problem because not only do they have a short lifespan but they also contain some nasty contaminants that need to be handled carefully. The value of these PCs makes it hard for organizations to treat them as anything other than consumables, although a number of organizations have grown up to help process these machines, recycle what can be recovered and now dispatch others to the Third World where they can help the education process.

The waste-neutral concept (WNC) is one that is starting to attract interest; it aims to provide within an organization a balance between the realities of business and the desire to avoid waste wherever possible. The principles of the triple bottom line must be part of the evaluation process for every business, whether environmental, financial or social, but in many cases often all that is needed is a little thought.

The Eden Project in Cornwall is an ideal environment to consider the practical application. The aim is to recycle at least 85 per cent of all rubbish. One example they gave was returning to china cups in the restaurant, since an evaluation of the economics showed that they saved over $150,000 per year, despite expenditure on a dishwasher and two part-time staff; no more paper cups and the customers get a better cup of tea! This simple story shows that with some forethought waste need not be a one-way process and contributes to the triple bottom line. They also utilize most of their rubbish as compost. WNC is about turning waste into value.

Waste is not simply about the rubbish we create, although this is perhaps the major focus, not least because of the implications for the environment and the clash between countries such as Russia and Sweden over the untreated discharges into the Baltic that have damaged many fish species. Waste should also be considered in terms of poor utilization of resources or exploitation of resources for no real benefit. It is also about recycling, which is a key aspect of waste management. It is unlikely that we will in the industrialized world ever get to the point where we have no waste, even excluding what humans produce. Thus recycling not only makes senses in terms of resource management but it offers the opportunity to create value from waste. Countries such as Belgium, Germany and the Netherlands profess to have recycling levels above 80 per cent of all rubbish.

For example, up to 75 per cent of UK landfill waste, 400 million tonnes, produced each year comes from aggregates, mining, sewage and sludge and construction waste, whilst 25 per cent comes from industry, commerce and households. In landfill sites much of this results in the creation of methane that adds to GHG. The UK produces enough rubbish each week to fill a major football stadium. Similar figures can be found for every major industrialized country.

One would therefore suggest that perhaps not only is this an environmental problem but also a large waste of resources. As landfill space becomes scarcer or less acceptable to the community, alternative approaches must be considered. We must also consider the implications of hazardous waste where contamination of the soil and frequently the water table are a danger to the wider community, perhaps for hundreds of years.

In the consumer society packaging probably represents the easiest of targets for reduction. The purpose of packaging is to protect the product and to attract the consumer; in the main it is probably the latter that creates the most waste. Thus the customer can start the process by supporting more functional packaging. Similarly in a business-to-business transaction the same principle should apply even more positively, since generally it is the product that's most important. In either case there are potential cost savings as well as environmental benefits.

In the western world vehicles perhaps cause the biggest problem since they are a wasted resource but also frequently a hazardous pollutant. There are pressures to build in recyclable elements to their design as well as in some countries creating regulations for manufacturers to pay for recovery. Perhaps of even more concern are the growing mountains of used tyres as these do not degrade but very often create pollution through fires and melting rubber. Finding a use has been a major challenge that is certainly not yet denting the backlog.

Electrical and electronic goods offer as many challenges in the waste equation particularly where again we see many purchases in order to adopt the latest model rather than to replace worn-out products. Dealing with chlorofluorocarbons (CFCs) was the first major attack on the waste mountains that in some parts of the world are now building to incredible levels.

With all this to consider one should not be surprised that there are many opposing views about the best solutions. Swedish experts opposed to separation and composting offer an interesting perspective, from a country that has a reputation for being green, promoting incineration. Many claim that incineration actually involves major transportation and is not very popular with those that live nearby. In most cases the views are limited by personal perspectives and fail to look at the bigger picture.

There is clearly a need for an integrated waste strategy and since this is only likely to happen if there is a driver from the business community perhaps that's where it should start. At the same time technological innovation will only come from the private sector. Waste must first be recognized for what it is in terms of an unused commodity and a costly environmental challenge. Zero waste may be a visionary concept but, for every business organization, there has to be value to be extracted from managed waste programmes.

In the future we may see resource recovery centres that could include separation programmes, incineration plants and composting programmes. There is a clear opportunity for energy plants being driven by integrated waste recovery. New technologies will be refined to exploit approaches such as pyrolysis, bio-mass power generation and bio-waste export programmes where waste can be used to help less fertile regions. Waste management organizations will take on the major responsibility for integrated programmes that may well link across national boundaries and into developing regions, so that we are not exporting waste and pollution but delivering new resources and benefits through processed waste.

The business community has the skills and incentive to look beyond the rubbish heaps and forward into the commercial viability of effective integrated waste management, as outlined in Figure 6.1, whether this is related to the individual operations or as part of a wider social community. The barriers to moving forward are ones which face many sectors of the business community, and which often start with public sector indifference or failure to recognize that the waste problem is one that affects everybody.

Investment and education will be the key to creating a new drive that can be both an environmental benefit and a commercial advantage. It also

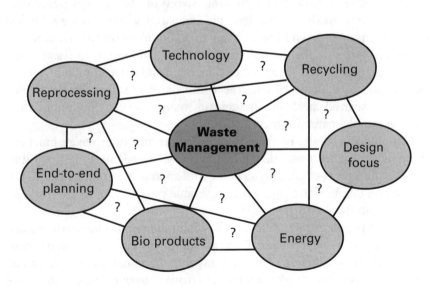

Figure 6.1 Integrated waste management

requires industry sectors to look outside the traditional boundaries and consider the implications of cross-industry knowledge, plant and resources.

Power and waste recovery processing plants make good partners, whilst perhaps worn-out off-shore platforms could become pumping stations for soluble waste. Bio-mass plants could be integrated into food-processing plants. Tyre pyrolysis plants could be integrated with conventional power stations or even nuclear plants to handle the emissions. Recycling plants need to be integrated with operations that can utilize raw materials, such as vehicle processing and steel plants. There will need to be greater exchange of knowledge and design between original manufacturers and reprocessing outputs.

Waste to power is perhaps the most integrated of opportunities since we have an abundance of one and a shortage of the other. Clearly waste products have always been used to generate heat going back to the arid lands where cow dung would provide cooking energy. Moving this to a commercial level should not be a technological challenge but is often constrained by local pressures and the problem of NIMBY's challenge. Across the world the balance between utilizing bio-waste for energy and feeding back into the soil must be watched carefully. However, refining the technology to generate energy efficiently and effectively from bio-waste would provide a valuable option in many poorer regions, as technology that helps one society handle its waste could provide an effective resource to another.

Waste must be elevated in order to address what is a major challenge for the industrialized world and a growing Sword of Damocles hanging over the developing world. In the past the industrial giants have established facilities in other countries to capitalize on low-cost production and frequently less stringent pollution regulations. This results in waste problems being established ahead of consumer demand-driven problems. In the exploitation of minerals around the world the waste deposits left behind have both scarred the landscape and in many cases left pollution waste seeping into the natural infrastructure.

Bio-products should be the aim of every manufacturer where practical. If we must produce waste then it has to be biodegradable and, if possible, suitable for reprocessing. The waste-neutral approach, as outlined earlier, is focused on taking waste through a recyclable programme, so the more we can get from the waste the better.

The short-term focus for the business community must be to concentrate on the easy wins which come from avoiding waste and eliminating non-value added consumption. This may involve the re-engineering of manufacturing processes or developing alternative designs that reduce the materials or potential for generating waste. These approaches are focused first on reducing the cost implications but, as a side-effect, they will also help to reduce the rate of consumption and environmental impacts. Reducing energy consumption has a direct impact on the production or operating costs and helps to conserve resources.

In the medium term the wider influence of the business process needs to consider the implications on supply chains and outsourced operations. Helping others to reduce waste should provide commercial benefits whilst reducing the overall consumption and waste creation. This may involve simple agreements to reduce packaging and optimize transport operations. Exchanging ideas across the trading boundaries may provide opportunities to identify opportunities to reduce inputs, materials and costs. This may well start to identify design changes that could simplify processes and incorporate alternative materials.

In the longer term we should look at the end-to-end whole life profile to ensure that products, processes and materials are optimized to minimize waste. At the same time they should be developed to integrate with recycling programmes and waste handling activities. Planning such a profile may create challenges for organizations that export their products and have little or no control over the long-term usage.

Responsible organizations would not ignore the long-term implications but less scrupulous organizations might. Thus in the longer term we must look beyond codes of conduct and address global standards that create a level playing field. The major implication is that countries such as China and India (which will be the major manufacturers and potential consumers) must establish enforceable standards if we are to create a balanced approach.

The overall challenge is of course to eliminate waste, but the practical implications of that are perhaps simply a pipe dream. We can only manage our own environment and frequently this is the business sphere within which we operate. What is important as a starting point is that waste should not be looked on as a troublesome side-effect but viewed as a commodity that needs to be exploited. The less we waste the more value we add to the business, and the more frequently we can recycle materials the more value we get from the initial investment. For some in the business world waste and new technologies offer significant opportunities.

Waste is about consumption, and enhancing the approach to waste management means that businesses also have to take their customers and consumers with them. Educating the customer is as crucial as investing in novel approaches. Reducing packaging and advertising can save much, but the value has to be appreciated by the consumer. Effective waste management has to be seen as part of company credit rating rather than simply challenging those that fail to act responsibly. We must recognize the stresses on the environment and consider that good management is a significant contribution to the community at large.

Turning waste into value ought to be a key strategic objective for every business and it is also important that legislative bodies and regulatory organizations provide the frameworks that encourage and enable organizations exploit the benefits. The growth in populations and the demands on resources mean that every practical benefit should be squeezed from the process.

CHAPTER 7

Social change

The biggest challenge from globalization has been the impact of cultural diversity. Not only do we trade across the globe, but communications have bridged the cultural divides that historically played much less of an influencing role. At the same time transfers of production have meant the breakdown of traditional communities built around manufacturing centres. The result in developed countries is that individuals and families have in the past two decades become even more transient. This in turn has in many cases contributed to reducing the commitment to community responsibility.

The traditional extended family has become significantly less prominent in the west, as has the nuclear family. In fact recent figures, for example in the United Kingdom, indicate that new residence registrations are outstripping population growth. This is likely to result in a culture that is more introverted, and perhaps the growth in online networks heralds some suggestion that we are seeing a significant cultural change. The employment profile is also undermining the stable community with greater flows and more dependence on freelance working, home working and portfolio careers. Reports from Japan also suggest that the core strength of their structure (the link between family, state and business) is also collapsing as the modern youth sees no long-term future within the old structures.

The other side of the equation has been the raising of awareness of other cultures and in the business world this has been perhaps the most volatile aspect of CSR and sustainability. Taking manufacturing or service operations to developing countries offers opportunities for business and the emerging communities. However, the local standards, growing needs, drivers and business culture approaches are frequently condemned by those who believe that these regions are being exploited. The question has to be asked, 'By whose standards?' Recently Indonesia indicated it would introduce the death penalty for illegal logging, so whilst taking the environment seriously we now have to understand the legal system; this represents a success for Friends of the Earth but a new challenge for Amnesty International.

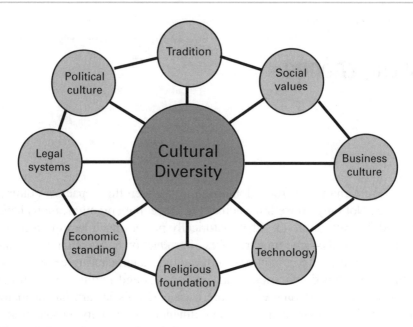

Figure 7.1   Balancing cultural diversity

We cannot separate business and industrial development from the community. For many the thrust of CSR has been to highlight the corporate support of community projects. What is at the root of a sustainable approach is how business works with the community to improve well-being, whilst balancing cultural diversity (see Figure 7.1). There have been many corporate sustainability reports that simply seek to capitalize on a small charitable donation in order to receive credit for being a responsible business.

One would not wish to stop these donations but the essence of sustain-ability for profit is to integrate the ethos into the whole operation. Clearly of course this is where the challenges start, particularly those coming from the NGOs, since cultural diversity may bring many opportunities, but it also brings many pitfalls. Understanding the social interactions that each community creates is a first step towards managing the complexities of globalization, although business leaders should not simply assume the challenges are overseas, since migrant populations are increasingly making national borders and characters very fuzzy.

There is some evidence that the way in which organizations are perceived in the market place does affect consumer confidence. It is perhaps, the hope of many that the customer will become more proactive and bring a sense of necessity to the CSR agenda. As the cultural mix becomes more apparent, one must consider that the actions of a company in one part of the world may well result in reactions in the linked community within traditional markets.

It is also worth considering the implications of Maslow's hierarchy of needs, which provides a valuable baseline from which to consider how people will react and respond to any given development. The Maslow approach envisions a ladder that starts with physiological needs such water, air and food. The next stage is safety, and concerns establishing stability and consistency. Love needs are focused on the need to belong to communities. Esteem drives the next phase, which highlights the ability to complete tasks, and the attention that comes from recognition. Finally one reaches self-actualization, which is the desire to become everything one is capable of. This simplistic profiling clearly works for all cultures and thus when we consider what our approach should be we must also recognize the stage that others may be at.

Considering these development stages in Maslow's terms one must look to globalization and its impacts on social change. Three major trends have been taking place during the last part of the twentieth century and appear to be accelerating into the twenty-first. Inter-state conflict is being surpassed by internal frictions, which provides an unstable environment for investment and development.

There is a growing disconnect between national governments and the people, with the result that internal frictions increase and in the worst cases there is an increase in ethnic conflict and refugees. Established governments in stable conditions are losing control in many areas due to increased globalization, with major corporations working outside national boundaries. A government's national economics policy is likely to be eroded through globalization and technology, whilst crime is likely to capitalize on technology and become more international.

This snapshot provides the landscape within which business leaders have to consider their investment and development strategy and within which they are also expected to focus on acting in a responsible and sustainable way. Clearly the challenge is a major one and this is complicated further by the desire of workers and consumers in the developing world to move up Maslow's scale. Their vulnerability is of course an opportunity for exploitation, but we should also appreciate that our standards may be in conflict with more immediate local needs.

The impact of demographic change on the social environment is one which is clear for all to see. The population overall is growing with an expectation of exceeding 7.4 billion over the next two decades. This growth, however, is not uniform and thus the social balance within the global market place must change. The west is an aging community, which will be less and less able to provide for itself though it will probably still control the financial markets and knowledge development platforms. Over 90 per cent of the growth will be in developing nations and this will create greater urbanization, which in less established political environments will lead to greater instability. These increases will also add to the pressure on health care, which may significantly affect the potential of some communities to capitalize on their economic strengths.

Whilst India's population will grow along with others, China's growth will be less pronounced and more level in terms of leaning towards the aging population profile, whilst Africa's population on the other hand is likely to decline as a result of the spread of AIDS. The old communist bloc is expected to see a declining population through mortality and declining birth rates due to economic pressure.

Diverging age patterns will clearly impact the drivers for different communities, bringing more focus on healthcare and training to maintain the workforce's capability. Less production capability reflects on economic growth so many communities will become increasingly vulnerable as opposed to seeing progressive improvement. This has already been visible in Africa due to HIV/AIDs. Organizations seeking to utilize the workforce in these infected regions will need to consider introducing more stable family-based communities to contain the spread.

We are also seeing the movement of people as never before, first of all from the drift towards urbanization and the cross-border migration that results from economic and political instability. These growing cities will surely test many governments' ability to provide the infrastructures to support a vastly increased population or to attract the investment to create these structures. This pressure will certainly increase the focus on any organization that chooses to trade or produce in these congested centres. Clearly the local working populations will be highly competitive given no other alternative.

These pressures on the community will probably lead to increased migration, which on the one hand may be away from low-income states and create employment pressure and unrest, whilst many low-income states will benefit from the remittances of incomes. In all these cases education and training must be a clear need and one would expect that in many cases the provision of such support will come not from local government or international aid but from the business community as a necessity in terms of building a sustainable workforce.

The downside in economic terms for the business community is that a better-trained workforce is likely to become more agile; thus retaining capability and achieving a return on investment will be a major challenge. Already in India we see that the skilled worker is ready to move on, and in some areas the local government has stepped in to control worker transfer but, without these controls, justifying investment in training and the social community may prove hard to bear on the balance sheet. The NGOs must realize that sustainability in a business context has to be balanced in terms of cost and investment.

Within the context of this population growth and increasing migration one must also consider the likely changes in communal identity and networks. The decline of traditional fixed communities, whether religious, ethnic or linguistic, will clearly offer some significant challenges to the governance of organizations. Globalization and improved communications capability has already opened the door to global mobilization of virtual communities as never before. These groupings may in the worst case be terrorist networks, but in the commercial sphere they present a major potential market force that organizations must consider. In fact they have the potential to greatly exceed the influence of current NGOs. They will provide fraternal groups that can focus on political, financial or religious issues and create pressure on business through consumer reaction or investment profiles.

Within the next two decades Islam and Christianity will be the predominant religious communities. Islam has been seen as being the growing political influence of the last decade and the most radical sects within this community have shown a complete disregard for established communities. This is not to brand all with this stigma; in the main these Muslim communities are industrious and are net contributors to whichever national state within which they reside. Christianity was seen as being in decline in the west but the population growth in Asia and South America is rapidly increasing the global head count. The decline of Marxism in China is opening the door to Christianity and Buddhism. Historically Christianity has shown it can be just as intolerant as any other religion or pressure group. These communities now span the globe and are active in the business and political spheres, whilst in many ways providing the only stability in the social environment.

The ability to mobilize these communities in a commercial context not only provides the linkages for networked business trading schemes but also pressure groups that can influence the market for or against major business investments. Linking, say, the investment capability of the Islamic community globally could significantly change the market profile of any business. Clearly there are religious perspectives to be considered where business approaches or products may offend cultural preferences.

Globalization makes the assumption that progressively there will be more international cooperation, but this must be balanced against traditional and historical influences that may well distort or crystallize opinions. Collective global communities may well take over many existing institutions or create alternatives, and although this level of interaction is perhaps too evangelical there will clearly be issues that will inspire collective action.

Certainly the youth bulge in the poorer Middle East and Asian states promotes the trend towards Islam and the involvement in trade associations, NGOs and institutions. The migrant community on the other hand may have followed economic drivers but still needs the security of a cultural homeland, whether real or virtual. Migration will not only involve the Islamic communities, but will probably be a trend that is reflected across all continents and cultures from North Africa and the Middle East to Europe, Latin America and the Caribbean into North America and southern Asia northwards. We are seeing the growth of the multi-ethnic community that shares economic growth but perhaps never drops its links to the homestead. Europe, for example, has a growing Muslim community through the accession states and Turkey.

The integration of India, China and perhaps Indonesia into the global market is creating the concept of an integrated world labour force. Education levels in these countries are improving and better communications are turning the market place into a common, agile and flexible labour pool. The rising Asian influence has prompted some pundits to suggest that western globalization is going to be replaced by Asian globalization. This clearly will change the balance of focus for many global organizations that will need to temper their approaches to match or merge with Asian approaches and values. This emerging Asian culture has already been seen reflected in the reduction of students heading westwards for education.

Current forecasts suggest that the major Asian players will see significantly higher growth rates than the developed countries, whose aging population will pull down their GDP. In time we will have to stop calling China and India developing countries because they are likely to be the market makers of the future.

There are suggestions that the globalized world of today will become more polarized in the future. The gulf will be between those that have managed integration of technology, economic and social approaches and those that have slid further into poverty and been left behind. Perhaps this is a pessimistic viewpoint because populations will still strive for improvement, and low-cost labour opportunities will keep the pot boiling. As the current low-cost market reaches a high level of economic wealth then the focus will shift.

Notwithstanding the various views and predictions, the economics associated with the middle classes in all countries will provide the stimulus for growth. Some estimates suggest it will take China 30 years to reach parity with western per capita incomes, whilst in India some 300 million live on incomes of circa $3,500 per year. This in a region where $3,000 per year is considered enough to buy a car, so we can see that an explosion in domestic demand is not far away. Having said this, there is still a large part of Africa and some Asian regions where people are living on a $1 per day.

This growth and development assumes of course that we do not see a health explosion such as SARS or the influenza virus of 1919, which killed over 20 million. Nature still has the power to put the human community in its place. Alternatively when we refer back to Maslow's hierarchy where economic or safety prevails to cause a degree of isolationism it can ignore the global impact.

Health and technology are likely to be the most important factors in developing social change. The combination of the two could radically change all predictions. Communications technology has already shown what can happen to the social environment and its influence on the business world. Biotechnology may provide many of the answers to the pressures of growing populations and reducing resources. Genetic modification has been promoted as the great provider of the future. It is, however, the merging of technology and health that will probably have the greatest impact.

HIV and AIDS are perhaps the most prominent of concerns for the global community. Current assessments of the next wave of HIV infection tends to follow the growth of many of the emerging economic powers and thus significantly impacts the business community and forward-looking strategic plans. We already understand what has happened in Africa and how this has affected the exploitation of minerals needed for growth. The spread in Nigeria follows similar exploitation of the minerals and oil reserves. Russia also faces a major challenge given its already declining workforce and economic dependence on energy supplies to the west.

The wider ramifications come from the spread of AIDS in China and India, which are predicted to be the economic engines of tomorrow. What is perhaps important to consider is that this spread has not come from the traditional hot spots of concentrated labour camps or low education; it has breached the community through plasma sales and drug use. Poor health foundations and low education contrived to allow the spread to increase in some regions. Some indicators suggest that in ten years the current epidemic proportions will be eclipsed.

The progression of the disease is also anticipated to spread outside the high-risk areas and into the mainstream populations. This will compromise the economic growth in a number of regions, including Latin America and many parts of Asia. Thus the technology-led health care advances could have significant impacts in the future. This must create some concerns for the business development focus.

Education and technology will, however, continue to be the differentiator for many parts of the global market and this too will influence economic investment and growth. The poor, one surmises, will always be with us, and business strategists must consider the implications and benefits of these deprived centres. Equality will be impeded by factors such as traditional approaches to allowing the education and development of the female sectors of the population.

The 'son preference' in India and China supported by population control policies is not likely to change dramatically in the coming years, though some progress is being made. This will cause a deficit of suitable female partners, which may increase the current assessments of a multi-billion dollar industry in female trafficking, along with the growth in prostitution.

For business organizations operating in these regions there must be concern for sustainable resources as well as pressure from NGOs with a feminist agenda. One can envisage a situation where business investors may have to take over the equalization process from governments, and this in turn will create ethnic challenges, not least because the one-child policy will also bring with it an ever-increasing aging population. India, on the other hand, is projected to outstrip birth rates in its Hindu population and this will increase the numbers left in poverty.

The standards of living in the rapidly expanding economies will not have to reach western levels before they establish a major influence on the market place. Growing demand for energy will place additional pressures on expansion and will force them to become more global, changing much of the traditional business culture, or perhaps exporting these approaches.

Migration from the developing world may help to balance the aging workforces in the developed countries. This will help in terms of the remittances back home to support struggling economies, but the downside of this will be further stretching of the cultural networks.

At the other extreme one can envisage that cultural integrity in Eurasia and Asia itself may also create a higher degree of separatism. At the same time, ease of communication and virtual networks may undermine governments' ability to retain control, forcing a more regulated environment for both nationals and foreign investment.

The growing consolidation of the Muslim community has shown the way for increased insecurity in some regions, and other ethnic communities are becoming more visible. Partly this is in response to oppression and corruption leading to instability for the business community in some regions.

These ethnic networks also provide the platform for the proliferation of criminal networks. This is not to suggest that crime is supported by ethnic or religious leaders or communities, but that common cultures do provide a communications level that enables criminal factions to exploit relationships. A common language or history will bring together communities that may then be preyed upon by criminal elements. This provides a significant challenge for the global business operation and those who would like to set standards for trading that are above corruption and exploitation.

Organized crime will blossom in resource-rich countries whether these are natural resources or labour-rich environments. As the one-party state opens its doors to a market economy, then corruption frequently follows. The same can be said where incomes rise and disposable income becomes prey to vices that previously had not been practical.

Thus as we look at the existing and predicted social change that is under way, the complexity of business strategies and relationships increases beyond what is currently to be expected. Cultural diversity brings challenges to traditional markets as well as clouding the perceptions of developing markets. Ethnic networks will increasingly provide the platform for commercial globalization. Increasingly cultural or ethnic groups rather than western developers pose a challenge for those who suggest that western exploitation will control the extended supply chain.

The vista for business leaders is one of increasing paradigms whilst those that suggest the business community should be more socially responsible must remember that much of this complexity is locally fostered. Cultural or ethnic groups may well drive market pressure in future. Exploitation may be the result of local structures and traditional approaches rather than commercial imperialism.

A sustainable business agenda must consider the social implications of investment and development strategies. Social welfare and health care may be a necessary investment factor rather than an altruistic consideration. Supporting traditional values within the local social community in order to ensure an effective workforce needs to be properly evaluated. Education and training may be the balance to what others view as exploitation, but is more likely to be driven by maximizing investment, productivity and retaining the workforce.

Integration of the global community will place considerable strain on the western business model and established socially ethical approaches. In many cases western standards will have to be readdressed in the light of new market makers and economic power bases that apply alternative perspectives. The concept of 'our way or no way' becomes blurred in an environment where we must also protect the rights of others to self-determination. Clearly we must maintain our own perspective, but we must also recognize that as the market balance changes, so too must the measures by which we judge those that work in those environments.

CHAPTER 8

Individual versus group

The fulcrum on which the whole sustainability agenda rests lies at the individual level. It may be easy to pass the responsibility towards groups such as the government or the business community, or even individual business leaders or companies. The reality is that individuals create the demand and many contribute to servicing that demand. The responsibility rests with the decisions made at an individual level and it is this pressure that business leaders understand. They can create a market demand but they are vulnerable to the influence of that market.

The individual concerned may be employee, customer, shareholder or socially responsible participant. Strategic conflict can cause internal pressures on an organization that may undermine business plans and profitability. It is also important to remember that when we criticize a company's performance, we ourselves may have influenced their actions.

The high-profile protester has caused considerable impacts on business projects and frequently its leaders. The result has been for many to ignore the validity of their concerns and seek to protect the economy and business community. In California they have passed a law that prohibits private citizens and public interest groups from taking legal action against companies unless they can prove financial harm. This Unfair Business Law will certainly not help open and constructive debate, but reflects the conflicts that are perhaps constraining real progress. As protest grows, so one can expect others to follow the Californian approach.

In today's more aware employment market many may well choose not to support organizations that do not reflect a responsible approach to sustainability. This impact on the skill base has already been reflected in the trend away from the traditional engineering and science-based industries. In part this is perhaps due to the reducing manufacturing base, but the dirty image is not one that appeals to many.

Corporate social responsibility was originally established with a focus to ensure that companies have effective management of people and processes and that these are aligned to measure the impact on society. As outlined

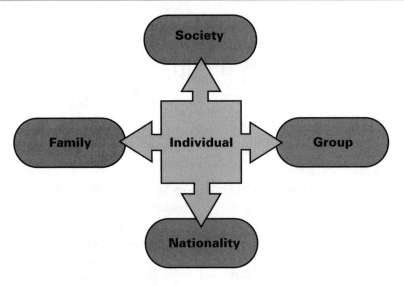

Figure 8.1 Individual connections

earlier, the CSR concept has in the main been driven towards financial propriety and the social impacts have been subjugated. Since we are all players as individuals (see Figure 8.1) the sustainability agenda needs to recognize the wide and diverse impacts of the individual in the multiple roles of employee, investor, customer, special interest group, family, cultural or ethnic participant.

The report 'Making Good Business Sense' issued by the World Business Council for Sustainable Development[3] defined CSR as 'the continuing commitment by business to behave ethically and contribute to economic development while improving the quality of life of the workforce and their families as well as of the local community and society at large'. Yet the same report produced numerous variations including 'building sustainable livelihoods' or ' business giving back to society'. It is this diversity that weakens the CSR agenda and dilutes the focus that should be on recognizing the business sector as part of a sustainable community.

There is clearly no one-size-fits-all answer and when one recognizes the individual as being the foundation of the community, and remembers that different states create differing priorities, it is no wonder we will perhaps never establish a uniform definition. The same difference will also affect individual companies by establishing a wide range of pressures.

It is perhaps less important to spend time trying to agree a common definition than it is to try to instill the sustainability ethos across the business community as part of its core strategic approach, whilst at the same time educating those outside that world to recognize that they will achieve more by working with the community rather than simply trying to pressure them. One of the dangers in agreeing a definition is that those less committed will then be able to manipulate the rules, giving us compliance rather than commitment. It is also probable, given the many failed attempts to focus world opinion and create meaningful UN directives, that they will be so watered down as to be useless. Compliance also fails to stimulate continuous improvement and thus, given that utopia is unlikely, it will never encourage development.

One thing is for certain: pressure on the business community will continue to grow. In the past decade institutions and NGOs have grown in power and, whereas the institutions are perhaps tied to nation states, the NGOs have been able to operate globally based on the energy of the individuals they represent. Yet many of the issues that concern them are frequently beyond the influence of national governments and perhaps real progress can only be made by business taking the lead. For example, Unilever introduced its own fisheries approach when governments had clearly failed to reach agreement, and used their supply chain to make a difference. However, we should not expect business to provide all the answers and neither should we abdicate responsibility to governments, which have their own priorities.

Since sustainability starts from the perspective that it affects every individual, it is important to consider the individual as the starting point. It is also important to understand that each set of circumstances creates a wide range of differing priorities for that individual to evaluate. Thus what may be a crucial issue for one person living in an economically and politically stable country may be far less important to someone trying to make a living in the developing world. It is often the fervour of those least affected that creates the pressure for change but frequently that change in policy or approach may disenfranchise those who rely on the status quo.

For many in the developing world what is considered exploitation is in local terms a good living. This is not a justification for exploitation, but a view that principles and prejudice should be balanced against the local needs. Child labour, for example, is something that has generally disappeared in the western world but remains a serious economic need in many countries for survival. Thus when organizations such as Nike are forced to withdraw from low-cost so called sweatshops the impact on the local economy is far more serious locally than it is for Nike.

What has to be considered in these cases is not the moral positioning, but whether some longer-term benefit can be derived from building on the relationship. For example, many companies now try to integrate support for children's education into the deal. The Royal Mail has just such an arrangement in Morocco where schooling is provided equivalent to the hours worked. Thus the local economy benefits, the commercial deal provides benefit and in the long term the children will also benefit.

The key to building a sustainable approach is to look at the individual level and then build up through the groups and national infrastructures. We must consider that the environment affects all inhabitants, and many who have a heritage of living off the land understand the inter-action of the eco-systems. The natives of the Amazon jungle or the Indonesian rain forests clearly inherently have a link to nature's balance. What they perhaps do not understand so well is the lessons learnt elsewhere that have resulted in deforestation, soil erosion and the failure to rotate and allow the land to rejuvenate. They are equally entitled to join the world market place and benefit from the supply and demand cycle. Forcing organizations not to trade with them is unreal, but encouraging education in forestry and land development will not only satisfy today's needs but also provide a platform for tomorrow.

There are those who suggest that certain trading practices around the world should not be tolerated. What one individual considers corruption another part of the world sees as custom and practice. Bribery and corruption is certainly bad, but frequently the challenge has to be made not at the individual level but at the systems level within which they operate. Too often corruption is institutionalized at the highest levels and trading with a nation state requires consideration for the rules of engagement. Thus one may take the moral high ground but must also understand that trading may not provide clean options in some cases.

There is much discussion centered around the principles of fair trade which promotes the concept of ensuring that local producers get a fair return for their labour and can continue to invest in a stable business. This makes sense only if individuals around the world are prepared to pay a premium for the produce. Some may describe fair trade as the right to buy balanced by the right to sell. The long-term consideration is that if producers have no reasonable return or the opportunity to maintain a living then either they will stop producing or in time they will band together to alter market prices. For the buyer there has to be a long-term strategic perspective that ensures good products, market prices and continuous supply. It makes sense not to bleed the market dry. At the same time the returns from the market are driven by the individual investors' expectations and the price individual customers will pay.

There are many who see the environmental challenges as being more important than business or the demands of the community. Frequently these individual protesters are only able to protest because they live in a society that protects their rights. In many parts of the world the environmental exploitation is driven by the state where capitalizing on natural assets is the only source of wealth creation. For example, the development of mineral assets such as gold and diamonds provides revenues and work. These particular commodities are perhaps the worst product of exploitation since globally there is more available than could ever be utilized industrially or would be needed to support the jewellery trade. Gold is perhaps the least practical of all minerals, so it is the value that is placed on these by individuals that makes them worth exploiting.

There seems to be a correlation between the level of protest and the distance from the so-called infringement. Again one must consider that in many parts of the world protest is not easy but isolation has seldom been seen to have any major impact on national governments. Local protest means real commitment to a cause and often is less attractive to the individual than a consistent living, which may or may not be less than others in the world but is better than nothing.

It may be worth considering that where business leads, eventually stability and development follow. Many would not accept that the East India Company made the most practical contribution to the development of trading infrastructures, education and economic growth. It is true that in some cases they did exploit the local community but, in the long term, they delivered a trading platform that eventually allowed local communities to stand on their own. Others would see this approach as commercial imperialism, but many would accept that business develops markets for profit while at the same time maintaining supply routes which requires investment in the community.

In many cases governments fail to negotiate conclusions to disputes based on ideology, whereas in business there is generally a compromise and a deal to be made. It is this aspect of the business community that needs to be developed and exploited in order to recognize the benefits of a sustainable approach. Those that sit outside the trading environment need to be focusing on their individual behaviour, demands from the market and working with business to find better ways of moving forward.

Invariably the whole question of sustainability comes down to one of individual choice. It starts with each individual assessing their personal needs and those of the families they support, whether this is the 4×4 driver promoting fair trade products but ignoring the environmental impacts of their lifestyle or the local worker in South East Asia who wants to improve his lot by working in a sweatshop. It may also be that education in many cases can provide the catalyst for developing more effective approaches that can benefit the local community and support the market-driven economy.

Education is crucial if there is to be long-term stability emerging from the exploitation of the market. Sharing past mistakes in many areas of environmental management may help emerging regions to avoid the same pitfalls. This of course needs to be supported by an integrated approach that does not penalize them for taking a more cautious approach. Education and training of a local workforce makes sense in the long term because this will provide further opportunities to expand the potential benefits of low-cost markets.

Helping children to earn and contribute to their families whilst also receiving an education should help create the next generation of a skilled workforce to provide continuity and further business sustainability. The more knowledge we share, the more opportunity there will be to deploy more stable and productive infrastructures that are not driven by corruption and power. This is perhaps a long way into the future but education is likely to be a more effective agent of change than excessive pressure which constrains our ability to live today.

In the industrial countries education is taken as read but frequently is based on traditional approaches, frameworks and platforms. These trading concepts have been created in an economic climate when the full extent of the potential damage being done was not fully understood. If there is to be a sea change of thinking in terms of sustainable business development being balanced with economic growth then we need new thinking for future managers and business leaders.

Special interest groups perhaps also need to consider their own motivations and the objectives which drive many of these NGO platforms. For many there has always been a clear focus on a specific aspect of environmental protection. For others their democratic protest has evolved into illegal programmes flouting the democratic rights that allow them to protest. Education should perhaps also be focused in these groups to ensure that they understand the relationship with the wider community, many of whom have developed extensive knowledge in their specialist areas; sharing this with the business community may establish approaches that share the mutual benefits of economics and environment.

The wide variety of focus groups creates confusion for those that try to balance their business operations with the realization that they also impact on the world as a whole. Frequently the response is to react to the group which holds the biggest protest or makes the biggest threats to the business flow whereas the correct and measured response should be to focus on another area. It is doubtful that any business operating in the global market place will be able to satisfy every pressure group.

What is even more important is that business takes a balanced approach and prioritizes where it can influence events. This requires the pressure groups to recognize that pure protest will only drive business to seek compliance or the protection of the law to which they are entitled. What they should be concentrating on is helping business to understand the challenges and contributing to finding effective solutions. Sadly what one suspects is that in many cases the more radical individuals within these groups are more intent on protest than they are on constructive development.

It is easy to sit at a distance and throw rocks at those who are committed to the process of creating wealth. There is no single group that has exclusive priority above all others, and for many in the business community their trading relationships will attract different pressures. It should be part of the education process to understand the integrated nature of the community within which we live, and where the benefit of creating wealth can be the improvement of the community. Clearly in many parts of the world the ability to protest is considerably constrained and frequently it is also these regions that are the focus of many protests about sustainability issues, from corruption, labour exploitation and over-development of natural resources to human rights and many others.

Whilst is important to try to help these regions evolve it is also important to understand that it is their country and their right to develop. Where business seeks to trade it must also be recognized that it does so to meet market drivers and deliver benefits to other sectors of the community. It is also likely that within some of these regions there will be groups trying to protest or change the status quo. Here we should be using all influences, including the business community, to find ways of accelerating change.

One sees the growing influence of non-state organizations creating a significant power in the global market. Whether these are religious, ethnic or focus groups they will become progressively more influential on the global stage. What is potentially dangerous to economic growth and wealth creation is if these groups can exert more power than elected governments and can damage businesses when they are not answerable to any community. Thus the responsibility of the individual and the group is to be mutually responsive to the industrial sector which whatever they may believe, will remain the engine of growth in the under-developed regions.

To continue to develop integrated strategies for economic growth, national governments will need to bring these non-state organizations into the wider dialogue or risk fostering protest that may be counter-productive.

The challenge for the NGOs is to decide if they really want to contribute to the development process and accept that not everything is possible, or whether they are simply intent on standing outside the creative process and remain protest groups that will ultimately become neutralized by communities across the globe.

The business community is crucial to wealth creation and therefore the growth and economic stability of developing regions. Their trading activities will naturally attract suggestions of exploitation in the name of profit. The right to make a profit is not one that can be removed from a free world and applies equally to the big corporation and the local farmer. The education and inclusion of the individual and the groups that grow from collective thinking is the only way to draw together the common threads that present a balanced perspective.

For the commercial leaders in the trading markets there is a considerable risk to both reputations and margins if they fail to engage effectively with the NGOs that, whilst frequently unaccountable to shareholders or the state, can influence developments. Governments must protect the right of protest and choice, but they must also engage with business and the community to focus on solutions. The NGOs must consider that while the vast majority of the public may acknowledge the importance of what is being promoted, they will probably do this only to the point where it impinges on their comfort zone or creates personal pressures. Thus goals must be reached by dialogue, debate and education.

Sustainability is a complex and integrated model that is likely to remain a major issue for the next millennium. What impact it has will depend upon the individual's choices in respect to their family and community, whether as a voter, an employee, a customer, a shareholder, a consumer or as a business leader. Business ultimately has perhaps more chance of creating effective approaches and perhaps then it makes sense to put the weight and knowledge behind the economic drivers rather than against them by trying to constrain the needs of others. It must also be recognized that many individuals do not enjoy freedom of choice and, as the trading community expands its reach, so cultural change will progressively open new channels of change.

CHAPTER 9

Pollution trading

We tend to think of pollution as a modern phenomenon and whilst it is likely that we are now creating more than ever before, it is a problem that has been with us for thousands of years in one form or another. The issue is perhaps more related to the fact that the more we understand about our environment the greater is our appreciation of the impact we are having. In some cases it is also true that technical advances have identified and curtailed some pollution whilst creating others.

As there is more appreciation of the potential dangers, so we have progressed to take steps to contain or eradicate some pollution. It is generally the high-profile events that bring pollution to public awareness, such as the Exxon Valdez (which was a manmade accident) and Shell's Brent Spar conflict with the green community. In the latter case Shell were completely wrong-footed by the public reaction to their proposals to sink the platform in the North Sea. It was perhaps the first major global case of public pressure changing a business strategy. There are those who suggest that Shell's climb down was more to do with public pressure than any scientific justification for rethinking the original strategy. Exxon Valdez was an example of the practical implications that have to be recognized when you move toxic products around the world.

We should, however, not consider pollution as being either a new issue or one which is solely the responsibility of the business community. Pollution is the result of technological advances and the demands of the population at large through consumption and choice. Those that have travelled through the less developed parts of the world will appreciate that pollution can be (and is) created in environments where there is no commercial exploitation. Clearly in toxic terms this is less damaging than some chemical pollutants but the impacts can be equally significant on the local health profile.

Thus as we advance so we release pollution or potential pollution, often without appreciating the impacts and chains of interaction we may be setting in place. Today the awareness in the industrial world is perhaps higher than it has ever been; we are paying for the ignorance of the past and trying to manage the challenges of today. It is easy to suggest that the problem rests with the business community but it should be recognized that without customer demand there is no business opportunity. Reports in 2004 identified Prozac in the water resulting from over 24 million prescriptions being issued each year in the UK. The drug is intended to help people, and whilst some may criticize the profits of the pharmaceutical industry, did anyone ever consider the long-term implications of this becoming part of the water table?

Pollution has been with us for a long time and it is perhaps to the credit of the environmentalists that we have now raised its profile in public awareness. However, long before the high profile of Friends of the Earth we understood that mine working conditions and waste outflows were damaging health and the environment. The effluent from factories created in the Industrial Revolution brought untold health problems. Smog and fog were clearly attributable to emissions from factories and power stations burning fossil fuels. Perhaps the extent of the problem was not fully understood but action to clean up the industrial centres started long before it became the vogue to be green.

The Kyoto Protocol is perhaps the first major breakthrough in terms of trying to build a uniform global approach to addressing GHG emissions. Sadly vested interests have failed to make the agreement all-inclusive, but it has also brought another concept to the fore: pollution or emissions trading. We have of course been trading pollution for much longer as part of the process of closing down manufacturing plants in the developed markets and relocating them into countries that perhaps have less stringent regulations.

This shifting of the problem through commercial development has not really changed the overall situation but it has helped the industrial countries to improve their lot and reduce emissions that have now grown as a result of other outputs, including car exhausts and increased power demand.

The concept of emissions trading in its latest guise is perhaps driven by a number of factors, not least of which is that in recognizing the challenge of changing people's habits, governments have looked to find a fudge that blends overall targets and outwardly presents a common front. It has also been adopted as a potential revenue stream so under-developed countries can share in the wealth of the industrialized world by selling emission credits. Pressure will clearly be on the business community when failure to comply with emission levels results in penalties that one doubts will be reinvested in environmental projects.

The idea that you can solve the GHG emissions issue by allowing countries or organizations to balance their excess outputs seems more like political manipulation than a practical long-term solution: in fact, one might suggest that the whole concept is akin to shuffling the deckchairs on the Titanic.

Take the concept a stage further and you open the door to the kind of initiative that Enron tried to introduce before its demise. The business model was very simple: it would insure power stations against emission penalties; at its option it would upgrade the plant, trade-off against other plants or pay the fine. This model would not actually reduce emissions but allowed the stations to continue operating. Similarly the World Bank insisted that loans would only be allowed for power station developments if they included emissions reductions systems. These systems added no commercial value but had high running costs; as a result they frequently never operated due to reported breakdowns.

Clearly industry has some way to go in terms of improving its public image and raising trust, but perhaps there is a need for a paradigm shift in thinking overall if we are really to address the growing problems of pollution. For example, instead of creating commercial offset programmes or establishing penalties and taxes to penalize polluters, there should be an environmental offset programme. This could perhaps be driven by allowing companies and developers to incorporate forest trusts that balanced the outputs. Thus companies would be planting or protecting nature's pollution filters.

Traditionally we always seem to take the approach that industry cannot be trusted to operate without regulation, and that the only measure of control is financial penalties. Perhaps some in industry deserve this burden but many would like to have a more constructive approach. The recent move towards 'polluter-pays' legislation in the EU is seen as being an inducement for more proactive consideration by the business sector through ensuring that the polluter pays the cost of cleaning up. This may be justice but is it really a constructive approach towards stopping the pollution problems? It also poses the question that unscrupulous organizations will simply try harder not to get caught, whereas the conservative organizations will increase costs by insuring against possible judgements.

The charges against Newmont Mining managers show how the environmental legal tangle can create challenges for the business community. In this case the claim was brought by an environmental group in Indonesia on behalf of a group of villagers for $543 million. This raises a number of issues, not the least of which is whether the company is liable if its employees flout company rules. If the company knew but did not act then it should pay, but is the compensation for the people, the environmental group or to repair the damage pollution may have caused?

The investment return on this mine may take a small hit if the company loses the case, and some of the managers may go to jail. They have created income for Indonesia and the local population in an area that is most inhospitable. It is a complex challenge to tie pollution down but clearly there is a need to improve awareness and consideration. Mining has always been the target for pollution protesters but, whilst there have been some very high-profile accidents involving leaching chemicals, the long-term predictions in many cases have been minimal.

Some organizations do not help themselves either in this pollution debate. Since the early 1950s the fears about nuclear power stations have attracted high-profile protests. One may remember being told that these clean energy plants brought unlimited cheap power. But in 2004 Sellafield announced a dramatic reduction in technetium-99 emissions after years of telling the public how clean the plant was.

Often the big players will be the targets for attack because they are more visible, despite perhaps being as careful as they can. In a high-profile case they will pay anyway to protect their reputation. Unfortunately the past suggests that the more you define the rules the more likely you are to see organizations trying to balance the risk. One must also consider that the source of pollution may lie outside the EU given the growth in global trade; thus the products we buy and then discard may be fine but the manufacturing process is attacking the environment in some other part of the world.

There have been suggestions that we should consider an environmental tax that is applied to every product we buy, since at least this way organizations would be less tempted to avoid controls. A development of this may be that environmentally clean products and processes would be exempt and thus create competitive advantage for those that act responsibly. It could equally be applied to imported products and thus level the playing field for the business community.

There are currently attempts to create a global league of countries that support ethical trading and we already have tables that identify human rights standing, so why not pollution or environmental management. The cynic will say it will be impossible to create such a platform given that even in the most basic of ways governments are frequently at the centre of the environmental problems. Friends of the Earth have reported that many countries in Europe, for example, do not appear to report as completely as the UK. It is also a view that revenues would never feed back into the environmental clean-up and support programmes.

It should also be debated what we consider to be pollution. The big issues of oil spills and chemical contamination from factories are clear targets for attention, but more subtle contaminations are potentially equally damaging and a lot harder to lay at any company or government doorstep. Take, for example the impacts of nitrogen wash-off from agriculture into the sea, which is creating reefs of algae that are absorbing the oxygen from the water. Some suggest that this is of greater significance than over-fishing.

The realist will acknowledge that pollution is an inevitable consequence of industrial development and that in time, if we have it, technology will eventually find ways of controlling pollution or even reversing the impacts so far. Technology may also be able to develop alternatives in many areas that negate the traditional pollutant drivers. This vision of the future is not likely to be a reality in the next millennium and, given population growth, consumer demand and economic expansion, pollution is clearly going to get worse rather than better in the near to medium term.

Pollution carries a cost to the planet, health profiles and also to the products we consume. It is therefore unrealistic to assume that we can demand a cleaner planet without accepting there is a price to pay. Companies that act responsibly and invest in controlling product impacts, whether in manufacturing or as biodegradable waste, face the dilemma of competing with lower-cost production that does not offer to incorporate similar contributions. Customers and consumers need to recognize that they hold part of the solution.

It is also necessary to recognize that long-term strategic programmes require funds, and these have to be generated from the market place. Market-friendly products are not yet at such a level of acceptance that premiums are generally acknowledged. Thus for commercial organizations the dilemma is clear: either they risk delivering a high-cost product and survive by marketing themselves as a good company, or they play at the lower level and try to balance the risk and cost implications against less scrupulous competitors.

For the business leader, pollution is no longer simply a question of paying for the clean-up or shifting the business overseas. The global market place is becoming more visible and the exposure (both legally and to reputation) can have a major cost impact. This minefield is not one to be left to chance and there needs to be a strategic approach that considers practical solutions, which are then developed effectively in the market place. Unfortunately the playing field is far from level in many sectors and those leaders that may wish to be more responsible still have to contend with the variables across national boundaries.

It is perhaps a forlorn hope that over time we could see the creation of the equivalent of the Kitemark for the clean producer. In the meantime companies should be encouraged to be aware and responsible. At the same, time they should promote their good performance and highlight their investments in improving pollution impacts. Customers and consumers need to utilize their buying power to ensure they are not indirectly contributing to the pollution arena.

The warning for the pressure groups and the regulators is that whilst there needs to be regulation in place for the minority of companies that fail to take the appropriate approaches, over-regulation will inevitably constrain real progress. Regulation taken outside a global platform will create commercial divides and periodic advantages that will by osmosis drag even responsible organizations into the void.

It must also be a consideration for those that choose to be the self-appointed guardians of the planet that spreading technology and economic growth brings with it the real potential to cause problems. What has to be the focus is the balanced view that whilst we can solve some of these pollution problems others require a breakthrough in technology. It is highly unlikely that such paradigm shifts will come without substantial investment, and that will require the business community to prosper and compromise along the way.

Enforcement of regulations must be robust to ensure that competitive advantage is not given to those that ignore the consequences of their actions. Thus the concept of pollution trade-offs being promoted at international level could inadvertently create a culture of fixes rather than effective solutions.

At a local level the more rules that are established the greater the likelihood of people focusing on compliance. It is easier to work on interpreting clearly defined rules than working within a more holistic perspective. The focus should be on looking beyond the current impacts and viewing the future with more concern. As we have repeatedly seen, many of the pollution problems of today reflect back on practice when there was less knowledge.

There are many areas that fall into the range of low-hanging fruit where the cost of taking action and the relative lack of complexity could start to make inroads into the pollution profile. Product assessment can frequently identify alternatives that can remove hazards and potential pollutants. This could be as simple as using lead-free solder in electronic and electrical equipment. Packaging, as we have seen, is a major contributor to waste mountains and thus results in pollution on a wider scale.

What does not make sense is the concept that by moving the pollution around (either actually, or virtually by trading it) we are in any way making a constructive contribution to its reduction. If the pollution is real then it needs to be addressed effectively. It may be that the approach is only seen as a mechanism to maintain political dialogue and that is perhaps a first step to global reorganization of a problem. However, emission management is largely focused only on GHG and there is much more pollution, some of which is perhaps more localized but infinitely more dangerous, such as mercury and toxins that feed into the food chain and either deplete food stocks or, even worse, affect the health of future generations.

Pollution is a factor in any developing society and whilst we may have inherited the consequences of earlier decisions it makes no sense to compound the problems or exacerbate them by further contamination. It also makes no sense whatsoever to suppress the problem by transferring it to others who perhaps do not yet realize the extent of the issue or who are economically vulnerable and thus susceptible to exploitation. The concept of pollution trading is simply hiding from the realities, which we must learn to manage and eventually overcome if we are to maintain the growth of communities within acceptable levels of risk.

Short-term financial solutions may help to bolster the balance sheet but they will inevitably come back to haunt the business leaders of tomorrow. Shareholders are also becoming more focused on the morality of their investments as well as the potential cost implications of being compromised. Companies operating in a global market will find it progressively harder to distance themselves from litigation either at home or abroad. Thus, as part of the sustainability agenda, pollution must be addressed proactively.

CHAPTER 10

Ethical trading

It would be easy to assume from reading the financial press and some of the more explosive daily papers that all business was corrupt. It is not hard from that point to make the further extrapolation that every business is exploiting everyone in order to boost profits. Like all things the truth is often a shade less black and white: the majority of businesspeople would like to operate in a straightforward manner. The realities of global trading are complex and thus so is the spectrum of issues that are inter-linked under the broad heading of ethical trading.

The past few years have seen a plethora of high-profile cases in the media that have shown the worst side of the business world. Some, such as Enron and WorldCom, do suggest that the manipulations of internal executives were driven by self-interest. Others, such as the reports of bribery associated with defence contracts, suggest that winning business in some parts of the world has to depend on joining in local practices. Those that have worked in the Middle East and South East Asia will understand that business culture. It might be fair to say that few parts of the world are exempt from practices which we would all prefer to avoid.

Ethical conduct is a requirement for all businesses, which means operating within the applicable laws, and respecting the rights of others in every sphere of operations. In the long term, operating in an ethical manner (as outlined in Figure 10.1) is a crucial part of maintaining relationships with customers, suppliers, investors, employees and the wider community.

Sustainable profitable growth depends on maintaining the confidence of stakeholders, which can so easily be damaged by being exposed to public or regulatory investigation. The labyrinth of issues that is drawn into the ethical agenda ranges over corruption, exploitation, manipulation and crime, but it also reaches to the higher ground of those organizations that choose to publicly declare and promote their individual standards.

Take, for example, the policy established by the Co-operative Bank. It has made a public commitment not to invest in any government or business that does not uphold human rights, and to avoid arms manufacture, animal

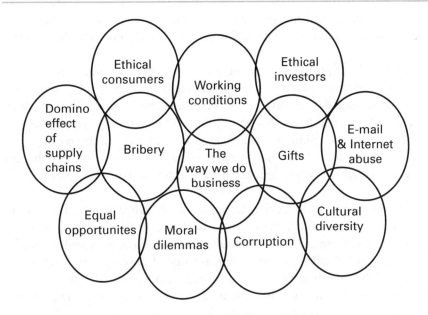

Figure 10.1   Issues of ethical trading

testing or the development of GM organisms. Some might argue that this means limiting the investment potential for its customers but it does not seem to have affected the bank's growth. It is also likely that some may criticize some of its practices since a bank that encourages customers to take credit is being unethical. But customers have a choice and the bank has positioned itself well in the market.

The World Bank in 2004 launched an initiative that requires companies bidding on large Bank-funded projects to certify that they have taken steps to ensure that no one acting on their behalf will engage in bribery. In their estimates bribery costs the global economy $1 trillion dollars per year and a substantial part of these funds is lost in government contracts. Sadly the cynic suggests that few organizations will fail to sign up, but at the same time one wonders if there will be a significant change to custom and practice in reality.

The faith and trust of the general public must be badly damaged when reading the reports on the Iraq 'Oil for Food' programme run by the UN. The former chairman of the US Federal Reserve, Paul Volcker, suggested that the programme was a shambles and that some actions were ethically improper and seriously undermined the integrity of the UN. Bribery will unfortunately always be a problem where large contracts are involved.

However, one should not ignore the fact that in many parts of the world local practice encourages facilitation payments right down to the smallest of sums.

Another high-profile case involved the international but British-based defence contractor BAe: it was suggested that large amounts of government-guaranteed funds were diverted to entertain and benefit Saudi Arabian officials. Those that know this part of the world are only surprised that this surprises any one. Similarly a Pentagon official was sentenced to jail in October 2004 for influencing a major contract with Boeing and the US military; greed is everywhere, but it should not be assumed that everyone has a price.

The dilemma for the business community is that if companies want to win contracts in some parts of the world (frequently this also involves governments) there are often conditions that have to be accepted. It may be true that in developing countries the real value of development investments may well be significantly reduced through corruption. But for the businesses trying to gain work in those areas one has to consider the pressures on them to accede to local demands.

If you take the example of Lesotho Highland Water Development (LHWD) Project, the biggest engineering project in Africa, this shows the extent to which such situations can arise and what went wrong. It is a case study in many respects of the worst type of exploitation. The project was set up during apartheid and was structured to ensure the breaking of sanctions. It was developed through a variety of consortiums and funded by the World Bank, backed by many of the major banks and underpinned by multiple government guarantees.

Many of the organizations involved had been the subject of previous corruption charges. Large sums were paid over to Lesotho officials and it is reported that the World Bank was aware of these transactions but could only take action when its own part in the project funding was involved. The case blew up when the Lesotho Government accused the LHWD CEO of taking nearly $2 million in bribes.

The project involved a number of other notable situations, which compounded the ethical dimensions of bribery. There was a violent access conflict to the water supplies; suppression of the workers who should have benefited from the construction work; environmental and social impacts from soil erosion were never considered in the project study; and many locals lost their livelihood whilst compensation was inadequate. For those looking to understand what can happen in such cases this is a classic profile of what to avoid and how not to present to the world at large.

The ethical trading environment is one that is certain to become more complex as ethnic issues are likely to divide the world and thus create a void in terms of consolidating the playing field. These will include the environment, technology, human rights, and international law. In this arena the ability of business organizations to find a clear and common platform will be greatly impaired.

With population growth the potential for local markets or migrant communities to offer themselves competitively will hold up the challenge to business not to be caught in the cross-fire of public opinion over exploitation. These issues are not just found in the developing regions as Laurel Fletcher, Professor at the University of California Berkeley's law school and human rights researcher, suggests that migrant workers across the USA are subjected to forced labour. She suggests that slavery is not a historical problem but is prolific today in many poorly regulated industries dependent on low-cost labour. It is also known that in many cases those within their own ethnic community are exploiting this labour so the cries of commercial imperialism should perhaps be tempered.

Typically there are many regions where internal ethnic conflict and exploitation pose a serious potential challenge for the business community. Sub-Saharan Africa remains perhaps the most fragmented region and one which also carries a poor reputation for institutionalized corruption. The human rights record across this region leaves little to the imagination but it also attracts many wishing to exploit its mineral resources. At the same time it is a region that is highly focused in terms of aid and development programmes aimed at lifting the economic growth potential.

Unfortunately even aid-based programmes in these regions tend to suffer from substantial levels of cash siphoning. Companies tendering for contracts find themselves faced with very clear options: play the game or get off the playing field. This becomes even more concerning when we envisage the G8 countries looking to write off debt and promote more investment and aid packages to address the social and economic problems. Unless aid programmes can be driven and controlled outside the local government infrastructures there is a strong possibility that past problems will simply be repeated. Development aid should perhaps be financed and directed by those contributing the money rather than simply handing it over.

In the global market place one must also consider the implications of organized crime. The attraction of stable governments is that they provide a relatively predictable environment, which may be why one hears that random terrorism gets little or no support from the crime organizations. However, institutionalized terrorism, as can be seen in many longstanding conflicts, actually promotes and integrates crime to fund its activities. On the other hand, countries that are unstable provide an environment where crime can be embedded in the institutions, making corruption politically correct.

Early investors in Russia after the economic upheaval found themselves negotiating contracts with both government bureaucracy and established crime bosses. In fact, some reported that these were often the same person but at different times. Given this complex infrastructure is difficult to see how business leaders can be sure of staying within traditional ethical practice. According to the European Bank for Reconstruction and Development between 4 and 8 per cent of a company's annual revenue is the cost of bribery in Russia.

In other parts of the world this figure would be considered low by comparison. This may be hidden within an agent's charges or a representative's cost but despite most states having legislation to prohibit facilitation payments, in many places every government employee expects a tip for doing what he or she is paid for.

It is a commonly held view that over the next two decades trans-national crime groups will become even more adept at capitalizing on cross-border trade. Criminal organizations will proliferate in parallel with the growth in migration and global trade, which again will offer little comfort for those trying to operate in a responsible way and avoid the pitfalls.

Estimates suggest that narcotics trafficking alone represents a $100–300 billion annual turnover. The funds and reach available to some of these crime networks will provide them with the capability to corrupt unstable states and their officials to the point where illegal activities will be legitimized, adding further concern that aid investment may be diverted from its targets. It must become a priority to structure trade, aid and debt programmes to ensure transparency and control.

Illegal toxic and hazardous waste dumping represents a black economy that turns over $10–12 billion a year, whilst theft of intellectual property and pirating is costing industry £1 billion per year. The CIA estimates corruption globally to have reached around one per cent of global GDP, or $500 billion per year. Whatever the figure really is it is substantial, and suggests that few (if any) major business transactions are proceeding without some form of financial influence being involved. The question that must be asked before the business leaders are hung out to dry is whether they are instigating the flow or simply being forced to respond to market trends.

Transparency International (TI) has established itself as a leading NGO focused on eradicating bribery and monitoring progress towards that end. In October 2004 it issued a corruption index based on 2003 findings; this identified and graded some 106 countries as having a rating of less than 50 per cent, whilst 60 countries scored less than 30 per cent, indicating rampant corruption. Amongst the most corrupt countries were Bangladesh, Haiti, Nigeria, Chad, Myanmar, Azerbaijan and Paraguay.

Corruption is a big risk to business but the solution is not an easy one to digest. TI suggests that the traditional argument of not being able to stop because of unfair competition is not valid since other countries claim the same principle; experience suggests they would say that. Validating local agents, representatives or joint venture partners is only practical to a certain extent and, where these relationships are embedded in local legislation, choice is limited. Facilitation payments and extortion during execution of contracts are realities, not myths.

TI proposes that these problems can be overcome by international agreement and by governments; institutions and companies should establish and maintain codes of conduct. Enforcing such an approach means that companies and governments must be ready to walk away from business and penalize companies that break the rules. The idea is to be commended but regulations are already in place in most countries, even those that are renowned for being corrupt, and still it happens even at the highest level.

Many anti-bribery conventions have been established in Europe, USA, Latin America and Africa. Codes of practice have been agreed in many sectors of industry but compliance remains the challenge. Simply defining bribery may be a significant problem given the confusions of political contributions, philanthropic contributions, gifts and hospitality, and facilitation payments.

Whilst the recognizable ethical issues of bribery, corruption and crime are important, they are not the only manifestation of ethical trading. The majority of business operations depend on external supply chains: on average this represents at least 50 per cent of the operating cost and in many cases will run as high as 80 per cent. Thus the impact on the bottom line from effective supply chain management is a crucial part of profitability. Little wonder then that pressure on price and delivery is frequently translated into downward pressure on the suppliers and producers.

The question is when does negotiation become coercion; when does a self-funding business model become an unfair trading relationship? Many will focus on the extremes and ignore the majority of trading relationships that are founded on traditional commercial interaction. Clearly many see that purchasing power provides significant leverage to ensure that suppliers operate within sustainable practices, do not use forced labour, comply with national employment laws and working hours; accept trade unions, pay living wages, do not abuse employees and operate within the local law. The challenge is, in a global trading environment, whether organizations can afford the investment and monitoring costs and remain competitive. It must also be recognized that given the diversity of many industries, setting benchmarks across regions and cultures is extremely difficult.

Supply chain power and management may seem a simple activity but frequently the production and delivery process is a complex chain that bridges many countries before reaching the consumer: one only has to follow the chain from African child labour harvesting cocoa through to the professionally operated chocolate manufacturers. What are perhaps more manageable are the intermediaries and global market traders who govern the commodities price structures and drive down labour costs, or the working conditions for products such as clothing and electrical goods where parts emanate from local sweatshops to eventually be combined in well managed and controlled assembly plants.

Many organizations have internal codes of conduct and several have contributed to programmes such as the Ethical Trading Initiative (ETI). Organizations such as supermarkets invest a great deal to try to understand the supply chain and help producers. Just taking this area of the market place offers a number of contradictions and challenges. It also highlights the difficulty for these organizations in trying to balance a price-driven market and the wider challenges of satisfying every NGO that has a protest to pursue.

Supermarkets are perhaps the pinnacles of supply chain management in the modern developed world. The big names, including Wal-Mart, Carrefour and Tesco, have brought value to the consumer through large-scale buying power, but the producers who supply them might offer a very different perspective on the success of these ventures. Clearly many suppliers would be reluctant to speak out but it does not take much imagination to consider the influence that consolidated buying power can produce.

When you control the outlets to the customer and take 90 per cent of the produce, dictating the terms is easy; and when this is set against a background of high street competition the short-term answer is obvious. This does of course lead to major questions about whether in the longer term these suppliers can continue over time to maintain output and quality. If they cannot, are there other competitors out there to take their place? The customer clearly is the real catalyst for change in that consumer choice can change the demand profile.

It does not only affect small local producers. The demand for flowers causes a delivery cycle that allows only 24 hours from order to point of sale. In Africa this means workers arriving without any idea whether they have work for the day and, if they do, they have almost impossible delivery times in order to meet planes the same evening. On the other side of the coin the major manufacturers, such as Procter & Gamble, declared their £30 billion take-over of Gillette would strengthen their negotiating position against the big buyers such as Wal-Mart.

In many cases the market has driven the exploitation of low-cost labour production, and frequently new competition has used this edge to open the market. The net result is that every other player has then to look for similar cost advantages and the exploitation spiral goes on. In China the economic upturn has resulted in regions such as Guandong facing wage increases to such an extent that many clothing factories import labour from villages in northern China. It is right that we do not accept human rights violations but it is more difficult in a business environment to govern the competitive challenge and maintain the ethical position, particularly when the perceived exploitation is an internal issue.

In the ethical market place we would never see people being exploited or human trafficking, either illegally or fashioned within local regulations. It should however, always be recognized that, given the alternatives, exploitation frequently offers them a better future. Similarly we hear much talk about the lack of equality for women around the world and, whilst not wanting to appear chauvinistic, it has to be remembered that in many parts of the world emancipation has still to happen and that requires a substantial cultural shift. In the same vein equal opportunities may be a desire but personal choice also has to be protected. Regulating for today's disaffected is likely only to create a new group tomorrow.

There is frequently a moral dilemma between what is locally acceptable and what other developed societies may consider acceptable. It will take time to change and during this evolution working within a community will probably be more influential than isolating those we do not agree with.

Perhaps one of the most influential developments in the past decade has been the proliferation of the Internet. This in many ways has helped to improve information flow and knowledge of others. It has also been used to build NGO networks and focus opinion on those working in the global community. At the same time it has allowed many more undesirable influences (such as paedophilia) to spread. We do not suggest that Internet providers should be shut down, but we must try to put controls and codes of practice in place. Unfortunately the worst elements of society will always circumvent acceptable practice.

What many in the business community (and frequently the less experienced buyers) are perhaps missing is that poorly paid or badly treated workers are not likely to be the most efficient. Poor factory conditions do not help in maintaining quality or productivity. Training costs are not optimized if workers are ill or injured and cannot work through bad health and safety arrangements. Whilst it may not be possible to immediately eliminate child labour in some regions, developing those children through education provides a better workforce for tomorrow.

It is interesting that in many predictions for the future including those tomes produced by the National Intelligence Council (NIC) (*Global Trends 2015*),[4] ethical trading fails to reach the agenda for potential international cooperation, even against a background of increasing economic growth and globalization. Perhaps the reason is that collaborating on legal and humanitarian issues does not impinge on the trading community.

Trade, as highlighted before, is driven by demand and fuelled by the differential between buyer and seller. Thus we should expect that some degree of so-called exploitation will always exist and in recognizing this it is also unlikely that governments and regional pressure groups will ever really seek to level the playing field. World Trade Organization agreements on trade are largely driven to avoid trading conflicts that may break down the platform of trade. However, for most countries the ability to exploit economic resources and balance the trade gap has a higher priority than focusing on a global ethical trading code of conduct.

In this situation the two major influences that have the power to impact on trade exploitation are the consumer and the investor. It is also important that the business community recognizes the potential of these groups to significantly impinge on their market strategies and global supply aspirations.

The ethical customer or consumer can set their own standards in respect to a wide variety of issues by introducing measures to demand that suppliers comply with a minimum standard and in special cases specific personal choices, such as women in the work place. These customers, however, will have to appreciate that in doing so they may have to compromise on price and choice. The likelihood is, based on the Fairtrade market, that we are a long way from this kind of power being realized, although on a product-by-product basis isolated cases may impact organizations that take their eye off the ball. One would hope that this pressure would recognize that most companies are trying to do the right thing, but will inevitably fail at some point.

The other side of the coin is the attitude of the ethical investor. As mentioned earlier the Co-operative Bank has made its position very clear. The big institutional investors frequently have some degree of focus on where they will and won't support companies in the market. Smaller investors may have less individual impact but collectively they can slew markets; frequently these are the same people who are members of some NGO.

In most cases one has in the end to take a view very much at the personal level, whether one is a consumer, investor, business leader or employee. The ethical dilemma is one that has no perfect solution. Standing for a principle may damage shareholders, employers, customers and frequently the local people that one is trying to protect or benefit. Most ethical decisions in the main will differ case by case and thus must be ultimately made on a case-by-case basis. Companies should be very clear to their stakeholders about what are the positions they will take and be prepared to defend them. Those outside the business world should be prepared to accept that others might have a slightly different perspective that is equally valid.

CHAPTER 11

Technological impacts

Since the Industrial Revolution the pace of change has been gaining speed exponentially. The advances in communications technology have opened up the global market place, whilst developments in many other areas have introduced benefits and potential dangers. As with most things, technology can be both benefit and curse in terms of sustainability.

New product development (NPD), innovation and research and development (R&D) are key factors in any business process seeking to build new customer offerings for the future. A study of FTSE 100, however, indicates that only 20 per cent reference sustainability in their development programmes. Exploiting technology may push the boundaries for one sector of the community whilst creating new challenges for the rest. One only has to look at the problems of disposing of electrical goods and fridges, not to mention the impacts of electronic and mobile phones. We have benefited from the use of these technologies but are now slowly being drowned in waste that is not easily processed. At the top of this pile is the heritage of the nuclear programmes, which provides significant impact but leaves us with a waste that will last over 1,000 years.

Technology must therefore be one of the key ingredients for a sustainable future given that we cannot go back to the caves. Additionally as more and more of the global population will be looking to increase their standards of living, in the future the challenge will be to balance this technological spread against the impacts overall.

Those who develop technology claim in the main to be driven by wanting to benefit society, although some (it is clear) are driven more by the challenge than they are by the benefits and others by the chance of financial return There has always been a love–hate relationship between society and the scientists and perhaps this is not a bad thing in that it creates a brake on what might otherwise be runaway developments. However, it often seems that the discussion phase takes place behind closed doors, then launches into developments with little chance of constraining progress.

Technology is only part of the equation and it should always be balanced

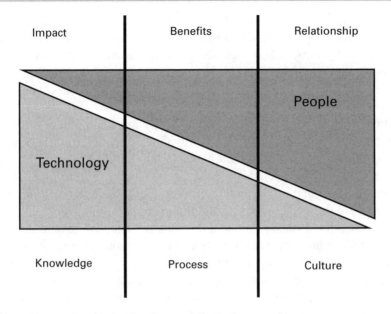

Figure 11.1   Balancing technology and people

against the community it is designed to serve (see Figure 11.1). The development and adoption of technology has to progress from knowledge to practical processes for delivery but it frequently clashes with the culture of the community. The relationship between people and technology is governed by two key aspects, the first being the benefit and the second being the impact. To this end one of the problems seen with the technologists is that they fail to spend sufficient effort on extrapolating the impacts over the longer term. Perhaps if they had we would be less concerned for nuclear power because we would have addressed the bigger issues. The impacts of disasters at Three Mile Island and Chernobyl have not dimmed enthusiasm for nuclear energy to fill the growing shortage. Given where we are, the future has to look to technology to provide some of the answers to the challenges of today.

With the challenges we face it gets a little disheartening to see NASA considering an asteroid protection programme. Certainly we are all aware of the potential impact if an asteroid crashed into our planet, but in the meantime there are a billion starving people who don't know or perhaps care. It is this kind of abstract technological investment that weakens people's belief in the scientific community.

Technological innovation can offer opportunities to reduce costs, create new niche markets by selling sustainability as part of the package or create new products with a sustainable contribution. Take as an example the Honda IMA programme, which seeks to sell technology, based on an integration of benefits linked together to save the customer money, whilst saving energy and contributing to the sustainable agenda. The green car is clearly a challenge but many other areas are looking to use technology to reduce pollution and improve efficiency.

Take, for example, the domestic gas heater that can produce electricity. Solar power and wind energy are being adopted by high-profile organizations, such as the FedEx in their Oakland hub building as part of a wider strategy, which also includes hybrid electric trucks. Future products will need to push technology even further to be able to address whole-life products that are designed to recycle and minimize pollution.

The latest enthusiasm following hard on the heels of genetic modification is nanotechnology, which involves the development and use of microscopic particles. However, as with genetic modification the implications are already starting to raise questions, as it has been reported that nanoparticles anoparticales have been found to cause brain damage in fish. Once again the quest to push the boundaries is perhaps outstripping the desire to understand the implications. Since many of these groundbreaking technologies are at the very edge of current knowledge, a little caution would perhaps be appropriate.

In fairness there have been moves at a more practical level to look towards environmental impacts being designed into products, such as the ISO 14001. These cover many aspects such as resource productivity which seeks to consider all materials uses, material intensity and mass balance analysis (mba), identifying where the material will eventually end up (say, for recycling and reuse). It involves lifecycle analysis as well as energy inputs to the production process, together with an ecological foot print analysis to consider the wider eco-systems. This at least starts to put a common focus into the material and product development process, though one fears its application may be more in compliance than commitment.

New technology can certainly help to improve the human challenges and underpin sustainability. Advances in medical technology and genetic engineering may well be able to create breakthroughs. A focus on food development and improvements in managing potable water will certainly address some of the current issues around population growth. The expanding wireless technology and perhaps translation capability will also help to level out the playing field. Some regulatory challenge will probably also be created by advances in technology in areas such as new materials, computers and communication. National focus on controlling and retaining technology is likely to lead to even more opportunities for a black economy and to a growing rift between the haves and the have-nots, but as global R&D activity spreads out, major organizations will be forced to look at how they control sensitive technology.

Biotechnology perhaps offers the greatest opportunity to address many of today's health, environmental and agricultural issues. Some would suggest that eventually it provides the ability to level many of the regional imbalances. Considering the impacts of HIV/AIDS, one would hope that technology could redress the current trends. Unfortunately these new technologies also have the potential to add to today's risks through poor management or even terrorist activity.

Technology may also provide the next global shift in economic terms as the historical technology leaders are now losing ground to the likes of India and China. The number of engineers graduating in the west is significantly down on those coming from China. This has both economic and cultural implications. On the one hand, those that traditionally held the technological lead also were able to influence economic trends and regional development. The focus in the future may tend more towards rapid economic growth rather than a wider humanitarian investment profile. We should also consider that the growth in communications capability and reach provides the platform on which global terrorists can learn, fund-raise and communicate. This creates instability when the business and governmental focus is on stability and sustainability.

India and China will no doubt lead the way in the future and become major players in the technological field considering that already they significantly impact global manufacturing. Advances will help in all the key areas that are currently constraining their economies, such as the need for alternative materials, waste management, energy and health. This change in the technological ownership profile could have significant impacts on the future sustainability platform since they will certainly have an alternative mix of technology and culture affecting the economic business model.

It is important to recognize that many of the new technologies developed for good may come up against ethnic barriers. Areas such as cloning, genetic modification and biomedicines could engender rejection in some communities in the same way as we have in the past seen food aid rejected on religious grounds. In some ways the industrial world's focus on environmental development may even be viewed as an attempt to constrain growth in the developing states and thus create pressure to ignore the knowledge that current technology has provided.

Information technology will continue to build on its impact which is perhaps the biggest shift since the Industrial Revolution, whilst GM crops may help to address the problems of the billion starving people in the world. The consideration then is once you have fed these people, where do you go next? If starving regions become well fed, the next step is industrial development, further compounding the challenges of today. They will represent future low-cost economies that will need industrial investment.

This potential expansion of demand in the Third World means that the pressure is on to find solutions to the environmental problems of today. There will be greater need for energy so potentially more pollution emissions and demands for resources like fossil fuel. The more products that are consumed the greater the need for new materials that have a life cycle design and biodegradable or reusable impact.

Innovative technology may well be focused on new ideas but this should not ignore the need to consider alternative uses for existing or 'old' technology (say, for example, computers and computer chips). As part of the drive for sustainable development is education, the redeployment of old PCs offers the potential to recycle machines that have been previously scrapped. Perhaps we should be looking harder at the consumer society and be developing ideas to share the waste to the benefit of others, introducing the concept of innovative holistic thinking as in Figure 11.2. Once again, however, the spread of communications technology will invoke concerns around culture contamination.

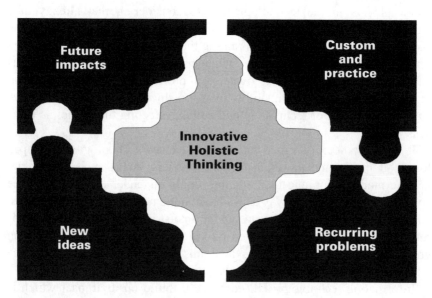

Figure 11.2   Innovative holistic thinking

The challenge for the business community is perhaps to look not simply at new technology and further advances but also to address some of the recurring problems of today. New materials may create new products but more importantly, they can effectively replace the materials in today's products. Industry also needs to look at past customers and practice to evaluate and adapt with a more sustainable focus. These same elements need to be considered when aiming to take new technological developments into the Third World.

Perhaps the most important aspect of technological development is to ensure there is sufficient focus on the future impacts. It is easy to blame current business leaders for many of the problems we now face. This ignores the fact that decisions made in the past were often limited by the knowledge of the time, though sometimes there are cases where the detrimental impacts were ignored, such as smoking. However, the leading edge of technology today is breaking most of the known knowledge boundaries and there should be greater control and concern for the long-term impacts.

Technology has the potential to change the face of the global community over the next 50 years. One hopes that not only will it find new benefits but it will also find solutions to some of the key challenges we face. Industrial development and economic growth demands more energy of which currently the only major source remains fossil fuels (oil, gas and coal), which have already had a major impact on the environment. Nuclear power or renewable energy creates a major cause for debate.

CHAPTER 12

Energy

The fundamental catalyst and ingredient for industrial development and the economic evolution of the developing countries is energy. Ever since the Industrial Revolution harnessed steam power the impacts have been enormous both in terms of the advances that have been made and the impacts on society and the environment. Even before the emergence of oil as the prime energy source coal was already driving the industrial engines of the world to create new industries, technology, employment and wealth, leaving in its wake scars on the communities it served. Much of the pollution and environmental impacts, which perhaps were not fully appreciated at the time, we now understand far better.

It is easy for those that stand on the sidelines to focus on the producers and consumers but their own futures and in many cases freedoms have come from this core of energy. The more we understand the implications of energy creation the more we need to adopt a more integrated and realistic approach (see Figure 12.1). For the business community energy is a costly commodity which frequently drives the potential for economic development. It, therefore, makes sense that reducing demand through greater efficiency would also benefit the industrial consumers as well as the environment.

Fossil fuel (oil, gas and coal) remains today the mainstay of current energy production and clearly will continue to dominate for decades to come. Estimates suggest that the growing demand for energy, which is expected to reach 50 per cent higher than today (particularly in the emerging industrial nations), will have a significant impact on the global trading environment with China and India at the fore. Despite the trends towards more efficient use of energy this growth reflects back on the 34 per cent level of growth in the last two decades. There has been considerable focus on renewable energy sources in recent years but even the most optimistic forecast suggests this will not exceed 8 per cent of need in 30 years' time. Those countries with a crippling need for energy to fuel their industrial expansion will tend not to use these green energy sources but will bank on conventional approaches and nuclear power.

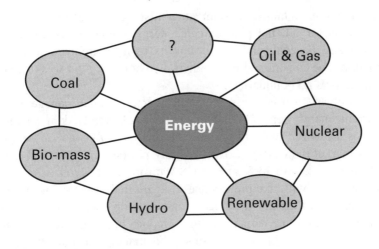

Figure 12.1 Integrated energy programmes

Whilst the International Energy Agency indicates that with substantial investment in new plant energy needs can be satisfied this relies on new areas of development being opened up. Estimates suggest that 80 per cent of the world's oil needs and perhaps 95 per cent of natural gas remains in the ground. Technology is supporting exploitation in more remote regions. Future oil production will increasingly go towards Asia and, with greater instability in the traditional supply regions such as the Middle East for oil, continuous availability must be a major concern for all and in particular the industrial business community. Given these potential economic risks and the implications for the environment of pollution increasing further, sustainability must maintain its focus on a balanced approach to energy needs.

Similarly those under-developed regions that are sitting on these resources need to be managed effectively to ensure that the mistakes of the past are not repeated. Increasing demand may create significant competitive challenges, and disruption in oil supplies may well drive new economic stresses. We cannot restrict what other nations do with their resources but, working together, these opportunities need not be turned into the next generation of environmental disasters.

India and China, for example, lack the domestic energy programmes to sustain their expansion and thus must rely on external sources. This has been reflected in increased overseas investments in projects outside their borders, which in turn will impact on trading and political policies. Some experts suggest that these countries will have to, at least, double their energy provision to maintain their development. Whilst they will certainly increase their demands for oil, the predominant energy source in the immediate future will still be coal, and this brings its own environmental impacts which will not be constrained within their own borders. As it was once put, 'the wind knows no boundaries'.

There is clearly a need for some form of international management of both current energy demands and the impacts of greater demand in the future. It is, however, more likely that the pressure of economic devolvement and market demand will over-ride any political international agreement. One only has to look at the USA position on Kyoto to see that national priorities will take precedence. It again makes sense for the business community to look at their needs and develop energy strategies that focus on the bottom line whilst helping to reduce the longer-term impacts. Certainly the reduction in western industrial demand, as manufacture heads east, will help as knowledge-based businesses have lower fuel needs, but consumer demand will continue to increase and this is where education and a collaborative approach will be crucial.

In the USA, for example there are many reports of the fuel economy of cars dropping by 6 per cent over the past two decades. These reductions have been challenged by many based on the measurement approaches being unreliable. But what is not in doubt is that the number of cars has increased exponentially and this is a common trend throughout the western world. So whilst cars may be better in terms of environmental impact the balance is far from beneficial overall. Add to this the fact that as the number of cars increases, so does the amount of road needed. Many drivers will share the thought that congestion is perhaps burning more fuel than actually driving. One thing that is certain is that individuals will not give up their cars: efforts to tax them off the road have failed so far, and would put most democratic governments at risk.

The fuel cell may in the longer term offer a real opportunity to reduce pollution and demand on oil but there is still a lot of development work to be done to address the range and performance issues. One hope is that its development is not constrained by oil producers trying to avoid competition, as was the case of Bryant & May and the everlasting match.

For years we have been told that diesel fuel is much cleaner than gasoline because it produces less lead, which is not good for people. NASA, however, recently issued a report saying that diesel soot is significantly contributing to global warming as it stops snow and ice reflecting the sunlight, which is contributing to melting the ice. It is of no surprise if we can't measure things consistently that consumers lose interest in the predictions.

Many business organizations have taken the step of suggesting they will become carbon-neutral as part of their CSR profile. HSBC announced, for example, that it would spend £4 million to introduce a programme that would include reducing energy consumption and travel, whilst improving green energy and energy efficiency programmes, participating in carbon trading and planting trees. All this is very laudable but many NGOs would suggest that it is little more than a publicity stunt when compared with their involvement in financing environmentally damaging projects such as dams, oil exploration and mines. What are perhaps not considered are the regulations that govern many of these projects, with which both HSBC and their partners have to comply.

The business of banks is to make money and as such one should expect that they largely have to follow the trends of the market. The fact that they are doing something should be applauded and not condemned as a PR stunt; on the other hand, perhaps HSBC should also declare its policy in the same way as the Co-operative Bank has done. The issue that many other organizations should consider is that saving energy is likely to be a good investment strategy as well as a benefit to the wider energy challenges.

Let us take as another example BP, perhaps one of the largest companies in the world, with a turnover that dwarfs many nation states. It has achieved a very high profile through its stated intention to adopt a more sustainable approach and become a sustainable energy company. This has clearly attracted a lot of comment from the NGOs who would like to see no oil exploitation; but one feels impelled to ask whether they drive to the protest in their cars. BP has a traditional end-to-end oil and gas delivery business from exploration to filling stations but many perhaps don't realize they are also one of the major solar energy manufacturing companies.

It might be easy to assume that BP has reoriented its business simply to shield its activities, which even it would agree has the potential to damage the environment. It would not, however, have any business at all if there were not a market for these products and activities. Years ago we worried if there would be enough oil; now we worry about emissions and environmental damage through exploitation.

As a major player in resource exploitation companies such as BP are perhaps better placed to manage the environment than many of the governments that want their help to exploit those resources, yet many would suggest that a sustainable profile is just a sop to the environmentalists. The reality is that we need the oil and gas and are a long way from substituting newer renewable energy sources so it makes more sense to work with such companies than simply stand on the sidelines and throw rocks.

Oil may be the most volatile of the energy sources but it should also be remembered that over the past two decades we have seen substantial shifts towards natural gas. In part this was due to the cost and availability implications of oil in many regions but also because gas is far more environmentally friendly although it is perhaps equally damaging in the wider context of sustainability. In the first place natural gas needs the same exploration approaches as oil but, once found, needs greater pipeline infrastructure to distribute it. The geopolitical nature of gas supply will force many industrial regions to become almost exclusively linked to supplies across borders. This limits its suitability in many of the developing economies as a practical energy source. It also unfortunately in today's volatile political climate makes its stable supply very vulnerable to attack. The dash to gas has already started to bite in many areas as costs, once customers are locked in, have started to escalate, which may change many people's views in the longer term.

Hydro-electric programmes offer a solution in terms of power generation and the emissions challenge, but it too brings a high cost in many other respects. Creating dams is a high capital cost approach and clearly is limited by geography. But perhaps more important are the wider impacts that such mega-projects can create. China's Three Rivers programme is totally changing the social and environmental structure of a vast region of central China. The cost in terms of human rights has frequently been the subject of discussion and protest. The Nile dam brought with it a significant problem when the Nile river flow was interrupted, creating an environment for parasites to breed. In most cases the development time for such projects will never match the increasing demand for growth.

Despite the fetish for alternative energy power sources (such as wind power), the immediate solution to energy needs remains nuclear power which, if managed properly, can provide the cleanest form of energy with minimum impact on the local environment. Thus almost all western countries are re-evaluating their nuclear generation capabilities and needs, whilst developing nations such as China and India are heading down the nuclear route (though some believe this is more to secure military benefits than power supply).

Many will contest this view by suggesting that we are simply building up problems for the future. Their view may be valid and clearly there are many issues to be addressed. The challenge is not to simply ignore the possibility but to invest in the knowledge base to find more suitable ways to manage the issues of contamination and long-term waste processing. Unless there is a breakthrough in areas such as fusion power there is unlikely to be a more productive alternative that has the ability to generate its own fuel source and thus provide clean sustainable power.

Fusion energy of course has been promising to come for years but so far the reports suggest that whilst the theory is there the practical proof has not been achieved in anything other than laboratory conditions, and is thus not repeatable. Existing nuclear plants are reaching their shelf-life and many of the skills have been lost as we swing away from nuclear energy, but, it does offer a solution providing it is properly managed. In Germany the green lobbies have got their wish and German nuclear plants are being decommissioned, whilst France has a high dependency on nuclear generation and will be processing much of the waste from these German plants. The risks across the borders (as was shown with Chernobyl) are perhaps less important to them than NIMBY considerations.

In the US up to 20 per cent of power generated reportedly comes from nuclear plants, and new plants are planned. None has been built since Three Mile Island but the cost and availability profile do offer an attractive economic solution to the growth in energy demands. It makes one wonder how they could possibly replace this level of energy from existing conventional generation. Like most things, when Oppenheimer created the atom bomb it was envisaged as being for good in the long term, so perhaps the real challenge is how we manage knowledge.

Strangely coal is perhaps the potential saviour in all of this. It was after all the driving force behind the Industrial Revolution and, given the global needs for energy, will continue for many decades to be the mainstay of power generation. The problem has been that carbon emissions and pollution are the by-products from these plants. Bearing in mind that major players such as India and China have substantial reserves of coal (and, in the case of India, limited alternatives), clean coal must be a consideration.

Coal-fired generation represents around 40 per cent of global output, and coal reserves are perhaps three times the size of natural gas reserves. Those that currently have pollution controls in place are limited and even those built under World Bank demands frequently do not operate the flue gas cleaning systems as they are costly. The answer would perhaps be green or clean coal super-critical technology, which operates at vastly higher temperatures and substantially reduces emissions. With development these plants could be improved to the point where they can equal the emissions of natural gas plants. Looking further ahead, carbon capture and storage as part of these processes could take the emissions to minimum levels.

For regions that require increased power generation to sustain their development clean coal approaches should be the norm. Not only are they potentially more cost-effective, but they require coal mining economies to be maintained where piped natural gas does not, and thus they contribute to the local economy. In the industrialized western countries clean coal offers a viable alternative to natural gas and nuclear plants where a balanced mix would perhaps give more economic stability.

It is suggested by some that clean coal technology fitted to existing plants could be as much as one-sixth the cost of wind power. That begs the question as to why such economic factors are not higher up the discussion agenda. Wind power is of course the great white hope for energy production. It is claimed to be totally renewable but has a high capital cost and a few other challenges to face. In the UK, for example, it is envisaged that wind power will in the foreseeable future not reach more that 8 per cent of generated power.

Wind power ticks all the right boxes for those that think fossil fuels and nuclear generation are unacceptable. They do, however, have a number of issues to address before they can be seen as the friendly solution that many would have us believe. First, they are expensive and frequently spoil the landscape in a way that conventional power stations do not. Vast fields of steel towers are not very attractive and as such cause just as much protest. Perhaps they could be built in less contentious places, but so could other solutions.

The wind may be a constant source of energy but many of these plants have to shut down in high winds for safety reasons. They seriously endanger wild life, and in particular birds, limiting the locations where they can be used. They have a tendency to interfere with aircraft radar and thus again sites are limited. The off-shore wind farm makes a lot of sense but one suspects this will significantly increase the capital investment and service costs. Those that live close to these plants may well be in favour of off-shore locations but one has to understand the potential damage to sea life, though reports do suggest molluscs do like them, which probably means more increases in maintenance costs.

Renewable energy is clearly a growth industry and one which should contribute to the overall sustainable agenda but, like many other aspects of sustainability, there are challenges to be overcome from the community and from an economic standpoint. Wave power has yet to prove itself though there have been some attempts to harness tidal flow, which may create more problems than benefits. Solar power has many advantages in areas where the infrastructure is limited but it is a costly approach that will probably be beyond local developing communities.

Perhaps the most unattractive approach, but one which offers multiple benefits, is investment in bio-energy power generation. It creates a cycle that helps to balance its environment since when you grow the energy crops they absorb carbon dioxide and, if burned efficiently, they do not add to the pollution. Even more effective is the fuelling of power plants from waste providing a solution to waste and energy into the bargain. In many parts of the world animal waste has been dried and used for cooking for centuries, but unfortunately in these cases the waste would have been better used as fertilizer.

Many governments have been and are still piloting waste to energy plants, and several have proved successful. There are investment incentives for companies that choose to integrate these types of approaches. Growing energy-based crops is another development that is being pursued, which is nothing new on sugar plantations that have used waste to generate steam for refining.

The interesting challenge for many in the business community would be the development of energy clusters where waste or energy crop producers develop programmes together with industrial users of energy. Integrated approaches offer the opportunities for one group to solve their waste problems and for others to benefit from energy creation that is truly renewable. Technology has also advanced in recent years towards mini-turbines which can be linked to heat generating processes. In this way manufacturing plants can start to harness waste heat recovery to generate power.

The major challenge to the business community is to take the wider social community with them when embarking on any development programme. The NIMBYs will fight hard to recognize the need for change but keep it away from their local environment. The demand for energy will not abate and it is unrealistic to assume that a few wind farms will make a significant difference. Continuous energy supply is a crucial part of the economic infrastructure and thus diversity must add to the stability. Even better, where companies can turn energy savings or energy creation towards their bottom line, everyone benefits.

Saving energy saves pollution and also saves on operating costs, but there needs to be a long-term strategy that recognizes the investment of industry. A recent report in the UK suggested that regional transport development programmes should be balanced against the potential loss of tax revenues by taking drivers on to public transport. If business develops proactive approaches then regulators and governments will look to harness the revenue streams.

Developing technologies that can fill the gaps in other regions may be as important as solving them at home. The US currently produces around 40 per cent of the CO_2 emissions, which is unlikely to be reduced significantly, but other regions are rapidly increasing their demand through economic growth, and thus helping them to achieve a greener profile would help everyone.

Energy sits at the core of industrialization and thus is an important factor in the business investment profile. At the same time it is potentially the biggest issue in relation to a sustainable environment. If these two factors can be linked to the benefit of organizations then there is a likelihood of making real progress.

This process starts with organizations taking a holistic look at their own operations and involving every tier of the business, then looking at other organizations to see who is doing things better or differently and (for that matter) who is doing things worse (not that this should be an excuse for doing nothing). Creating a corporate policy that is visible to all the stake-holders sets the tone for making things happen.

Implementing an energy programme that is properly resourced and, where practical, involves other businesses, helps to share the load and often the investment, though investment should only follow careful evaluation. In the main many improvements are likely to be made simply by looking at the operations and processes from an energy perspective and seeking out savings. Reduced energy costs relate to higher profits, improved competition, secure jobs, enhanced reputation and frequently improved products. The side-effect of these considerations is a positive contribution to reducing pollution and more sustainable energy profiles generally.

Global economic growth will certainly demand more from the energy sector and, although transport and industry may become more efficient in the coming years, population growth and the emerging nations will fuel substantial increases in demand. Whilst current energy sources are likely to be able to provide these needs, the impacts on the environment overall will be significant unless action is taken to temper them. Fossil fuel will clearly remain the backbone of energy supply despite the pressures to shift to renewable sources, which are unlikely to offer economic benefits to sufficiently shift thinking.

Predictions suggest that Asia will in the next two decades surpass the USA as the major energy user and thus the emission challenges will shift from established corporate names to some who will be far less concerned about reputation. Education and transfer of technology offer the only real hope of building an international energy profile that supports the environmental concerns of global warming. Nuclear fuel obviously offers some benefits but carries with it a number of concerns, both from a perspective of waste management and a radiation disaster. We may see fuel cells and so forth but, for the foreseeable future, oil, gas and coal will be the mainstay of energy production.

In the main the burden of the management of this challenge will fall not to governments and political diktat but to industry and business leaders. It is of little value to make savings at home if you export the major production and energy consumption. Companies that undertake energy programmes need also to look at how they can influence their external partners and suppliers globally. In the case of exploration and exploitation of fossil fuels, major developers have a duty of care to ensure that whilst national governments may seek to benefit from their resources this is done in a responsible manner. Those seeking to finance energy-based projects should be looking to ensure that environmental evaluations are effectively integrated.

Sustainable energy is a major concern to the whole business community and how they manage the issues affects the wider social community. It is unlikely that governments will ever reach a fully integrated global programme but, in the meantime, they will bring about more and more regulation nationally which will create differentials of approach that business must traverse.

CHAPTER 13

Regulation

In reviewing the sustainable landscape of the business community it would be easy to make the assumption that business leaders are uninterested in sustainability issues. Certainly that is the inference that comes from many of the NGOs who believe that corporations are simply looking for loopholes in order to avoid doing what is right.

It might be perhaps even more emotive to suggest that the primary driver for most business leaders is keeping the regulatory pressures at bay and satisfying the compliance requirements. In discussing this issue with business leaders they all agreed they had personal concerns around the future environmental impacts. They do, however, see the growing mountain of regulations as such a drain on their businesses resources that focusing beyond these challenges is not practical. It is then perhaps understandable that the current ethos is largely one of compliance rather than long-term commitment to sustainability.

More and more regulation is becoming global, or at least regulators are ensuring that organizations cannot abdicate compliance obligations by transferring activities overseas. This can be seen, for example, in the current pressures in the financial sectors where off-shoring may be a cost advantage but brings with it the need for extended responsibility. The OFR (operating and financial review), for example has established clearly the reach and roles of directors regarding subsidiaries, environmental matters, social and community issues. Successful companies will be those whose directors who look at the long-term as well as short-term issues and take all factors affecting companies' relationships into account. Much of the current thinking is also being driven by FTSE4Good and the Dow Jones Sustainability Index (DJSI), the question is whether these fine principles hold sway when they affect profits.

For those working in the global market place, either directly or indirectly, the complexity of the regulatory maze is a major challenge, particularly because lack of consistency creates a minefield of opportunity and risk. The regulatory framework that business operations have to contend with includes:

- industry sector guidelines;
- regional controls;
- national regulations;
- multi-national agreements;
- international conventions.

Any reader who has travelled will recognize the simple problem of connecting electrical equipment to local power supplies. Of course today this problem has been recognized to some extent through multi-phase units and plug adaptors. Unfortunately the same adaptor approach cannot be created for the regulatory maze. It should then not come as any surprise that when the business sector is challenged by new regulations it protests and the NGOs claim self-interest.

What also has to be recognized within this environment is that regulations are far from consistent globally, creating competitive advantage for those ready to lower their standards or those who have not recognized the benefits of best practice. Thus when business can follow local laws in one country, and can do what would not be acceptable in others, it is likely that it will become a target for criticism. The biggest danger with over-regulation is that it promotes a need for compliance rather than commitment and a duty of care for sustainable development.

There is no doubt that regulation must be in place to control the criminal performance of organizations, but even here the differences between what is legal can create anomalies country by country. It is also commonly the situation that regulation tends to be reactive, responding to crimes and environmental challenges that have already occurred. Thus it is frequently running behind the evolution of economic development rather than shaping the future focus. It also has to be acknowledged by those that want less regulation that voluntary management has frequently led to some exploitation which self-governing industries have not been able to contain.

Clearly then we need regulation to govern for the worst cases but perhaps we should be looking within the sustainable development agenda for some form of responsibility-driven framework. Unfortunately here again one sees a situation where defining rules will preclude any focus on the forward-thinking organizations that are stretching current knowledge. As discussed earlier, many of the pollution problems of the past came from ignorance not spite, and as we push the boundaries then we need some over-arching commandments which focus thinking. Certainly we are a long way from this utopian position, although the UN Global Compact launched at Davos in 1999 did try to set in place nine principles concerning human rights, labour standards and environmental issues.

Whether voluntary or regulatory, no business will be able to ignore the implications of CSR; unfortunately, this will no doubt lead to agreements based on the lowest possible common denominator in order to gain acceptance. This is still only the start of a complex journey for business leaders, but one they will not or should not ignore. In 2000 a UN survey established that 60 per cent of those questioned wanted companies to do more than simply follow their traditional role of paying taxes, creating employment, obeying the law and making profits. Given the increase in globalization in the same year, at Davos Mary Robinson (the UN Human Rights Commissioner said: 'Harmonising economic growth with the protection of human rights is one of the greatest challenges we face today.'

Multi-nationals make up more than 50 per cent of the top 100 international organizations and as such they are directly involved with the unprecedented changes in political profiles and privatization of economic power. With this involvement that cascades to the majority of business operating in the global market place they are progressively being pushed more and more into the spotlight. Thus voluntary approaches will continue to be exposed by those pursuing a specific cause. Increasing regulation may in the longer term have a detrimental effect.

Human rights have been high on the agenda for a number of years and have been incorporated into legislation across a broad range of nations, but not all. Unfortunately the trend has been more towards a US compliance culture by imposing criminal charges. The implication is that organizations will devote their time to ensuring a legally defensible position rather than looking to integrate human rights into more efficient business processes. The Turnball report in 1999 recommended that risk management include health, safety, environmental, reputation and ethical issues. Despite political recognition that we should keep CSR outside the regulatory arena, we are seeing more and more regulation advancing on aspects of sustainable development.

The UN approach of creating the Fundamental Human Rights Principles for Business Enterprise could, if fully adopted establish a common platform for good whilst levelling the competitive playing field.

Establishing regulation could have the effect of dampening continuous improvement towards best practice unless the market place was prepared to reward companies that exceeded minimum requirements. Of course governments could also influence trends through tax incentives and support to ethical investors.

The progress towards legal accountability is increasing and reflected in the number of domestic claims being upheld. In 2001 Shell and the Nigerian government reflected the growing focus on multi-nationals and host governments. In this case the African Commission upheld a claim on behalf of the Ogoni peoples that both Shell and the Nigerian government were complicit in breaching human rights. Other examples from Nigeria, Myanmar, Sudan and South Africa have implicated companies including Uncol, TotalFinaElf, Talisman and Cape. There is also a growing acceptance that home countries (such as the US, UK and others) will be prepared to recognize claims against registered companies operating overseas.

All of this brings to the fore the implications for companies working in countries where there is conflict, unreasonable use of security services, poor labour standards and land rights. Human rights have been broadly accepted today to include rights to justice, political participation, reasonable living standards, sustainable environment, labour regulations and equal rights.

There is also a growing trend towards the concept that business must use its influence to improve conditions in local countries if it is not to be guilty of human rights failures. The real question that business and its stakeholders must ask is, to what level should we assume companies can take over government policy in host countries, and what level of blame should they face if they fail to influence those practices that are considered unacceptable? Standing on the outside it may seem black and white, but for those involved the lines may be a lot less clear.

The energy giant Enron's huge black hole has led to a worldwide shake-up in accounting rules. The results will be far-reaching and will affect the way companies account for acquisitions, and this is turn will skew profits and inject more volatility into profits. The International Financial Reporting Standards are designed to avoid nasty surprises such as Enron, but they are not commonly adopted globally and thus again we see the potential for risk trading across unequal boundaries. The trend (particularly in terms of financial services organizations) is that the trading foundation of 'caveat emptor' is being eroded in favour of making sellers more accountable.

The problem is that regulatory differentiation does in fact provide exploitable opportunities for many organizations. It is also a significant risk that businesses need to understand and manage. Given these challenges, organizations are seeking to establish processes that clearly define their approach to ensure that whilst problems may still arise the implications cannot be put down to poor management. These include:

- a clear corporate vision and values;
- recognition of board responsibility;
- clear accountabilities and delegated authority;

- objective and performance-driven management;
- unequivocal and public business standards;
- improved focus on risk management; and
- external audits.

All of this is a structure to drive towards changing the face of compliance, which is a term that is widely used by business but its interpretation can be extremely limited. For some it involves all legal and industry requirements, together with recognition of how the business conducts its affairs and its interfaces with stakeholders. In addition, how the business is managed internally and the effectiveness of its processes and systems should be considered, with above all a clear focus on effective corporate governance. For others compliance is about minimal commitment to regulatory demands to ensure protection from prosecution.

Companies do need to ask themselves if their view of compliance matches up to the objectives and values of the organization. All businesses, wherever they operate, are constrained by cost and thus effectiveness and business benefit will always be measured against the cost of compliance. Frequently the responsibility for ensuring a sustainable approach is delegated to an individual or group which is then not adequately resourced for fear of creating a monster. In fact the sustainable development culture should be an internal partnership where compliance and best practice are part of the operational ethos.

We also need to consider where regulation is necessary to defend the business community. In today's market place the dependence on information and communication technology (ICT) and the Internet has become virtually irreversible. Cyber warfare is the growing terrorist weapon, and even some environmental groups have resorted to using the Internet to promote their positions, and have used viruses to damage companies they are opposed to.

There are billions of dollars lost each year through attacks on individual corporate systems or more general Internet viruses. This, in addition to Internet fraud, costs industry dearly and, as has been said before, the less wealth that is created the less there is to fuel improvements globally. Thus if there has to be a common focus for all sectors of the community then regulation and control of the Internet must be high on the agenda.

Economic growth will inevitably mean even more dependence on the Internet so as a means of spreading sustainable ideas we should protect this medium from commercial or political control and from exploitation by pressure groups. If there is one feature of modern technology that should be governed, controlled and policed by the UN it should be the Internet. It is a common platform that will progressively pull down boundaries and barriers to sustainable development

So where does all this leave the corporate strategy and the business leaders? The simple answer is under a great deal of pressure and faced with a very complex jigsaw puzzle in which to do business (see Figure 13.1). Trading in the global market place, or even being connected to the market through imports, companies are challenged to maintain a competitive position, respectable margins and to satisfy the numerous focus groups that are constantly prowling for the opportunity to promote their individual causes.

As mentioned before, the differential between organizations or countries is what creates a competitive environment. This is perhaps even truer today where technological advances are almost ubiquitous and their deployment in the market faster than ever. Thus in both production and services national cost advantages can be reflected in any number of aspects through which regulations, rather than culture, may define compliance for the business community. At the same time the responsible and forward-looking organization should be looking at the disparities and assessing where introducing best practice may bring more benefit than compliance.

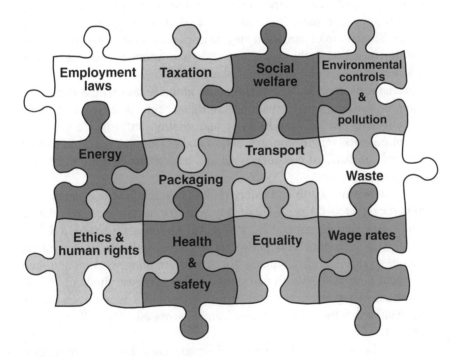

Figure 13.1   Regulatory jigsaw

Across the developing world the view of employment law is very akin to Europe prior to the Industrial Revolution and certainly before the rise of the trade union movements where work was a daily (or, at most, weekly) commitment; there was no long-term employment, only performance-based payment. Thus local businesses carry limited overheads and certainly no long-term liabilities for job security. This profile is common but takes no account of the potential for organizations to build up employee loyalty and attract the best workers.

Taxation is a common regulatory differentiator and can encourage organizations to transfer production or service support into specific regions. This happens even in the developed world where regional incentives for economic regeneration are available. This can be attractive for inward investment programmes but is not a sustainable model.

As outlined earlier, energy sits at the core of most business ventures and thus regions that have low cost and indigenous fuel suppliers provide attractive manufacturing locations. The exposure is more about what that exploitation of fuel can mean for the long-term environmental infrastructure. Frequently this exploitation raises the vista of ethical practices and human rights. Relocating business or outsourcing activities does have a backlash on the previous communities. A feature of recent off-shoring programmes is that these relocations are short-lived as the cost base increases. Short-term exploitation may be unethical but may also be a waste of investment, particularly where education and training was necessary to exploit the human capital in the first place.

Human rights are clearly a major issue globally and whilst it may be acceptable locally to operate within the limited regulations it is not likely to be delivering the best productivity and quality performance. The fair treatment of workers will improve output and performance, which overall may balance initial cost considerations and help to develop a longer-term sustainable programme.

In the same way health and safety (H&S) is something that is taken as given in the developed world. There may be the occasional scandal relative to exploitation but in general it is accepted by business that H&S is a contributor to efficiency and performance. It may also be that workers would not work in an unsafe plant, but actually training workers and then losing them through ill-health and injury makes no sense. It should be no surprise that in regions around the world where H&S is not even on the public agenda that the same principles should work equally well and bring productivity benefits.

Evidence from organizations such as Fairtrade and common sense suggest that even nominal investments in working conditions can considerably improve overall output. This in turn means greater profitability for the local manufacturers, and more dependable production and delivery along with increased quality control. Overall H&S is morally important, but it also has a direct influence on business performance.

Packaging and product identification is something that varies across the world. It is an area that frequently comes up in terms of regulation in the developed world. The main focus is on identification of the ingredients but what we have seen recently with Soltan 1 contamination is that a complex delivery chain can fail with significant cost implications. At the same time the demands of organizations for packaging standards often involves destroying local resources such as timber simply to transport goods.

The challenge that AIDS has brought to many organizations operating in under-developed regions highlights the business impacts that come from poorly supported social environments. Alongside poor health and education infrastructures there is the impact of a low-grade workforce that limits future development and business investment. A robust social climate means the potential for improving the overall business case is itself robust and sustainable.

Transportation is a major factor in the global trading network and as such poorly developed regional infrastructures often result in accidents, delays and increased costs. Clearly the high cost of transport and the implication for added pollution again provide additional factors in the whole cost profile.

Business is often challenged on issues such as equality, particularly in countries where women and children are not fully integrated into the political or cultural structure. This is a major exposure for the business community but often one which it is hard for the organizations involved to master. However, help with education and increasing the respect of the workers must help to improve performance compared with using slave labour. In time one may hope that these barriers will come down, but in the meantime employment revenues may be crucial to the local economic stability and frequently make the difference between life and death.

Assessments by those outside the business community tend to make comparisons on labour rates. This ignores the reality that low cost is what makes these regions attractive to business and, in turn, the consumers. However, as in the case of the Fairtrade coffee programme, if producers are not paid a sufficient return then eventually there is no further investment and the resource and advantage is lost. Paying the going rate may be a short-term benefit but paying a balanced wage can develop greater stability in supply.

Waste, environmental controls and pollution create major concerns for us all but this is no excuse for exploiting regional environments where the regulations may be weaker. There is an expression that 'what goes around comes around', so if we transfer our problems by exploiting regulation variables then eventually we are only adding to the overall challenge of sustainability. Countries that turn a blind eye to exploiting the natural resources (or, worse, which actively promote such developments) are simply adding to the problem. Influencing a focus on resource management, whether it is forest management or fish stocks, means that these commercial advantages can be sustained.

It is easy to see that whilst regulation advantages are short-term commercial advantages they will ultimately lead to an unsustainable business environment. Best practice transferred to these under-developed regions ought to be part of every business strategy given the potential to benefit all stakeholders in the long term. There is often a financial drive towards lowest price and this remains a core aspect of commercial trading, but more recently there has been a realization that the total cost of ownership and delivery are more important.

Governments and cultures in these developing countries may not be focused on the bigger picture, and they may even be opposed to 'managed programmes', as was the case with B&Q and the Malaysian government over forest management; but progressive investment in health, education, social welfare, environmental awareness and best business practice can deliver benefits to all. Taxation, aid and trade are tools that can be used within a regulatory framework to help promote effective approaches rather than encouraging business to find loopholes.

It should also be recognized by NGOs and governments that regulation, whilst necessary, can also be a major factor in preventing sustainable development and therefore requires a balanced approach. The business community may have pockets of exploitation but effort should be directed to encouraging the positive attributes of business contributions to under-developed communities. It should also be apparent that whilst we can place expectations on the business community, many of the criticisms they face are not of their making and provide a difficult challenge. Not every issue can be addressed at once and they should be encouraged to look beyond compliance through support, not demands.

It is not realistic to assume that we can pass regulatory responsibility on to the business community, but it is equally unrealistic to assume that we can expect business to uphold a sustainable development focus if the majority of its spare resources are focused on ensuring compliance. Regulatory environments will not go away and there should be a wider dialogue around deregulating aspects that are better handled by responsible organizations.

It is also important to recognize that the more detailed the regulatory requirements, the greater the difficulty in promoting best practice. The more rules you write, the more lawyers and accountants that need to be employed to manage them, deflecting resources from constructive approaches that support business objectives and wealth creation.

CHAPTER 14

Corporate governance

The last decade of the twentieth century and early into the start of the new millennium presented us with a large number of news issues related to the question of corporate governance. We of course assume under this barrage of news that the corporate executive community has become totally corrupt. This is far from the truth in the majority of cases but brings down on honest business leaders increasing pressure to prove their openness and trust in order to create or maintain stakeholder confidence.

The business press and frequently the general media is littered with high-profile cases that underline the need to raise the game in terms of creating greater confidence in business leaders. The performances of Enron, WorldCom and Parmalat raise questions for the security of investors, customers and employees. Royal Dutch Shell had to own up to its over-stating of reserves, which damaged share value and confidence, whilst US Vice President Dick Cheney found himself under the spotlight over bribery allegations involving Halliburton. There can be little doubt that if we promote the idea that we are to trust our business leaders to adopt and integrate sustainable concepts then there also have to be benchmarks for corporate performance.

We have tended to lump many if not all these issues under the banner of CSR and (as discussed earlier) the wider profile of sustainability. This often gimmicky approach clouds the whole subject and creates confusion between the legal obligations of corporate directors and the broader issues and approaches we often hope to see reflected in the performance of business leaders.

This lack of clarity is frequently what drives CEOs into a corner as they are between a rock and hard place, since in the same way as every individual has a personal slant on the world, so too does an executive or corporate board. Thus outside the legal frameworks, which vary state-by-state creating even more confusion, the focus for responsibility and accountability are reflective of these personal drivers of those in authority and those positioning themselves to be critical of highly focused crusades.

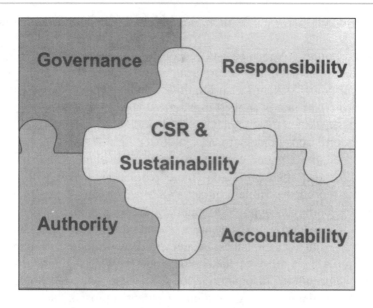

Figure 14.1   Balancing corporate governance

This is in no way intended to be a case for increasing the levels of legislation: we must have a balanced approach, as in Figure 14.1: first, because defining laws will generally dilute the overall aims and create disparity between states, and secondly, because what will promote a sustainable focus is personal aims and choices not regulation.

Corporations have invested considerable sums in endeavouring to address this dilemma by presenting a more responsible profile and substantial PR budgets to address the challenges that come from the market place, whether from customers, consumers or NGOs. In many cases these pressure groups gained their successes by shouting loudest, and often creating a focus that in the wider scheme of things was not perhaps the most important.

Part of this corporate profiling has been the drive towards producing reports on sustainability. The FSTE4Good and DJSI offer investors a perspective on the organization's commitment. How meaningful these reports are in relation to their real performance is another matter. It is good that companies are trying to promote their good works and responsible approach side, but these programmes are more PR than corporate ethos. This in turn provides an excuse for those in the protest fraternity to attack these reports rather than accept them as a stepping-stone to the next level of responsibility. If such reports were promoted rather than criticized then perhaps the pressure could be more effectively directed to those that don't report.

True corporate governance and responsibility can only grow from an integrated system that links executive authority, financial accounting, board accountability and stakeholder aspirations to transparency, which entails a code of principles that is applied in practice. This offers a challenge when one also has to accept that the playing field globally is far from level, where it may require stakeholders to accept lower performance in favour of returns based on a wider evaluation profile. Developing this balanced perspective rather than promoting more regulation, which will tend to constrain a more responsible attitude, should encourage corporate leaders to share the journey as opposed to guarding the wagon train.

Sound governance approaches are a crucial part of developing business sustainability but many business leaders find themselves surrounded by attacks from a wide range of stakeholders and growing regulations. These pressures can result in personal litigation from these same stakeholders and thus, despite perhaps wanting a more transparent approach, they are forced to act within a legal minefield.

We have witnessed a number of high-profile cases where clearly governance broke down but, looking in from the outside, perhaps the biggest failing was not the legal regulation but the executive commitment to responsibility. Thus it was not the rules that needed addressing but the attitude of executives and non-executive directors to pay attention to the 'tone at the top'. Corporate responsibility and commitment must be captured by the executive and blended into the business at every level.

The problem in cases such as Enron was not the external image that was being projected but the reality of focus internally at the top. The development of corporate financing models and changes in business modelling generally means that regulation will follow rather than lead. It is thus essential if the boundaries of innovation are being pushed that those in authority have an ethos rather than a rulebook. Enron had all the right procedures in place but there are major questions about how these failed to operate with adequate independence to provide control and challenge.

Enron grew from nowhere in 15 years to become a major player in the energy industry and the seventh largest corporation in US, employing over 21,000 people in 40 countries. It was seen as a major success story, judged to be *Fortune* magazine's most innovative company for six years, consistently in the top 100 best companies to work for and on the all-star list of globally most admired companies. It regularly issued its social and environmental report outlining its approaches to the environment, its anti-corruption stance, social programmes and employees.

The company's vision, defined by CEO Kenneth Lay, was based on respect, integrity and excellence. It was people that failed, not the rules of engagement. As a seemingly successful company they enjoyed connections at the highest level and perhaps this also contributed to practices being adopted unchallenged. What clearly emerges in this story is that whilst financial reporting could have been more robust, in essence the corrupt people will always find ways to bend the rules. If organizations are to be trusted then a more responsible ethos must be embedded in the organization.

It would also seem that the remuneration approaches of the senior executives provided the impetus to drive up share value and benefit from option deals, thus clouding other judgements. It is easy to focus solely on Enron but it worth recognizing that this phenomenon is neither new nor purely a US practice. History is awash with examples of similar business collapses: Robert Maxwell's pension fund raid, the Polly Peck collapse, the BCCI banking failure, WorldCom, Parmalat and Tyco in more recent times all reflect not a failing of the rules but a failure of the corporate culture.

Clearly no two organizations are the same and over time even individual companies change. It is, therefore, important to get the focus on building the appropriate culture and ethos that will ensure a balanced perspective. The problems arise when, for example, Scott Sullivan (the former finance chief of US telecoms firm WorldCom) admitted that he used to lie to fellow board members. The big question in this case is to what degree did the CEO choose to ignore evidence of a major financial hole? Similarly, Qwest started to face claims in 2004 of fraud in respect of under-recognizing expenses in order to boost profit ratios.

Oil companies have frequently been in the public eye in relation to environmental problems and Royal Dutch Shell has enjoyed its share of notoriety. Many will remember Brent Spar. More recently, however, it hit the headlines again but this time due to having to reduce its calculations of proven oil and gas reserves. Much of this appears to have been due to the problems of assessing when reserves can sensibly be exploited and (perhaps more importantly) the structure of remuneration packages colouring more optimistic views. Interestingly the problem seems to have arisen because two other oil companies working in partnership with Shell declared different calculations for their shares of the same oil fields. A complex management structure and poor corporate governance are blamed for the crisis that seriously impacted shareholder confidence.

These situations are a global phenomenon, as can be seen in the Parmalat case, which started in October 2004 in Italy. The collapse of the dairy company brought 32 executives plus Deloitte & Touche (the accountants) and Grant Thornton (the Bank of America subsidiary) into the dock. It is also interesting that Parmalat sued Bank of America for assisting in transactions to hide insolvency. The UK Serious Fraud Office is said to have joined the investigations into the activities of US oil services business Halliburton; whilst Vice President Dick Cheney was running it, adding to the participation in the inquiry of France and Nigeria. Global business and trading means global focus on corporate governance, but this must also recognize differing legal and regulatory systems.

Considering the range of issues and the challenges for corporate leaders, what should they be doing to redress the balance and help to build stakeholder trust and confidence? The traditional approach has been for corporate boards to focus on legal obligations and regulatory compliance. Clearly this narrow perspective is what provides the culture for those ready to push the envelope and test the current accountability rules.

Many have made the first step to establishing themselves back inside the most regulated environment. News Corp, perhaps one of the biggest media organizations in the world, decided to reincorporate the company in the US and bring it under the Financial Services Authority regulatory umbrella. The approach is designed to present an absolute confidence profile to stakeholders and, in particular, investors.

Every company is different and must consider a number of factors in developing an approach. This includes variables such as the industry sector, stage of development from start-up to long-established company, structure of ownership, operating markets and legal systems, regulatory and environmental conditions and, most important of all, the personalities involved. The skills and capabilities of corporate leaders are crucial and the experience of non-executive directors becomes an important check and balance.

A survey in Canada, for example, suggest that corporate governance is now a significant factor in the business community affecting increased workloads, additional operating costs, staffing levels and consultancy costs. Insurance premiums for company directors are certain to rise, as are the number of litigations aimed at corporate executives. Insurers have clearly focused on the Sarbanes–Oxley Act in the US in order to retain their cover. The ramifications are clear and the pressure is on in terms of financing governance, so what can we expect from the wider CSR agenda?

What then do we see as CSR and, more importantly, what do we expect of corporate leaders and the organizations they lead? Certainly we expect governance, regulatory and fiscal compliance, but beyond this we look for good relationships with all stakeholders reflecting a consideration for the community and the environment. We look for leaders with clear visions and values that are apparent throughout the organization's practice and operations. These must be focused on a sustainable development programmes, lifecycle management and continuous improvement. Openness and performance that promotes confidence and trust should be the mantra for organizations seeking to enjoy a dialogue with the wider community.

Where does corporate governance fit within this wider picture? It should be a robust system by which companies are directed and controlled across four key areas. The first of these is financial accounting, which has been the main development post-Enron. The configuration and competence of the executive board, along with recognition of the stakeholders in the business, are key factors. The fourth element is transparency. The key drivers behind this need are brand protection, investor relationships, employment trends and capabilities, and risk management.

Corporate governance is now a major consideration in the context of global trading and development. The World Bank in October 2004 expressed serious concern over the slow pace of implementing new corporate governance regulation in India. Certainly, as we see the growth of India as an economic power and at the same time a beneficiary of World Bank development programmes, establishing a sound structure to manage companies is crucial.

For similar reasons young business leaders in China are already exerting influence both in the regional infrastructure and business culture, having been trained in western international standards in governance. This reflects awareness that as China builds its international influence it will also seek wider stakeholder support. Human rights will also come to the fore, eventually being driven by economics rather than ideology.

It is generally agreed that Africa has a major challenge to implement economic reform and good governance in order to support high economic growth. The African countries need to reposition themselves in terms of negotiating future trade and aid. Even at a charitable level a joint report by Oxfam and Action Aid estimates that 80 per cent of global aid goes missing through over-priced products, administration and poor management. If future development depends on investment confidence, then corporate governance must be a major consideration.

Thus across a global community corporate governance sits at the core of developing a wider sustainable development programme. If we cannot create the trust for the business community to manage the key elements of their operations, why should the community at large trust them to support the environmental and social aspects of the community?

At the heart of good governance are the corporate values that create the ethos and culture of the operation. Every company is different but it is generally reflective of the management style and approach cascaded from

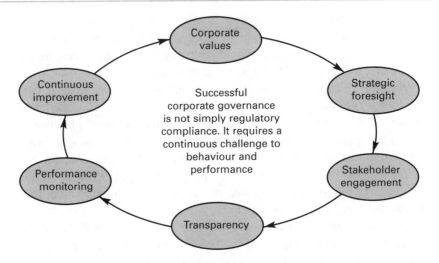

Figure 14.2   Governance through behaviour and performance

the CEO down. The values of the organization should be supported by the stakeholders, including investors, customers, employees and the wider community. This support will provide the framework for strategic development and be reflected in behaviour and performance, as in Figure 14.2.

Strategic foresight is a crucial part of the board's role in leading the organization and this frequently benefits from non-executive directors who are able to bring a wider perspective and knowledge. At the same time they must also be able to understand the business and bring balance to strategic initiatives. Many organizations proclaim their role and purpose but often fail to live up to the rhetoric by establishing objectives without considering what they mean and how to measure them. In this context it is worth remembering that what we know is an opportunity; what we don't know is a risk. Balancing pace with understanding is a crucial requirement of developing strategies that support visions and objectives.

In all of this the role of the multiple stakeholders is key to being able to move forward without a continuous drain or direction change driven by external or internal pressure groups. Successful companies of the future will be value-focused and operate within a disciplined approach linking financial performance and strategic positioning. By managing risk and measuring shareholder value they will operate within a framework that includes all stakeholders and brings sustainable development within the corporate strategy. This more enlightened governance model means that executives must consider the wishes of all their stakeholders.

Improved transparency is a fundamental part of building stakeholder confidence. Financial reporting is only part of the equation and sustainable reports, such as FTSE4Good, provide an opportunity for organizations to openly declare their commitment and approach to the community and the environment. However as was the case with Enron, unless this is supported by action it is worse than doing nothing. The European Commission is aiming to introduce a voluntary code of recommendations to provide shareholders with more information about directors' remuneration as a clear way of opening the background to developments.

The rhetoric and PR are of little value unless they are supported by action and performance. The Economist Intelligence Unit reflected that, in 2004, fewer than 40 per cent of companies had effective measures to report non-financial information, whilst 75 per cent acknowledge that their companies were under pressure to provide and monitor non-financial indicators. If business leaders are to promote their organizations to stakeholders then they need to be able to measure the health of their business operations. The challenge is that as each company is a unique entity, outside high level categories it will be extremely difficult to reach consensus for key monitor indexes. What would be more practical would be to develop an approach such as the excellence model to provide a measurable profile.

The final phase has clearly to be a programme of continuous improvement that is embedded in the organization. Globalization, or even its impact at a local level, is producing a continuous evolution in the business landscape. As such it is important that organizations remain adaptable and responsive to market change. The challenges of maintaining market competitiveness demand that organizations are continuously pushing the envelope of performance, design, cost and processes. This evolution will stretch and test executive strategy and governance and must be monitored and kept in check to avoid compounding these challenges through internal management and governance.

It is also worth considering that whilst it is easy to focus on the major multi-national organizations and brand leaders, these issues also apply to every business whatever its size. The assumption is that this group largely comprises companies of fewer than 250 employees, but they actually represent the major portion of the business community. Efforts by many governments to support this community are often in conflict with the regulations such as those driven through in the wake of Enron. Recognizing that Enron was once an SME is perhaps the best reason for promoting a more open approach at every level.

We have been looking at corporate governance and its role in CSR based on historical examples of failure. In fact, as mentioned before, most regulation is reactive based on evidence of wrong-doing rather than anticipating future developments and challenges. As the market place becomes more dynamic, so must the corporate thinking that drives organizations through the morass of complexity.

With the increase in globalization and the growing economic developments and regional breakdowns, there is a growing new challenge to governance which, together with dispersion technologies and information technology, provides a background for greater connectivity. Organizations are becoming multi-national, multi-cultural and operate within virtual communities. These communities operate outside national boundaries and regulatory constraints, creating an environment where governance has lower accountability. It also means that many organizations can and may utilize elements of a business outside the frameworks of corporate governance. The other challenge is that virtual organizations operating across national boundaries will possibly be functioning within different cultural regions, adding to the risk in terms of corporate practice and governance.

As governance principles become more recognized and perhaps even harmonized in some regions, so we must also appreciate that population and economic growth are both likely to change the complexion and possible balance of the global business community over time. Corporate governance standards of acceptability may need to become multi-national in structure in order to be effective or useful. This will pose a potential conflict for organizations that create their corporate visions and values from the perspective of non-western cultures. Thus many of the external pressure groups may find themselves contesting the business practices of global organizations that do not share the same ethnic foundations and thus have differing values.

Within this corporate governance debate we also cannot ignore the growing potential for organized crime to be progressively more influential in many parts of the global trading landscape. The participation of criminal elements either actively or simply as investors can have a major impact on organizations' performances to an even worse extent than the occasionally misfocused executive. Economic and cultural migration is progressively shifting the balance from national communities to social, ethnic, religious or political borderless communities that carry their own codes and practices into the business community.

This must be a consideration for those trying to create a more open and transparent market place and building trust between investors, customers and the corporate leaders. Continued globalization will probably take the role of governance outside the direction of national governments as it becomes more apparent that business sustainability and durability will be dependent on multi-national stakeholders. Thus if a company wants to attract investment it must rise above the regional regulatory influences and satisfy a much more dynamic market.

The corporate community will be better suited to provide a harmonized perspective than national governments or even world trading organizations. As one might suspect, in the future the power of the multi-national corporation will increase above that of most governments. It is at this stage that the business community will be most vulnerable to abuse, but at the same time strongest in terms of delivering practical solutions. The risks and opportunities are there to be exploited.

The creation of corporate governance is essential in maintaining investor confidence and increasing shareholder value. It does, however, go beyond compliance to regulation which is at the heart of corporate ethos and performance. If we are to have a sustainable community then corporate governance must both protect the rights of stakeholders and inspire them at the same time. Corporations with sound values, robust governance and transparent performance should be the focus for sustainable investment.

CHAPTER 15

Risk management

One cannot look at the issue of sustainability and CSR without raising the spectre of risk management and the risk involved in ignoring the warning signs. Business is about managing risk, and the principle cannot be ignored that the greater the risk, generally the higher margins. It is perhaps this factor more than most that drives organizations to over-reach themselves and find their business strategies, plans and reporting seriously exposed to the rigours of government, NGO or community criticism regarding sustainability issues. The challenge is to navigate between the benefits, corporately and individually, of facing short-term risk and the potential benefits of taking a longer-term view that builds on sustainable approaches and reduces risk. Even in the short term, effective and responsible management of sustainable issues can add value and reduce risk.

The United Nations Environmental Programme review 2004 highlighted the fact that many organizations are not disclosing to investors the true risks that exist in their sustainability reports. These risks can cover a wide range of factors from environmental impacts, social impacts, ethical impacts, sustainable development and the more fluid concepts of what external parties consider as part of corporate responsibility, which can damage reputation and investor confidence.

In every business venture there is always an element of risk and it is the skill in managing that risk that distinguishes successful organizations from the rest. Risk is the potential variability in the future outcome of a stated situation due to uncertainty. In the global environment and with a focus on the implications of sustainable development, risk is a major consideration (see Figure 15.1), yet, as intimated by the UN, many organizations fail to report or manage this risk effectively. The greater the level of risks the higher the potential reward, and thus the temptation to ignore the warning signs and focus purely on returns.

The major focus for business today is regulatory expansion. In the era that is now referred to as post-Enron many countries have instigated more financial regulatory controls. This growth in regulation has also been

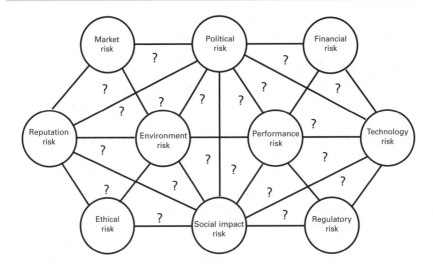

Figure 15.1   Sustainability risks

instrumental in creating some wide international agreements. At the same time many organizations (in the financial services sector in particular) have looked at off-shoring but are now appreciating that not only do they have less control, they have not abdicated any responsibility. Driving developments towards establishing a more collaborative approach in order to maintain integrity of information is crucial in managing relationships and performance.

It is also important to recognize that the changing geopolitical landscape and expanding global economy is offering the prospect of business opportunity and perhaps greater risk than ever before; at least, it is certainly more unpredictable. Business communities, stakeholders and investors are all now faced with pervasive insecurity on a global basis. Terrorism has changed the business profile which has in turn influenced the views of future trading relationships, which may support or host unethical or criminal approaches.

Developing a corporate strategy must be linked to the creation of a risk management approach that addresses the concerns of all stakeholders. This does not mean that every risk or situation can be managed or that the investment is justified in every case. Few businesses operate in an area where every eventuality can be addressed, but at least those that are identified and recognized can be considered.

Risk is about loss, uncertainty and choice and should not be left to luck. Developing a robust risk management programme as part of the business process is a crucial factor in being able to build strong but flexible operations. The exploitation of collaborative relationships with stakeholders is part of the mitigation process.

The essence of effectively managing risk is the ability to distinguish between assumption and actuality. This challenge is amplified when the parties involved are focusing from a diverse number of starting points across the stakeholder profile. In many cases competitive edge is lost through the accumulative impact of risk contingencies throughout the business process, and thus perception of risk may in itself be a significant risk factor.

The key in any organization is the development of risk profiling as part of the strategic development process. The earlier a risk is identified, the more opportunity there will be to manage the situation. What cannot be seen is unlikely to get managed effectively, and the more fragmented and global organizations become, the more important it is to ensure that all those involved both understand the risks being faced and, more importantly, allocate responsibility for action.

Analysing risk that may be likely to affect future development can often highlight many opportunities that not only eliminate risk that previously had been based on assumptions within the organizations, but also raises the profile of situations that would perhaps have been ignored against the concerns of the wider community. What is often more difficult to establish is the risk management culture that accepts the principle that risk is a joint responsibility and does not simply ignore risk on the basis that it is just a corporate or government problem.

The advantage that can be derived from a collaborative approach is that many risks are a result of the interfaces between organizations, and once these are open to joint assessment they can be managed more efficiently. Effective risk management is a crucial advantage in a market place that is becoming more volatile in many aspects of its business culture. Risk represents in most organizations a significant cost consideration, and by developing an appropriate approach organizations can gain competitive edge.

Risk can be classified in many ways, as outlined below; the first step in establishing a risk management strategy is to focus on a clear structure. The key challenge for business is to acquire better resources than the competition and then deploy them more effectively. The harder organizations try, the higher the levels of risk they encounter.

Loss	Liability
Interruption	Waste
Technology	Social impacts
Environmental impacts	Political impacts

The wider aspects of risk involve the social impacts of extended enterprises where the performance of one partner, or their suppliers, can have an immediate backlash on the other partner. The risks, for example, in outsourcing can often be mitigated through greater integration and ensuring that the aims of both partners are shared and projected through their business dealings.

Classifying risk enables organizations to evaluate the most suitable approach, at the same time as identifying who is most suitably placed to manage that particular issue. Without a risk management programme the decision-making process is hindered by a lack of data.

All risk has an impact in terms of cost, time and profitability. To establish an effective approach it is important to analyse what the potential risks are and, more importantly, what are the potential effects. This analysis may be focused into three main areas of attention, the first being those issues that can be identified by source in terms of where the risk comes from. In many cases this may provide the ability to reduce some risks by changing (say) supply options. Others may be natural risks, which generally are subject to insurance cover or, in certain cases, the need for design adjustments.

Then there are the risks that come from the actual operations, whether this is an internal function or an external source of supply. They may result from production processes, and the ability of collaborating organizations to share working knowledge can often provide a wider range of solutions. Operational analysis must also focus on the environmental and social implications of the operations. In today's market place the regulatory and investment impacts of poorly managed operations may bring major risks to the fore.

The third area is that of effect in terms of being clear what the repercussions may be. These would generally sub-divide into effects on people, property or earnings. In each case the risk manager seeks to find the most cost-effective mitigation and then tries to balance future actions to reduce the profile to acceptable levels.

Risk may not simply be an issue of cost against today's business: it can also be an influence on tomorrow's potential business. The biggest risk to any business is to lose customers through poorly managed processes. The range of risk issues that confronts any business venture is extensive, and the need for organizations to consider and develop effective approaches is crucial.

It is important for every organization to recognize that whilst many risk issues may have common bases across all commercial ventures, others will be very specific to a given industry sector, location, customer or contract requirement. Risk management is by its nature a dynamic process and must be approached with a clear programme that recognizes the need for constant validation and is adaptable to change, at the same time evaluating the undertaking of increased risk to enhance competitive edge.

In most business operations external expenditure is between 50 and 80 per cent of operating cost. It is therefore not surprising that one should consider the supply chain as a major potential area of risk in terms of every aspect of the business profile, from profitability to long-term reputation. Customers will tend to look at the prime seller rather than the supply chain that supports it. Therefore the whole process of risk management has traditionally focused on passing risk down the food chain through tight contracts and penalties for poor performance. What is often ignored is the real ability of the supplier alone to influence the outcome, the impact of poor performance or the risk to reputation arising from exploitation.

The supply chain is the most under-rated asset of a business and the potential it can deliver into organizations to improve performance and reduce cost is significant. However, clearly the greater the level of exploitation the higher the risk potential, so high on the risk management agenda must be the development of sustainable strategic procurement approaches.

There can be few business ventures today that are not directly influenced by the spread of globalization. The multi-dimensional nature of the global landscape creates an environment that inherently generates an ever-increasing profile of risk which must be addressed. The quest to exploit the opportunities of the global market and the volatility of the many factors that can change the platform of a business deal engenders a need to focus on managing the risk. In addition, the growing risk of facing new competition highlights the need to develop a flexible strategy. Technology has further complicated this business environment by providing faster communications and raising the expectations of customers who now anticipate the benefits of global pricing, whilst still focusing on traditional quality and performance.

The pressures of regulation and environmental liabilities, together with the wider and more indirect ramifications of global trading are factors that every organization must recognize. The political and cultural challenges of working outside the comfort zone of traditional business networks are complex. The implications for organizations are far reaching and necessitate an increased focus on risk mitigation to ensure successful ventures. The attraction of low-cost sources and manufacturing is certainly a potential opportunity for all organizations, but the implications and risks should not be under-estimated.

Outsourcing has become an accepted methodology to capture competitive advantage but this extended enterprise approach brings its own level of risk through interdependence and reputation risk. The need to ensure that external suppliers share a common focus on the business objectives is crucial to long-term sustainability and maintaining a perspective on CSR. In any business venture the key ingredient for success is the development and exploitation of the relationships that govern the interfaces between organizations.

In today's business world the importance of relationships is often subjugated in favour of improved technology and communications links. The development of effective relationships, or simply the recognition that these interfaces have a major part to play in the whole venture, is a critical feature of any risk strategy. People are the biggest asset in organizations and the way in which they work, or even appreciate their role, is a key factor in the overall success. The view of each group and individual has to be considered and managed to avoid conflicts or simply abdication of responsibility, which in turn may allow more conventional risks to go uncontrolled.

The risk to any organization of failing to recognize the impacts of its people can be significant, and especially so in cases where the business strategy is being developed within the concepts of widening the enterprise through globalization. At the same time, dealing with people in different business cultures is also a factor that can damage the overall possibilities of success.

There can be few in the business world who are not constantly aware of the many pressures from the environmental objectives of individuals, NGOs and governments. In many cases these are not simply the impacts of regulatory change but also the ever-growing desire to adopt a long-term perspective on our business activities.

The thrust for business organizations is often to focus only on the legislation and compliance. Unfortunately the playing field is seldom a level one and the temptation to export problems in the short term is high. The danger is that seeking suppliers who may be prepared to take on risks within their own national regulatory frameworks is likely still to have potential negative implications. Improved communication now puts very effective and speedy pressure on organizations resulting from the failings of their supply network.

Managing the risks associated with environmental pollution and social exploitation is a major factor for most businesses. What is often missed in the quest to maintain competitive headway is the potential benefit that may be derived from a proactive approach to integration which exploits the savings from waste and energy conservation. Improvements in training and education in the longer term will provide more effective supply opportunities.

Developing an environmental strategy is a significant element of implementing effective risk management, and working the programme through a wider collaborative network may provide new opportunities. In many cases the risks are not just related to the obligations and penalties that can be imposed: the wider implications may lie in the effect of delays on the venture that ultimately may be more costly to the business.

Risk management is a process that must be developed over the whole lifecycle, and often this is ignored on the basis that risk only arises once a contract has been put in place. The reality is that in many cases the risk issues were generated in the pre-contract stages either through error or lack of knowledge. Developing an effective risk management approach has to be integrated into every facet of the business venture. Lifecycle management is now a major factor in business development strategy both in terms of customers extending their requirements and investment analysis, and also in the marketing profiles of businesses seeking to extend their range of products and services.

The primary objective of every commercial venture is to generate an acceptable level of return for the investment made and the risk carried. As explained before, the higher the risk, the more likely it is that the rewards will be proportionally higher. Thus it would not be practical to consider a risk management programme that was not focused on the financial risks. In a more linear structured organization the traditional approach has been to concentrate on passing risk down the food chain. The potential downside of this approach is that those asked to take on, or coerced into accepting the risks are often not the most capable of managing that risk.

Every facet of the delivery process has a direct effect on financial management, but these aspects are often overlooked against the background that the responsibility lies with others. In fact a more holistic perspective would suggest that a more collaborative analysis would shift responsibility and management to those best able to maximize control and optimize results, to the benefit of all the players. Cost planning that looks beyond the traditional interfaces may provide more effective management.

Change is generally viewed in a negative light but often changes can be introduced to improve performance or to add additional value to the operation. However, the impacts of such positive changes may well have negative effects at other points of the process or within the activities of others.

A more open approach to change may introduce alternatives that could be mutually beneficial and create less of a significant impact. Change is the number one risk area for any business but the way in which it is effectively processed and incorporated can be a major bonus to future business opportunities; each case needs proper evaluation and appropriate risk assessment.

There are many who would suggest that sustainable relationships are more risk-inclined than traditional contracting arrangements. It may be true that for the buyer and seller relationship the division of risk is much clearer and the responsibility defined. Furthermore, they will often infer that bringing external suppliers into the heart of the business is itself an unnecessary risk.

The perceptions of risks that may emerge from these relations are in the main driven by those who failed to understand or appreciate the full benefits that can be exploited. The concern often comes from a traditional background that has a culture of deferring risk to others whilst in reality often these are only superficial transfers of liability in overall terms.

Having earlier identified the various areas of risk it is then important to develop a strategy to find the most suitable approach towards mitigation or management of the issues. Risk must be assessed and balanced to ensure that provisions, contingencies and resources are not loaded into the proposition to such an extent that it becomes non-competitive.

The application of risk management and mitigation strategies must be assessed to focus on the market value of the risk profile and the potential for winning and executing successful business. The creation of a risk management strategy must address every facet of the operation. The full extent of risk can only be assessed and managed against a background of the total business relationships and stakeholders, whether these are with customers or supply chains. How these elements fit together and interact will have a major impact on the overall success.

The deployment of risk management strategies can often encompass many facets of the overall operations and therefore any strategy that ignores the impacts in other areas may ultimately dilute the solution or waste the effort by not reflecting the domino effects of other actions. The development of effective risk profiling should be done in order to ensure that every practical implication is considered and incorporated as appropriate. Finding the right balance is an important part of developing a business strategy, and the extension of this to consider the external contributors to the delivery process provides a sound basis for the development of risk and reward contracts.

It is often easier to identify potential risks outside the organization, when in many cases there can be risks that in fact are the result of internal practices and culture. The initial stages of developing an effective risk management strategy should proceed from a baseline of understanding the internal issues and then prioritizing actions related to these and the external issues.

The targeting of risk issues is an important factor in being able to take appropriate action. Often, due to financial pressures, the focus is directed towards the high-cost areas but these can in many cases be relatively simple challenges that have a lesser contribution to the real risk profile.

Assessing the internal impacts on risk is often related to the ability of the organization to work in an integrated manner. This aspect of risk management is one, which many organizations prefer not to address but, as many will appreciate, the internal boundaries to overall success can often be greater than those which may be considered external to the operation. The larger organizations may have many divisions or functional departments, each with separate targets and objectives. These may be considered as having a common focus but in reality may be risk barriers. Many organizations will place high levels of expectation on external companies, which they would not normally place on themselves. The net result is that risks are built up internally whilst efforts are being focused outside.

The traditional business model which promoted the concept of one organization owning all the requisite functions, resources and facilities has been in many ways neutralized by the increasing evolution towards a global approach, which creates for the business world the need to find alternative operating models that can provide the degree of flexibility required by addressing the multiple variables involved. The risk created by the dynamics of the changing environment can in many respects be overcome by the deployment of collaborative ventures and the move towards partnering, providing a basis to evaluate and apportion risks to those best qualified to manage them effectively.

One aspect of risk that often creates a great deal of activity is the assumption of risk based on a background of unrealistic expectations. This may seem a strange concept in the whole picture of establishing a risk mitigation strategy, but in many cases effort is expended in order to prevent losses or potential risks that have no real basis.

Too often careful planning and creation of strategies is lost once the enthusiasm of the real work starts. Even worse is the situation where at the development stage risk issues may be identified which are not carried forward into the contract negotiations, and thus the first major opportunity for mitigation is given away.

In a similar vein the implementation of isolated mitigation approaches is undertaken without first considering the wider perspective of the whole risk profile, resulting in the use of opportunities or resources to counter a specific circumstance and failing to recognize the even bigger problems only just around the corner.

Proceeding to the development of a risk profile requires a structured approach and many organizations will already have their own risk management teams and processes. Sustainable risk management must be built around the process for developing stakeholder partnerships, but it also provides a value guide to the development of risk profiling. Each stage of a relationship journey has very distinct processes and these in turn give rise to the evaluation of the risk that may be encountered and exploited along the way.

The question to be considered by the corporate strategists is whether CSR and sustainable approaches are risk management or a responsible focus for the common good. The hope, of course, is that it is responsible corporate governance that is combining with risk management to benefit stakeholders and the wider community.

CHAPTER 16

Brand management

The evolving business models of the second half of the twentieth century and the prospect that these will further evolve in the future are founded on the concept of brand rather than production. To move from the traditional Fordist monolith structure to a virtually integrated fluid structure presents a major challenge in terms of recognizing and managing sustainability within the supply network backing a brand-based business model.

There can be few that have not seen the pressures applied to leading brand managers such as Nike, Coca-Cola, Adidas, McDonald's and others. They are the classic new business models where integrated use of third-party organizations has become the key to business delivery processes, although more traditionally-based organizations have now focused more on core activities and developed global supply chains. The brand name of a product is perhaps less and less a representation of its manufacturing origin. The increasing pressure for cost competitiveness has forced greater use of outsourcing and sub-assembly to the point where often perhaps only the product badge retains the traditional image. Thus the impacts on brand increase as seen in Figure 16.1.

This brand-based model carries with it a new interdependency and risk that is perhaps not yet fully integrated into companies' operating approaches. Any successful brand name is continuously open to becoming the focus of all the numerous NGOs that see high-profile names as spring boards to promote their cause rather than specifically trying to change their business practice. The general public may never have heard of the many producers and processors in the supply chain but focus, say, on Nike, BP, HSBC or Marks & Spencer and you are certain to get media coverage. Thus for many the challenge is not only to promote the brand but also to protect it by limiting the exposure potential from not fully understanding the supply network or ignoring the growing pressures for corporate responsibility.

What makes a brand strategy is the focus on building growth through creating market demand and product recognition towards sustained

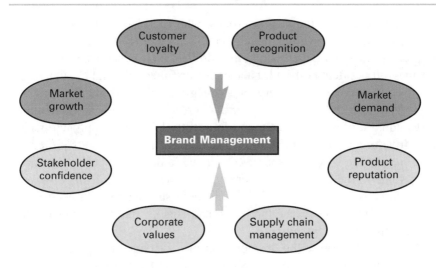

Figure 16.1 Impacts on brand

customer product loyalty. The counter-balance is that the higher the focus on the brand the more vulnerable it becomes to issues of product reputation and shareholder confidence. The extended supply chain creates commercial benefits but leaves organizations exposed to the behaviour, culture and ethos of parties in those networks. What has to be part of this process is the visibility of corporate values. These set a defence for random problems but at the same time these values provide a stick for organizations to be beaten with when they fail or are caught out by lapses in control and management.

It is also apparent that as organizations strive for growth they depend on both the market opportunities and investor valuation. Financial structuring can be extremely vulnerable to investor fluctuations, which can leave organizations exposed. Thus any situation that impacts the potential standing of their brand reputation can destabilize business strategy and development plans. Those involved in industries that are frequently considered dirty, such as construction and mining, often find their strategy seriously impacted by local pressure groups of many differing beliefs and causes, from the eco-warriors to the NIMBYs delaying or prohibiting developments.

Thus as a first step maintaining a profile in the market for being a sustainability-focused, responsible organization helps to maintain investor and customer confidence, recognizing that reputation is an organization's most valuable asset and that one poorly considered action might damage years of effort and investment. In the worst case this pressure could hit the bottom line if the public could be mobilized to vote with their feet.

On the other side the protest groups, who each have their own special cause, should recognize that negative publicity will tend to draw resources to protect the brand rather than perhaps reflect their concerns back into the business. It is often a difficult balance for organizations and as such meeting the requirements of every pressure group may eventually convince organizations to be defensive rather than proactive towards sustainability.

Building a brand is a costly and frequently long-term approach, which can drive organizations to spend considerable effort and funds protecting that investment. Clearly resources expended in defensive programmes add little value to the business. Harnessing these resources to focus on proactive and constructive approaches is far more sustainable. Thus those that seek to promote their cause through brand attacks may in the longer term be defeating their own aims.

Many, however, see the development of a sustainability programme as an effective way to promote their business and protect their long-term strategies. AMEC, as an example, is a multi-national in construction and mining, which proudly promotes its reputation and performance through their sustainability report entitled 'In Touch', with the strap line '*sustaining our reputation*'. A sustainable company is clearly one that does not sacrifice long-term interests for short-term gains and has moved its corporate focus from a conflict between profit and the community towards an integrated approach that recognizes the need for balance.

What many are coming to realize is that the traditional ethos of 'profit at all cost' was wrong, in that good health and safety supports efficiency, environmental consideration supports community commitment, and responsible management provides investor confidence.

BSkyB, coming from the world of media, take a similar view, suggesting that social activity and responsible corporate behaviour aren't bolt-on initiatives to make people feel good about their brand. It's in a company's interest to make its brand as attractive as possible to the widest market to deliver shareholder and stakeholder value.

What is often interesting is that whilst many organizations strive to improve their image and approaches they are frequently bench-marked across industries. Thus, whilst there are clearly some common issues you can't expect a development construction organization to measure up against the Body Shop, which has its own specially structured approach to developing a sustainability based market value. This lack of realism is what frequently dilutes the impact of the NGO and perhaps encourages some organizations to focus on compliance rather than commitment to sustainable approaches. On the other hand, companies should be prepared to declare openly their visions, values and codes of practice, and acknowledge that they won't get it all right at once. Of course these approaches are assuming a rational approach from protesters and NGOs rather than from almost illegal environmental terrorists.

This may all seem very straightforward but it takes a limited amount of research to realize the depth and breadth of brand attacks that are part of our everyday life. What is clear is that the bigger the brand, the wider the protests' focus. The question that keeps coming up is whether the focus is a serious attempt to alter a corporate board's approach or just the vehicle for promoting the cause. What is very hard to find are the hard facts about the commercial impacts of these campaigns, where certainly the animal rights groups have grabbed the headlines but have they really changed anything or, on balance, should they have changed anything? The issues come down to personal opinion and legal processes and, whilst we should protect the right to peaceful protest, we should not condone illegal attacks on legitimate commercial business.

The consumer boycott has in recent years become a very powerful weapon where organizations have failed or (more importantly) continue to fail to address public opinion. There are a multitude of cases that have hit the headlines and it is difficult to consider the implications of the brand minefield without bringing some of these to the fore. They should not, however, be considered in isolation, as certainly there will be many companies around the world equally open to criticism but not as high profile. What some of these major cases highlight is the need for all organizations to consider their sustainability strategy and decide whether to invest in being proactive and become vulnerable, or defensive and lose the opportunity to develop.

Take, for example, Shell which has hit the headlines several times over the past few years for cases of exploitation, false reserve accounting and the fiasco of Brent Spar. Interestingly enough, of these the one which evoked the most notoriety and forced a change in approach was Brent Spar. The concept of causing pollution through dumping the production platform in the North Sea mobilized the green lobby across Europe. Boycotts of Shell petrol stations created a financial backlash that forced a climb-down by the management. Public opinion had been seriously under-estimated and the power of the consumer was clearly demonstrated. The other issues failed to evoke the same level of reaction in the public domain but clearly cost Shell in the investment market.

BP, on the other hand, has invested substantially in a strategy of presenting itself as a sustainable energy producer. This has invoked many greens to attack BP even when they invested in renewable energy developments. Clearly in the field of oil exploitation there are going to be few supporters in the green protest groups but the public would generally seem to be more favourably disposed to those trying to improve. Some suggest these green investments are purely a sop to the market and that being a substantial R&D investor allows some degree of control over market development.

Exxon Mobil has perhaps been less successful in maintaining its image by being seen as the major supporter of the Republican Party in the USA: some claim they wrote President Bush's clear skies speech, and they are opposed to the adoption of the Kyoto agreement. It is suggested that contributions to lobbying Capitol Hill by Exxon exceeded those of Enron, and perhaps this lobbying investment might be a measure of the robustness of an organization's sustainability programmes, in that the more they spend perhaps the more they have to hide. In all these cases it is hard to see any prolonged impact on their business strategy, profitability or development. One may suspect that we actually have little loyalty to what petrol goes in our tanks as long as it is available. Thus protest and brand are limited to short-term specific issues, though Greenpeace maintain the boycott hurt Exxon (but then they would).

StopEsso has brought legal disputes and active support from organizations recommending boycotts including the Body Shop and various universities. Major organizations have declared they do not or will not use Esso petrol, a common practice across brands and retail outlets.

Find any kind of sustainability report expressing concerns over corporate focus and you will certainly find Nike being pilloried by many ethical consumer groups as the symbolic representation of all that is bad in business. Human rights, child labour, labour exploitation and workers' rights are some of the challenges continuously laid at Nike's door. Considering the market reach of Nike (over 140 countries), and a complex production network stretching across all five continents involving over 700 contract factories, it is little wonder that periodically they shoot themselves in the foot. In a competitive production market, switching suppliers is inevitable, which clearly results in job losses and local difficulties.

Nike has, however, owned up to some of its blunders: it has introduced a code of conduct and claims to be working towards greater integration of sustainability issues. It continues to bear the brunt of sustainability attacks and perhaps it could benefit from advice rather than reactive protest because of its profile. It is also worth considering the competitiveness of these production markets and the local impacts of walking away from contentious situations. The classic case of the children sewing footballs eventually did little damage to Nike, but their withdrawal from production regions has damaged the local economy.

Adidas caught a similar backlash and pressure over the use of kangaroo leather for football boots. Many may dislike the idea of farming these animals (and they are entitled to their opinion); however, the kangaroo industry of Australia depends on this trade so we need to introduce balance into the overall thinking.

Boycotts, then, are seen as a major weapon of the NGOs with which to provide some form of restraint on the activities and antics of disreputable companies. Whether they are actually disreputable or simply responding to market demand probably depends on your personal perspective, but what must be recognized is that if public opinion can be marshalled then it can impact significantly on strategy and profitability. The growth in awareness of the sustainability and CSR agendas has prompted many to look at how the potential damage of brand boycotts impacts companies. Recently there has been a move towards promoting investor attraction to companies that display a sound approach.

This has been taken further in the creation of the boycott vulnerability ratio (BVR). The idea is that where share values and sales are equal then any drop in sales would have a similar impact on stock value, but a company where the stock value is higher than sales would thus suffer to a greater extent from sales reductions through boycotts. The aim, then, is to target companies where the BVR is high so that they will probably respond quicker to pressure. Considering this balance may influence investor strategies, but one wonders if dividends will still be the major influence. KarmaBanque think this is so valuable that they are considering launching hedge funds to exploit the differential.

We often ask if boycotts of brands really have any impact and it is true that frequently the claims of success by the NGOs are often not reflected in the reports of profits and dividends of the companies. The Co-operative Bank's Ethical Purchasing index suggests that petrol retailers lost over £450 million in one year through boycotts, but since there was no reduction in overall consumption it would seem that some degree of pressure works.

De Beers had a confrontation with Survival International over its lack of policy towards indigenous tribes in Botswana, whilst working in a 50:50 venture with the local government. De Beers reversed its public view despite the fact the Botswana government had not changed its position and is facing legal action from the relocated bush men. Kraft, on the other hand, decided to take the initiative with its plans to curb advertising to children for its snack food products. Faced with a growing concern about obesity in children they have reacted by looking at what they can do to avoid criticism, but at the same time they have a $30 billion business in a highly competitive market. They are still under pressure to take cartoon characters off their packaging. It would be nice to consider that advertising was our only challenge.

In 2000 Mitsubishi elected to open discussions with the Rainforest Action Network rather than fight off continued boycotts and protests. By committing themselves to alternative policies on wood and paper consumption, Mitsubishi faced over 40 Californian cities passing resolutions condemning the company. They also pulled out of a seawater salt extraction project to avoid further protests, which would suggest that many organizations do take the boycott potential seriously.

Nestlé, on the other hand, seems to be at the forefront of fighting the boycott arena judging by the diverse column inches that get written by both sides. The big challenge came from exploitation of baby food, which was certainly emotive enough to attract support across a wide public circle. These protests have included Baby Milk Action, which enlisted stars to boycott sponsored events and even advertising projects. Nestlé was accused of flouting World Health Organization regulations to promote the benefits of their baby milk to avoid AIDS transmission. Despite supporting charitable actions, Nestlé often faces criticism that it is cynically positioning its products irrespective of the implications for the Third World. An organization of such a size and complexity must struggle to switch to suit every pressure group and, as the biggest in its field, defence is perhaps its only choice.

As the lists of boycotts and protests grow from Australian kangaroos through to Unilever animal testing, it becomes a constantly increasing minefield for organizations. The higher the company profile, the greater the chance they will be implicated in protests for some oversight or failure to manage the supply chains. This situation grows even worse when one starts to look at the protests and brand attacks that reflect political drivers rather than company failures.

Anti-genetic modification protesters have targeted Starbucks for using GM products and Bayer for their involvement in developing and exploiting GM organism production. Protests stopped Bayer testing in the United Kingdom but surely this means that development will increase elsewhere.

Animal rights have caused no end of difficulties for many commercial organizations, and frequently the most violent attacks on property and people. Animal testing has always been a major cause for conflict, which has over the years steered many organizations towards alternative testing programmes. There often seems to be a lack of reason when it comes to animals, perhaps even more so than exploitation of people. Procter & Gamble (P&G), like many diverse product organizations, faces protest over its testing for pet food. The anti-vivisection groups have not only targeted P&G but also Colgate-Palmolive, Unilever, Nestlé, Reckitt Benckiser and Pedigree: in fact, virtually every mainstream producer, which is perhaps more likely to bring about a coalition than major movement.

Canadian companies and the tourist industry come under pressure every year because of the emotive spectre of seal culling. Coco-Cola has been consistently associated with the spread of American influence and as such frequently comes under the microscope based not on its value proposition but its political heritage as well as some of its business decisions, such as the suggested linkage with union oppression in South America. Growing competition from Mecca Cola stems from the Muslim backlash to American policy overseas.

The challenge, then, for organizations is not only to mange their own activities but also to be aware of the political environment within which they operate. Clearly the major USA organizations, such as Coca Cola, have always been associated with the spread of US policy; but when the US President decided to attack Iraq, the protest spread to the boycotting of US companies. Surveys have suggested that up to 20 per cent of consumers in Europe actively boycotted US-based products as a direct result of the invasion of Iraq.

Few nations however in recent times have evoked as much boycott activity as Burma based on the human rights record of the government. Company after company has found that for the sake of its wider business sphere, withdrawing from Burma was a sensible choice. From British American Tobacco to Triumph motorcycles, the pressure has been applied to pull out. Not only has this pressure been applied to direct involvement, but also to any major corporation with shareholders in companies that have a presence in Burma. The arm's-length approach is often one deployed by organizations to circumvent national sanctions.

Burma produced perhaps the first significant coalition between industry and the NGOs; major organizations including Body Shop, the Co-operative Bank and Friends of the Earth joined forces to build the campaign. Major retailers pulled Burmese products from their shelves along with tourism, which is perhaps the most vulnerable of industries to political boycotts. Many organizations found themselves being forced to validate their supply chains, which included Burmese suppliers in the third tier. Again the challenge is often not one's own actions but those of suppliers further down the food chain.

An interesting phenomenon that comes from the creation of a 'dirty list' (the companies that continue to work in Burma) is the 'clean list' of companies that have pulled out. This reverse boycott concept is one that many organizations are now starting to consider as being far more positive. Promoting companies that do things right is perhaps more proactive than just chasing the bad boys. A South African reverse boycott has been operating to promote the sales of products to help improve economic development and employment.

Moving to a proactive approach does require many in the NGOs to consider their long-term objectives and to be prepared to think outside the box. If the motivation were to attack organizations to promote their particular creed then shifting to a brand credit would be a major transition. Helping to promote organizations in the market place because of these companies' policy and practice would set a benchmark for those that should perhaps improve. Adoption of ideas such as the Fairtrade mark has created more interest for the consumer, as has the Forest Stewardship Council (FSC) in terms of forest-managed products.

The overall issue, however, for the focus on sustainability and brand management programmes is that organizations must take care to protect their investment. First, as the global supply network increases, the risks of being compromised by second and third tier suppliers increases. Second, companies need to consider their internal policies and develop effective management processes to take those policies beyond corporate boundaries.

Obviously the overall aim is to build a more sustainable approach into the operating ethos of the company and to promote these policies to attract the customer and consumer. At the same time the high-profile players need to consider how to engage with the NGOs and how to establish a public policy that is practical and workable in their business environment.

The brand minefield is one that offers so many potential risks that many commercial organizations have chosen to develop a protectionist approach which frequently encourages the NGOs to become more aggressive. For many, the prospect of being unable to enter constructive debate prompts them to raise their protest beyond public debate. It must be recognized that brand protection is a crucial part of any business organization's responsibility and there has to be some balance between the Body Shop's exploitation of a valid sustainable brand approach and the Nestlé concept, which many would suggest is based on forceful marketing and maintaining critical mass and market share.

Looking to the future, and perhaps towards a more proactive approach, we see the creation of a sustainable reverse boycott approach that promotes organizations that are pushing to improve and integrate effective policies. This will have to acknowledge that problems will surely still arise but would reflect how companies respond to challenges or changes in the market place. Consumer acceptance will certainly be a key factor, shifting the brand defence funding towards a sustainable investment programme that puts the effort to positive use.

Clearly corporate actions or political positioning, whether this is anti-USA or pro-Palestine, can drive the boycott. The multiple pressure groups can range from animal rights to human rights, and none of these one would suspect would consider their cause less important, but for the company there will almost certainly be a degree of prioritization. There is perhaps no major brand out there in the market that is not exposed in some way to one or more special interest groups.

UK surveys have suggested that around 20 per cent of consumers choose a product or boycott it on the basis of ethical reputation, whilst 30 per cent would support products with charitable connections. It is, however, not only the customer or consumer reactions that need attention: employing the right people means attracting the best and that too is a factor of the brand image, as people do not want to work for condemned titles and names.

Thus it is clear that sustainability and brand management are inter-linked and present a key risk or opportunity for the business community. An exposed brand can be costly for the bottom line, and may require a heavy spend to counteract market opinion. Protecting the brand is perhaps more about effective corporate responsibility programmes and visibility being integrated into the business process. When companies consider the exposure they may face, the cost and implications of adopting a proactive approach is more practical than fire-fighting problems. Sustainability can be cost effective and this should be exploited through development of brand integrity and trust.

CHAPTER 17

Stakeholder values

The sustainable community landscape, whether at a local or global level, encompasses a wide range of perspectives and opinions. These vary from personal greed to an almost saintly focus on some aspect of human development. In some cases the extremes are seen in both corporate exploitation and eco-terrorism. To develop a long-term approach there cannot be one single driver or group focused on delivery. The holistic nature of any community creates an environment where everyone is to some extent pulled in various directions as stakeholders.

The values that we apply both as individuals and groups directly influence the way forward. We cannot place pressure on business without changing the expectations of customers and consumers. It is unrealistic to raise the expectations of the developing world before establishing the ability to deliver on the promise of a better tomorrow. It is perhaps unreasonable to apply industrialized western perspectives to Third World manufacturers without realizing that those that suffer most in the short term will be the workers that the protest is trying to protect.

The growing influence of stakeholders (as shown in Figure 17.1) is gaining more importance at the corporate board level, but to move forward to a more sustainable future means their recognizing that governance must move from compliance to commitment. The challenge of this inclusiveness is that it has to clearly focus on shareholder value whilst balancing increasingly conflicting demands. The is a growing acceptance that whilst their primary duty and responsibility is to long-term shareholder value, this can only be achieved by having regard for the many stakeholders. Some may see this change as enlightenment, but the reality is that taking a more inclusive perspective makes common sense in a strictly commercial business arena.

Take, for example, the B&Q story that started back in the 1990s when the company embarked on a programme to address the criticisms being levelled by environmental pressure groups. The company acknowledged that the protest was affecting their competitive business. As a result of the

Figure 17.1   Integrating stakeholder values

initiative, B&Q established new buying rules that dictated the principle of managed forests. This approach came under considerable criticism from the Malaysian government which objected to the pressure that the B&Q approach would put on the local economy. The programme was successful in quietening Friends of the Earth and was generally accepted as positive by consumers. In later years, having established a consistent approach, they then went back to the NGOs to see what to do next and were met with confusion. One wonders if the NGOs want to keep their protest platforms or really make a difference. More recently the buying policy has come under increasing pressure as price competition has not been supported by consumer commitment.

Corporate reputation has many impacts on the effective development of any organization. There can be few CEOs who would not want to protect the reputation of their organization but, despite the growing trends in the market place, many still see only compliance. They are, in the majority of cases, failing to recognize the potential benefits to overall performance from deploying improved social and environmental policies and approaches. It is perhaps only a mind-set change to appreciate that there should not be a conflict between responsibility to shareholders and to the wider stakeholder community. A responsible sustainable approach can focus on eco-efficiency, which in turn can deliver value to the bottom line.

We are in many organizations seeing a step change from a limited paper recycling commitment to a much wider and future-focused strategy towards sustainability. The real social impact is growing beyond the annual contributions to charity. This change does, however, need greater commitment from the top and this has in any business to be rationalized against the demands of shareholders and the influences of the market. Take the approach of Diageo plc, one of the major drinks manufactures and distributors, whose declared corporate core values are outlined below:

> Passionate about consumers, Freedom to succeed, Proud of what we do, Be the best

They benchmarked themselves against the GRI and took these core values into the policy and practice of the company. This focus was driven directly by Paul Walsh (the CEO) and specialist working groups. Regular consultation with stakeholder groups – both internally with employees and externally across investors, consumers and regulators – helps to maintain balance and visibility.

Many other organizations have taken similar approaches, recognizing that if you stand up and declare a position you also need to validate it and frequently defend it in the market. Unilever's corporate motto, for example, is 'We believe that to succeed requires the highest standards of corporate behaviour towards our employees, consumers and the societies and world in which we live.' What is equally important is to demonstrate that policy and performance are inter-linked. A report in November 2004 by the Sustainable Energy Institute in the US suggests that many corporations across a range of industries are moving ahead with GHG reduction programmes despite the US government staying outside the Kyoto Protocol. This shows business leaders taking the initiative over compliance and in the long term will perhaps draw environmentally focused consumers towards these organizations.

Perhaps driven by a poor image in the consumer market, the coffee companies have established a voluntary code of practice aimed at improving conditions and environmental standards for employees in producer companies. The signatories included Nestlé, Tchibo, Sara Lee and Kraft, but the code itself falls short of committing to buy certified coffee although it does focus on supporting premium quality producers. Given the many challenges faced by the likes of Nestlé, perhaps a stronger commitment would help change reputation impacts in many areas of their operations.

Starbucks on the other hand committed over $1 million to help establish the Conservation Coffee Alliance in order to provide economic incentives and technical support to small producers. Given the boycotts and pressures on Starbucks this shows how the market influences companies, and may over time help other communities. The coffee market has been continuously attacked through organizations such as Traidcraft and Fairtrade where big players use various means to maintain their place on the supermarket shelves.

As companies come under more pressure to make public their policies and approaches to sustainability, stakeholders feel they have the right to judge how companies perform. Many investment managers and (as we have seen) investment banks have established a greater focus on analysing how organizations operate and manage sustainable issues. This is perhaps partly driven by a desire to promote best practice in corporate governance but there are also practical considerations.

As sustainability gains more visibility in the market place, it also introduces increased vulnerability in terms of financial performance. One socially responsible investment fund, Citizens Advisors, announced in October 2004 their top ten corporate citizens in environmental stewardship. These were drawn from over 300 companies that had been screened for both financial strength and corporate responsibility.

Investors have their hands on one end of the corporate tug of war rope with the customer or consumer at the other. The need for corporate leaders to deliver dividends often clouds the wider perspectives of responsibility. With only a mandate for financial performance they have little room for social positioning. The introduction of the FTSE4Good, Dow Jones Sustainability Indices and the Ethical Investment Research Service (EIRIS) has started the process of developing a more rounded view of corporate values and performance. The reality, however, is that if sustainability is to be embedded in the corporate business process then part of the drive has to come from the investor community.

Clearly many aspects of the social and environmental considerations can be adopted, integrated and converted to add real value. Other aspects, however, may need to be driven and supported through a more pragmatic and responsible investor approach. It was an interesting challenge to a corporate board to see Caterpillar facing a resolution by its shareholders focusing on the use of its bulldozers by the Israeli army to flatten Palestinian property on the West Bank. Shareholder power can never be under-estimated by CEOs.

There is certainly a balance to be struck between commercial benefits and the longer-term sustainability and social programmes that will not provide short-term, high-margin dividends. These situations mean that both customers and investors need to consider their own policies and aims. As we have seen some organizations have set themselves up to exploit the attraction for socially sustainable and environmental business models. These will probably touch only a small fraction of the market place and, if we are to see real progress, then there needs to be a cultural change that induces investors to join the arena of responsibility.

An innovative approach will clearly not come overnight. On the one hand, corporate organizations need to be able to demonstrate that sustainable responsibility can be harnessed to deliver additional value and performance; on the other hand, the investor community needs to be looking towards the longer term and recognizing that a sustainable future means less short-term exploitation. It may be that regulatory and governmental incentives could be consolidated to help bridge the investment gap, say, in terms of green tax benefits and sustainable investment advantages. Considering what is currently invested in overseas aid, for example, perhaps sustainability-friendly programmes in the private sector could attract offset support.

Before considering the customer/consumer pressure on corporate strategy it is also important to look at the employee within the stakeholder network. It is becoming frequently apparent that sustainability considerations are already affecting employee expectations. The past two decades in particular have seen a trend in the industrialized world away from the dirty industries towards those that are viewed as more environmentally friendly (although given the implications of, say, the ICT community and its waste/exploitation globally, one wonders if they are simply chasing the money).

It is clear that employee performance is greatly affected by the working environment and fair labour considerations. Thus at every stage of the business delivery process, how employees are treated and managed affects output performance and quality standards. It makes sense then to integrate responsible policies into the business operation if only to optimize performance, and if this also reflects a more socially responsible approach, then so much the better.

Health and safety, wherever in the world the operation is carried out, has a major impact on quality and performance. Companies have to protect their own staff and contractors and the communities they are operating in. Poor H&S reflects directly on performance and frequently can have a major impact on the cost profile and bottom line of an operation through lost time incidents, litigation or market protest. So not only does it make sense, it also has significant commercial implications.

Delivering a corporate sustainability programme is not simply a case of creating corporate vision and values; tt depends on the approach and commitment of the employees at every level of the operation who have to translate these values into practical applications and maintain them throughout normal operations. The best way to accomplish employee buy-in is to educate employees about the values and benefits of a sustainable approach. In many cases employees are perhaps already enthusiastic about a better future but are constrained by corporate performance drivers and incentive schemes.

In the wider context of the sustainable agenda the implications of globalization have brought additional strains to the relationship between corporate boards and their employee base. As the commercial pressure builds to relocate and rationalize, this impacts the employees and the local communities.

The balance in the corporate tug of war is the customer or consumer, although we will look at customers separately later. The consumer is a stakeholder when buying products, but frequently also as an employee, investor, NGO supporter and member of the community. It is spending power that influences most corporate considerations. Strategy, product development, marketing and future investment are driven by understanding what the consumer wants or what they may be induced to want. In the same way it is within the power of the consumer to strongly influence responsible corporate performance.

The frequent dilemma, however, is that whilst consumers may well want corporations to behave more responsibly, they still expect best value for money. Strong feelings may occasionally prompt an effective boycott that forces a brand to take stock or change course, but in the main product price and quality will have a greater impact on sales. The feel-good factor may allow some to feel encouraged to support charitable or Fairtrade products but, as soon as the economic cycle dips, the commitment wanes.

The real power to effect change, then, rests with those that buy the product or service and seek to support companies which have sound sustainable principles integrated into their business model. Adam Smith, over 200 years ago, outlined a key justification for free enterprise capitalism when he said that organizations survive and prosper through meeting the needs of customers. If the concept of corporate responsible performance is merged into these needs then the consumer will ultimately drive improvements and change. Companies that ignore this pressure will not survive, and in the global market place this vulnerability is easily overlooked.

Take Tesco withdrawing whale meat from the shelves of its stores in Japan because of pressure from the wider market. Now whilst one may not support whaling given the shrinking stocks, is it right that local customers should not have freedom of choice? Despite international law it is also doubtful that Tesco's action will significantly reduce the local demand.

Supermarkets are frequently under the cosh from numerous sectors because of their buying patterns, yet they are growing their customer base and have significantly changed the purchasing habits of many established nations. Freedom and increased choice balanced against competitive pricing helps to underpin the growth. So whilst we may applaud Tesco for acknowledging the demands of Greenpeace, the Friends of the Earth (FoTE) have continued their opposition to supermarkets in general. They maintain that in providing a consolidated sales outlet to the consumer they are damaging the wider community by not offering best prices whilst bullying producers to sell at low prices to the extent that they are putting small producers and shops out of business.

It is unlikely that the consumer will want to see the demise of the supermarket approach but still FoTE maintain the approach is totally out of balance with sustainable drivers, destroying communities and small businesses while increasing waste and pollution through distribution. It is perhaps time to focus on the realities of what could be improved rather than trying to reverse the tide.

The notoriety of the eco-terrorist and animal protest groups have taken centre-stage in terms of stakeholders in the arena of sustainable responsibility. In many ways this acts against the aims of the many constructive groups that would like to be part of the proactive debate with the corporate world. It is also the diversity of these pressure groups that frequently lowers the profile of their concerns. There are so many organizations protesting and (in their view) defending aspects of the planet that most corporate organizations have little chance of staying in step or even in dialogue with them. The result is that their pleas are not heard until they react in a confrontational manner, which then arouses the worst conflict between commerce, the community and the pressure groups. Certainly everyone is entitled to their opinion, but corporate leaders and other stakeholders demand a balance between need and impact.

These groups have in more recent times expanded to include religious and political as well as environmental and social targets, even constraining corporate developments and performance. It is perhaps not possible to find a commercial company anywhere that is not offending some segment of the community. What has to be recognized is that if companies cannot go about their legal business without interruption then they will not seek to consult

NGOs unless it is business-critical. The disappointing aspect of this relationship is that in many cases these specialist groups do have a wide knowledge base and perhaps can offer constructive alternatives.

Part of the business community that is frequently ignored in terms of sustainability strategy is its role and relationships with suppliers. Many companies sit at the top of complex supply chains that may spread across the globe. The performance of a supplier who may be several tiers removed could be totally undermining the efforts and values of the prime company. For those organizations that purchase significant elements of their product from other suppliers, the creation of corporate values and policies is wasted if those downstream are not equally committed to the long-term future.

This becomes particularly pertinent when the buyer is looking for short-term cost savings and has limited need to commit to a long-term supply relationship with that supplier. The valid and constructive aims of corporate leaders may be completely negated by the performance of suppliers further down the food chain. It, therefore, becomes important for those committed to a sustainable future to ensure that appropriate processes, controls and monitors are in place to underpin the overall values. It should also be remembered that when it comes to external criticism of mainstream brands that problems at the supplier level could reflect on the big name.

Suppliers, on the other hand, may have their own values and developing these into reputation attributes may well help to consolidate relationships with customers. Progressively organizations are moving towards a more agile business model that relies on network clusters of complementary suppliers. Focusing on core skills, major organizations are frequently ringed by tiers of suppliers and service providers. It is likely that the stronger the relationships between these players, the more effective the operation. Thus it is also likely that similar values will help consolidate these relationships.

The growth and diversity of legislation and regulation adds a further dimension to the stakeholder network. Many would suggest that we need more regulation, whilst others clearly see rules as being definitive and thus it is easier to facilitate compliance as opposed to agreeing to capitalize on sustainable approaches. Regulators have to be part of the stakeholder dialogue but frequently they focus on responding to politically sensitive issues without understanding the impacts and negativity that may be created. The more regulation, the greater the tendency to look for commercially attractive solutions that may be short term and not support long-term programmes. The essence of a global approach to corporate responsibility is that each nation has its own values but, whilst idealists may want to see all equal, this is not likely. As such it must also be acknowledged that operating within the regulations is often the best that many organizations are able to achieve in the short term.

Overall one must consider in the business-to-business community the customer, who may be the interface with the consumer or end-user but is certainly the driving force for change and evolution. In most if not all business operations we are both customer and supplier at some part of the process. What is frequently apparent is that the majority of organizations distinctly segregate these functions, so that the way in which they react to customer demands and values is seldom reflected in the way they treat and interact with their suppliers.

An intelligent company should be looking for intelligent customers and suppliers since, unless there is a common acceptance of common values, the impacts of sustainability strategies will be limited. The customer or consumer has the power to dictate a clear focus on sustainable approaches but must be prepared on occasion to prioritize the longer-term value over short-term cost savings. Investors need to balance their return on investment and focus on companies that are balancing value and sustainability, which may require more time to return full credit for the investment.

The community, local or global, has a wide variety of stakeholders, each with their own agendas and drivers. What should be clear is that to build sustainable solutions there has to be compromise and consideration which blends the values of each stakeholder. Many will be involved as stakeholders at various levels and must understand that their demands and the demands made of them should reflect a common focus in order to deliver value.

What is perhaps even more important is that talk is cheap, and it will be the measuring of performance that helps to build confidence across the stakeholders to acknowledge that others have values which should be considered where practical.

Value is relative and the community is diverse, and thus it is inevitable that groups will frequently find themselves challenging specific actions. What needs to be understood is what is driving that action and how alternatives may provide solutions with equal benefits. Principles are easy to maintain until one is faced with direct conflict, given the range of issues that fall under the sustainability agenda (from ethical trading to environmental damage). All stakeholders should consider what is practical, what is possible and what is the majority rule that companies have to follow.

There can be few corporate organizations that are currently not exposed to some form of protest or sustainable challenge. The first step in making a difference to this negative use of resources is to engage in the debate and try to understand who are the stakeholders.

CHAPTER 18

Sustainable development

Numerous corporate reports carry the words of CEOs who claim they are making good progress towards a strong, sustainable business. But what is sustainable development? Sustainability is the capacity to continue operating in the long term. It is also important to establish that sustainability is not just about protecting the environment and taking a more measured view concerning the use of natural resources; it must also incorporate consideration for ensuring stable economic and social growth for the whole community.

Sir Peter Mason, CEO of AMEC, describes it in terms of three pillars of sustainability, people, the planet and prosperity, each of which is equally important. To a large extent they are also interdependent. The ability of business to create wealth and employment is crucial to sustainable development and key to building long-term value for all the stakeholders.

In December 2004 the World Bank issued its annual publication, *Environmental Matters*,[5] which is based on the theme of long-term sustainable growth. It promotes the idea that the environment is an issue for both developed and developing countries and called for the developed countries to reduce subsidies, ensure appropriate pricing and tax environmentally-damaging products adequately. As an example every European cow is subsidized to the value of $2.50 per day, whilst one billion people live on less than $1 per day. With potentially 1 per cent of the world's population consuming 80 per cent of the world's resources, the equation is not sustainable. Employees, customers and business partners are increasingly aware of global inequality and it makes them uneasy. Corporate leaders, therefore, have an obligation to develop strategies that acknowledge and influence some of these challenges.

Reviewing public reports would suggest that the majority of FTSE 350 companies are addressing aspects of sustainability. A review by Article 13,[6] who specialize in advising companies on the risks of sustainability issues, analysed 20 per cent of these to find evidence of socially focused innovation and established that the majority were actually directing efforts towards compliance.

A few forward thinking companies are demonstrating real innovation in this area. In these cases the innovation is mainly in the areas of business processes, channels to market and product offerings; the main changes are incremental with some transformation of products and process. These changes include a food processing company that introduced new processes within sustainable guidelines for key crop production; a waste management company that introduced new products from recycled waste; and a major retailer that decentralized its CSR policy to allow each business unit to develop its own sustainability programmes within the local communities.

The Arthur D. Little January 2005 presentation, entitled 'A turning tide' focused on its research into sustainability-driven innovation. It found that to date the main emphasis of companies had been on the control of risk and adaptation of current approaches to meet sustainability objectives. A trend was emerging, however, of companies starting to look for ways to take sustainable issues into new business opportunities, new ways of working and new markets. Though the report was developed around a global group of technology companies, the findings and concepts should be considered by every business (some adaptations may be necessary).

The main reasons to implement sustainability programmes involve the need to reduce cost and thus resource demand. At the same time there is always a risk to the brand and reputation of a business, but developing a responsible approach is viewed as the route to customer preference. Innovation brings forward the concept of creating new products and markets.

The shift from responsibility to opportunity is the first sign of business adopting a proactive approach to sustainability and in turn creating a greater likelihood of real sustainability being developed. We have already discussed the implications of stakeholder interaction and focus, which sits at the core of true sustainability because it must be a compromise between today and tomorrow, focusing on development, as shown in Figure 18.1.

The recognition that sustainability may be good for companies and business ventures in the long term has prompted a new channel of strategic development that is being integrated into business processes. All businesses are centered on continuous growth, and the pressure from NGOs has in the main created a reactive approach from business. What is suggested by the Arthur D. Little research is that there can be real benefit, much of which businesses can drop to the bottom line to help to improve competitiveness.

Cost and risk were the early leaders and we shall look more deeply at eco-efficiency later, having already raised the issue of risk and reputation. In the main this is an internal question, but supply chain interfaces can also contribute. Externally the whole issue of stakeholder value and debate is one that again we have addressed at length.

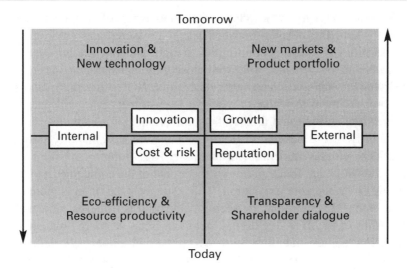

Figure 18.1 Focusing development
Reproduced with the permission of Professor Stuart Hart

Business sustainability is clearly an issue of growing the market and then maintaining it. The key to this is to understand what the customer wants, and then develop new markets or introduce new products that create their own demand. In this external activity the crucial focus is on understanding the customer's perception. Innovation then becomes central to building a growth-driven business. New technology, adapting or innovating current propositions with a sustainability driver, provides both a responsible approach and a new opportunity to be exploited.

Mapping social trends is a crucial part of understanding future needs and desires, and provides the opportunity to build up alternative approaches. The environmental, economical and social pressures within all markets will define the effects on corporate strategy. This trend analysis also enables organizations to look at the potential risks that may arise through less predictable aspects of the trading landscape. Thus much of the new technology is either being driven by social change or is actually driving social change.

The mobile phone, for example, was an innovative toy that has swamped the industrialized world. The latest generations are now providing capabilities that build on the notion that once people have a mobile phone, companies should exploit it. It is suggested that we are already seeing reductions in travel through greater use of tele-working. With aging populations the development of tele-care for the elderly by BT is responding to trends and providing new business opportunities.

The Arthur D. Little research provides one aspect of sustainable development where the balance between social pressures and environmental considerations is creating opportunities. It highlights the fact that customers remain the major influence, followed closely by legislation and regulation. One company surveyed responded that whilst NGOs and the media may have brought them to where they are, it is customers who will take them forward. It also suggested that whilst some organizations are clear leaders, the majority of businesses are failing to integrate sustainability into their operations, with investment in sustainability R&D running at below 10 per cent of development funding. Some 40 per cent of the companies had teams working on sustainable innovation, which suggests the trend is increasing.

Those that have invested are seeing value returns from real-time asthma diagnostics (mmO2) to free digital meters to improve energy management (Enel). Companies including Sony, Vodafone and Dupont all claim to be driving sustainable innovation because they are seeing real benefits. The biggest obstacle is pay-back time, which is not surprising when considering the conflicts of sustainable programmes.

Sustainable development for business is about attracting investment capital and talent to create innovative new products and develop new markets. This innovation can also be focused to reduce the cost of processes and consumable resources for existing products. In the longer term there can be differentiation through the growing demand for environmental and community impacts. Creating a business development plan that embraces sustainability can lead to exploiting traditional benefits and contributing to future value.

Sustainable development may require a greater focus on innovation, and certainly one would argue that to address many aspects of these challenges we must think outside the box. However, in a great many cases the drivers can be seen as being far more practically based and focused simply by looking differently at what we already do. Take, for example, Anglo-American, whose investments in its African operations as regards health and the community are seen as taking a positive step towards improving the local community profile. It is perhaps driven more by the economics of sustaining mining operations in a community where HIV/AIDS is depleting the workforce almost as fast as it can be trained.

We cannot and should not hold Anglo responsible for the disease, though unknowingly perhaps their labour utilization programmes have not helped the integrity of the family structures that might have contained the spread. However, their needs and those of the community have now come together and, by raising and supporting health awareness, they are contributing to providing help. In December 2004 Alco announced it was investing

$250,000 in Guinea to support family planning programmes and one wonders what the business driver was; not that we would contest the action, but sustainable business requires true motivation. It would certainly help other organizations to share the business logic rather than the goodwill image.

At the November 2004 Birkbeck lecture by James Smith, Chairman of Shell UK, his premise was based on establishing that there was a sound business case for sustainable development based on meeting customer needs, attracting talent and gaining strategic insight. However, to achieve the benefits companies need to integrate sustainability into the way they run their business.

He also voiced a spirited defence of CSR against those who maintain that the business of business is business, and that profit is the only motivator. The reality is that these views are not in conflict with sustainable responsibility if the drivers and pressures from the market place are demanding a socially responsible company. Customers create demand and poor customers do not build strong economies. Thus those that might suggest we stick our heads in the sand need to go back and address basic economics.

As a bolster for sustainable development it is interesting to see Shell promoting its policies against a background of some high-profile sustainability negatives. It is, of course, in the prime target industry so one should not be too surprised at the negativity. The clear message is that business couldn't operate in isolation and achieve sustainable outcomes. Business needs to be open to new ideas, new ways of doing things and working in partnership.

In a global market place the role of the SME is a key part of the economic structure. As the developing countries see economic growth, so they too will see a need to foster the SME community. Yet the sustainability profile of major companies may be important: if we are to have an effective business community and sustainability then we must also engage the SMEs. Many fear the social impact of big organizations pushing CSR demands down the food chain as a result of their concern for the potential vulnerability of a dispersed supply network.

Smaller businesses are perhaps frequently more socially aware than large ones, but the competitive pressures can often create demands that force good sense into the background. Sustainable development means not only working to support the social and environmental impacts but also considering the infrastructure implications, and that includes the economic actions of the SME community. The major players need to quality manage the value chains that support them and ensure that transfer of responsibility does not lead to dilution of sound strategies at the top. Perhaps whilst we pursue FTSE4Good we also need a small business responsibility programme that includes mentoring and support.

SMEs may not yet see the pressing need for participating but in the bigger picture their input and action is equally crucial to true sustainable development. As globalization increases and developing countries grow so the multi-nationals will rely more and more on local sourcing networks which in turn can create their own economic, environmental and social impacts.

Sustainable development rests on two main thrusts: the first is sustainable production, and the other is sustainable consumption. Both phrases have been utilized regularly in the sustainability debate but to most they are just buzzwords and sound bites, as well as a regular feature of global policy discussions. The UN Environment Programme defines sustainable consumption as one which attempts to find a balance between our rights as free consumers and our responsibility towards others, and encourages the simple practice of questioning the need for the product and then challenging how and where it was produced in order to ensure minimum impact.

Sustainable production starts with R&D and NPD. If the sustainability focus is to be maintained then clearly the investment must start at the point of origin; yet research suggests that the majority of companies don't have a sustainable policy in their R&D programmes. It may be possible to tweak current processes but fundamental change needs to develop progressively through the innovation process. This includes evaluating more efficient production processes, with lower costs through reduced energy and material consumption, modifying existing products and transforming product offerings to attract new customer focus.

CSR may currently frame corporate thinking but sustainability is far more wide reaching and there must be inclusion at every level. Every community is a combination of stakeholders and, whilst family businesses may be ready to innovate (and frequently, by their very nature, they are more attuned to the local community), they are also responsible to major global players. This cannot be effective simply on a compliance basis; it needs to be interactive and self-supporting. When in January 2005 it was reported that two Thai officials of Donghwa Digital were arrested and that the President had disappeared, it transpired that workers had been exposed to toxic chemicals in the production of liquid crystal displays, leaving them with crippling injuries.

This clearly begs the question of whether the customers knew but, more importantly, what is the impact on the local community? Beyond the health issue, which is clearly grave, the future of the plant must now be seriously in question. The impacts of the collapse of a significant local employer will ripple through the community in every aspect of local life, economic and social. The supply chain is also disrupted and eventually everybody loses, except those no longer having to working in dangerous conditions. The case highlights the clear impact of short-term opportunism and lack of a sustainable business approach. For a limited investment in safety clothing and ventilation, a viable business and community contributor could have been established.

Sustainable development must be integrated into every aspect of the business and industrial world, with technology playing a major part and offering opportunity. Take the case of a small company called Romag Limited which has developed a product called 'PowerGlaz' using solar cells to allow the integration of energy-generating glass products that can be integrated into all buildings, providing an alternative source of energy and contributing to the wider sustainability agenda. Certainly we will continue to put up more buildings which drain the resources of the planet, so why not balance this with less demand for energy?

Given that demands for water as well as energy will be a governing factor in the developing world another innovative idea is the Seawater Green house. Its polyurethane structure enables seawater to evaporate and be transferred to irrigate crops. Working with the natural energy of sunlight it is green in every sense except, of course, for the oil-based polyurethane, but perhaps this is a reasonable compromise in creating alternative ways to help arid coastal regions to produce food through a sustainable programme.

One of the major green developments in recent years has been the Eden Project in Cornwall. It is a living theatre of plants, people and possibilities. It was created in a disused, ugly and useless clay quarry with the intention of establishing a self-sustaining attraction, and is now the fourth most visited site in the UK. The biomes, huge transparent structures, house an extensive variety of plant life from across the globe. As well as clearly boosting the local economy, what is perhaps more interesting is the ethos and philosophy of the Eden Project team.

Whilst focused on delivering an enjoyable experience for its visitors it is highly tuned to ecological balance. Thus, for example, their waste-neutral programme is designed to achieve at least 80 per cent recycling and every investment follows this direction. From a business perspective, however, this project also offers some insight in the process of evaluating economics and vision as outlined earlier the simple process of serving tea to visitors could provide the blueprint for many organizations to look again at what and how they operate. Often our drive for a fast disposable operation is draining resources and building up costs, without considering the overall impact.

One imaginative project undertaken was to produce an eco-surfboard made from natural products grown within the biomes, which has proved a popular alternative to the traditional petrochemical-based boards. On the downside, the location of the Eden Project means that in the main visitors have to travel by car and, as it becomes more popular, with 5 million visitors over four years, there is a counter-balance to their vision. Over time one hopes they will succeed in improving the transport links and getting a better balance.

Another business model is that of Traidcraft, whose aim is to fight poverty through trade and over a few years it has created a multi-million-dollar business by working with producers in developing countries and providing a marketing outlet where the benefits flow back to the local communities. Fairtrade products are becoming progressively more readily available and consumers take up the increases year on year. The focus of the Traidcraft model is pure sustainability using trade; it provides support and influence to improve production methods whilst ensuring the benefits are reinvested in local producers to provide an ongoing development programme.

Campaigning against unfair and oppressive approaches by the short-term focused buyer complements this business-based approach. Many will recognize the Cafédirect brand, which was started by Traidcraft but has now floated a £5 million share issue and continues to grow, buying the high-quality beans at premium prices directly from the producers and providing support for continued sustainable growth and development.

The business edge is clearly the consumer interest and their feel-good factor, but it has to be acknowledged that stability and quality from producers must be a key element in every business programme. However, one must also ask how, whilst the consumer or customer may not always be prepared to pay a premium for an ethically produced product, it could still provide a competitive edge? Trade can either be a force for good or evil in terms of exploitation; if it can be used for good without losing competitive edge, then it must make sense.

One could not think of writing in this area without a mention of Anita Roddick and her Body Shop chain. The success of a business that in many ways flew in the face of conventional thinking at the time shows that sustainability, together with investment and support for the developing world, can be integrated with profitability. It is largely a question of choice on the part of the customer and also the proprietors and shareholders.

To argue that everything done by big companies is bad would be stupid. Companies create jobs, develop new products and provide services that we all need, and they also invest in communities. It is the sustainability of that investment, whether at home or abroad, that needs to be rationalized to ensure stability of supply and thus maintain a foundation for local economic growth. Adam Smith suggested that the baker was not there for the benefit of the people but was driven by self-interest. However, since a poor community does not provide customers sustainable development must also look to future trading balances, opportunities and benefits.

It is clearly not possible for every investment, development or operating decision that a company makes to be locked into a long-term sustainable outcome. Market pressures, limitations of alternative resources and technology simply constrain many decisions. What should be part of the business planning analysis and evaluation, however, is consideration for possible options that may not be part of the current approaches. Costs and profits are driven by availability and customer demand, so if short-term exploitation of resources means short-term stability then it can't be the best strategy. If customer demands are not recognized then there is no market, which is similarly not a sustainable approach.

Developing new products or creating innovative uses of current materials, products and technology can create new opportunities for organizations. Exploiting these developments can create a competitive edge, new markets and long-term stability for the business stakeholders.

The ultimate sustainability challenge is reflected in the development programme currently under way in the Utah Desert. The Mars Desert Research Station (MDRS) is being sponsored by business and NASA and is manned by volunteers for short periods to simulate living on Mars within a hostile environment. The programme may seem trite to many but it provides the opportunity to test ideas and approaches that may benefit a potential Mars landing. Replicating an environment that perhaps mirrors some of what many suggest we are pushing our own planet towards may produce innovations that can be adopted or adapted locally. When the teams recognize that they are all interdependent and breathing the same limited air supply, perhaps this microcosm will hold some message for sustainable development business programmes.

CHAPTER 19

Eco-efficiency

The key to implementing sustainable strategies is to understand that the benefits of exploiting a structured approach can build alternative options that deliver value as opposed to depleting margins. Sustainability is frequently viewed as being a nice-to-have ethos that wealthy society and businesses can afford to invest in. There is certainly evidence to suggest that the feel-good factor can influence both expenditure on fair trade products and charitable donations. However, organizations and business leaders should look beyond the rhetoric and address the potential savings, opportunities and benefits that sit within current business processes, which will contribute to sustainability objectives as a by-product.

A programme run by Iceland Frozen Foods sought to engage customers by introducing the concept of sustainability in the simplest way and perhaps this offers the first insight to eco-efficiency. By focusing on the frozen garden pea they started to address waste and save energy. The idea was for Iceland to deliver rather than for customers to drive, with obvious savings in energy and pollution. The second step was suggesting alternative ways of cooking while at the same time promoting healthy eating.

Customers being drawn into the programme by sustainability issues also reinforces customer loyalty. At the industrial end, as outlined by the Arthur D. Little report, many organizations are beginning to direct R&D and innovative developments towards sustainable opportunities. This may in part be driven by corporate objectives and commitment to the future but it would be unrealistic to think this did not have a business motive, and why not? The idea that we can not develop a strategic approach that is both profitable and rewarding is perhaps what keeps sustainability as a second tier issue and target for NGOs.

An interesting case was that of Beacon Press, a small family printing company that was challenged by a schoolgirl to identify what it was doing for the environment. This challenge launched a programme that resulted in Beacon Press implementing changes that delivered £100,000 savings per year. Revolutionizing its printing processes to eliminate water and alcohol was not only green, but it delivered richer colour. Using film-free printing plates reduce waste. The reputation they built up attracted major clients who also had a socially responsible approach. Thus Beacon created a model approach that was environmentally friendly and profitable.

This begs the question of why other companies don't adopt similar practices and approaches to the benefit of the stakeholders. On the one hand, it is probably apathy or fear of the investment profile, though in the case of Beacon it clearly was worth the effort. The second element is probably traditional thinking which underpins the view that what has worked before should not be changed. It is also possible that a further contributor is the inherent resistance caused through continuous pressure from green groups which fosters a negative attitude and a compliance culture.

This unfortunately loses sight of the fact that the benefits are real savings and contributions to the bottom line. These advantages come from simply using resources more efficiently and avoiding the generation of unnecessary waste. Using materials more effectively is crucial to overall sustainability as there can only be a finite supply, but frequently it is a fear of investment costs that prevents a proper focus being applied. Extrapolating from pilot programmes suggests that manufacturing industry could save billions of dollars simply through environmental improvements and developing eco-efficiency approaches (as seen in Figure 19.1). Many governments in the

Figure 19.1 Developing eco-efficiency approaches

developed world actually run programmes to help smaller companies understand the benefits and identify areas for action.

Whether using external advisers or implementing internal initiatives, the first step towards eco-efficiency is to undertake an audit of the current operations with a focus balanced between cost improvement and sustainable issues. Over many years the implementation of cost-saving programmes has become a common feature within organizations. Frequently the reaction from the workforce has been guarded because cost savings generally translate into job losses. Sustainability, however, engages most people to some greater or lesser extent but is seldom seen as a personal threat. Thus for most organizations the process should be one that can be proactive and positive.

There has been a procession of initiatives since the 1960s aimed at developing robust quality programmes. Right-first-time approaches clearly have a place in the business culture, but more often than not quality control rather than management becomes the main focus. The Six Sigma quality programme looks to reduce the percentage of errors delivered by a system, but perhaps what is not appreciated with all these systems is that each time we have a failure we initiate reprocessing, scrap, waste, energy consumption and pollution. Boots Group identified in one small programme $500,000 savings by working with suppliers on quality.

Thus part of the sustainable agenda should be a focus on eliminating quality failures rather than simply constraining them. This aspect is one that clearly stretches beyond the organization and into its supply chain. As the supply network becomes more global, so the impact of errors and faults becomes more costly. It is therefore perhaps worth considering that low-cost labour exploitation not only conflicts with sustainable objectives, but may also be harming upstream processes and programmes.

Packaging is perhaps one area where we have become hooked on the need for supporting all manner of waste, energy and resource exploitation. It has to be accepted that attractive packaging remains a major factor in consumer selection; however, the business-to-business aspect of packaging is simply a question of providing suitable protection during transportation and storage. Experience suggests that customers look for special requirements and suppliers invest in making their products stand out in the warehouse. Reusable packaging should be the standard and, wherever possible, organizations should avoid complex specifications that do not add value to the process.

Technology obviously offers a multiplicity of opportunities but may also require investment and a longer pay-back period; but in many cases the simple solutions to current needs can be addressed by technology that is already available and tested. The everlasting light bulb is just one example but how many organizations have them in place? In many areas the technology already exists but, through poor or limited maintenance, is not operating to optimum efficiency. Look at what in the process contributes the most cost, and assess whether this is currently delivering value.

It is commonly accepted that the advent of the word processor has allowed more reprocessing, which together with a PC that is seldom used to more than 10 per cent of its capabilities means cost, time and energy being wasted. Even e-mail, the bane of most in industry, offers several opportunities to waste time resources and frequently paper for those who find reading a screen difficult (not to mention the multiple chains of people being 'copied' and forced to participate).

Alternative materials offer opportunities but this may require some redesign and perhaps customer testing and acceptance, although frequently material selection is based on availability and cost and is seldom assessed for its sustainable impact. Offering the challenge to look at current approaches may introduce new ideas and options. Those who have been through a time of shortage soon realize that other materials can be utilized. The Eden Project's eco-surfboard is a clear example that lateral thinking with a green objective can challenge current thinking. The growth in organic food demonstrates that the consumer will pay more for something they believe tastes better or which appeals to their concerns. It is also important to recognize that traditional approaches can be replaced by the availability of improved manufacturing methods.

The growth in road transport and the decline in rail traffic reflect the fact that we have now moved towards the convenience and flexibility that business believes it needs. There are certainly experts in this field who can develop and justify complex and economic distribution networks; but when in the USA it is reported that cornflakes have travelled some 2,500 miles to the customer's bowl, we must ask if we have lost sight of social impacts and economics in place of control and flexibility.

Transport is a costly part of operational economics and it is clearly also a major factor in the fight against pollution. One group of small companies outside London recently discovered that they each sent a truck into town each day and, even worse, they generally covered a similar route. It did not take long for them to work out a plan whereby each went only once per week and networked deliveries for all five. We frequently hear about 'just-in-time' delivery programmes but one wonders how many times 'urgent' deliveries get left in the warehouse for a couple of days. Looking at collection and delivery programmes from a sustainability perspective may highlight prioritized schemes that reduce frequency, improve load carrying ratios, reduce operating costs, limit trucks on the road or even the number of required trucks and, yes, reduce pollution.

Resources (whether people, equipment, materials or consumables) are a key factor in managing any business and offer a wide range of opportunities in a balanced sustainable approach. People may be the most significant asset any company has but how they are deployed affects them as individuals and also the bottom-line operating costs. Travel is tiring, time-wasting and costly but business travel does not seem to abate. Technology allows greater flexibility for home working but commuter traffic remains congested; a balanced approach could reduce travel and improve personal performance.

Efficient equipment is a major consideration but, for many organizations, the capital cost investment prohibits taking advantage of the increased output and power consumption that it could deliver. This is certainly more of an investment consideration but what may be more important in the short term is to look at operational use profiles. Can equipment be utilized in more concentrated periods; can it be adapted to be more multi-functional; or could operational downtime be rented out? Are there other organizations that operate similar equipment where the investment could be amortized to mutual advantage? If it is true that it is cheaper to leave a water heater full and hot than reheat periodically, then perhaps the same advantages could be found in operating equipment.

The third element of resources is material and consumables, and here experience suggests some simple production mapping to optimize material use could provide immediate results. The work of a material cutter in a dressmaker's never ceases to amaze by the complexity of the arrangements to maximize the use of materials; yet in many industries the same care is not as common and when visiting a factory a quick review of the scrap bins will shed light on the ethos of the business and the potential production/delivery problems that may be encountered. What is even more concerning is the wastage of resources as simple as water and compressed air through leaks that could easily be fixed.

One of the most viable areas for looking at cost savings and eco-efficiency is a review of the business processes. Production planning is a valuable skill, and optimizing a product line and the operational ergonomics can be very complex but highly productive. Similarly, effective design of warehousing can reduce picking time and damage. In both cases the aim is to produce maximum efficiency, but frequently organizations evolve rather than grow through design with the result that efficiency is lost and, along with it, waste and cost. A simple programme at one small manufacturing plant saved $100,000 per year, which at a 10 per cent margin equates to $1 million in additional turnover, and this contributed to environmental improvements.

In this age where outsourcing has become a more fundamental part of many business processes these inefficiencies are complicated by external interfaces. Production and delivery flows are complicated by interdependence on others. Bringing these networks together could provide valuable options to improve flow, sequencing and perhaps reduce duplication. Investigating the overall process may suggest alternative consolidations of sub-activities and thus reduce time, cost and (of course) environmental benefits.

Top of every environmentalist agenda is energy but strangely enough it is probably equally high on the business agenda as a major cost. Thus it should come as no surprise that in the context of eco-efficiency audits, energy-saving offers the most immediate return from low-hanging fruit. A PC switched on for 24 hours a day emits one tonne of CO_2 per year. If it was switched off it would save \$100–150 per year. Equipment on standby just in the home wastes 8 per cent of household consumption which could be \$250 per year, so what are the impacts of equipment in the business environment?

Such is the value of this uneconomic use of energy that the American Council for Energy-Efficient Economy (www. aceee.org) has launched an on-line guide to energy-efficient commercial equipment. The aim is to help organizations select the most economic solution when buying new equipment. It is particularly focused on the construction of new buildings to ensure that they are more efficient. An energy audit of any business facility is almost certain to deliver immediate proposals and simple ideas to cut cost. Extending this into operational process reviews is likely to provide even more significant contributions.

If we assumed that every business in the country wasted just \$100 on power then we are wasting billions across the business community. This means more pollution, which has its own costly by-products.

The final element of the eco-efficiency audit would be waste, and whilst few businesses would openly admit to being waste producers they clearly create it through operational performance and frequently as a by-product of the packaging and delivery process. Waste is both a risk to the environment and a cost factor to business in three ways, the first of which is waste through inefficient production operations. At the next level the waste that organizations produce has to be processed which includes transportation and disposal costs, occasionally pollution protection and also clean-up costs. The final stage is the waste that the product itself produces from its packaging, operational output and eventual scrap disposal. In Europe the motorcar manufacturers will be expected in future to incorporate the cost of eventual disposal. This will no doubt progressively encompass most white goods and even other items.

A waste cost profile, then, is not only a short-term cost-saving opportunity: it will be an increasing cost factor for all producers. As a result the long-term competitive consideration must be the addressing of waste up-front to reduce levels and cost impacts. Overseas production may not be the solution either as importers will probably also have to accommodate these cost penalties. Waste has no value except to those that create businesses dealing with it so for the majority of the business community, a waste management approach is not about good works and social responsibility: it is about bottom-line cost and competitiveness.

Biodegradable waste products should be considered since in the end these will be recycled with less impact on the environment. Customers and consumers will eventually have to be part of the debate and will perhaps even encourage supporting products based on their waste impact rating. How we buy products, both in business and privately, also reflects a culture of ignoring the waste impacts; bulk buying reduces the packing cost and waste profile.

This initial focus for eco-efficiency is only the starting point and has been kept in simple terms to avoid over-complicating a concept that should be understood in every organization at every level. What should be obvious is that whilst most organizations would consider themselves to be optimized and efficient there is always some area that can be improved. If you ask the question of any group of business people there will seldom be one that would admit to being better than 75 per cent efficient. In truth the real level is somewhere between 80 and 85 per cent, which means that (excluding external interfaces) there is already room for improvement.

Sustainability may be a hard sell in terms of being proactive as opposed to being defensive, but in reality the focus should be on commercial benefits that support environmental and social impacts as a profitable result. Taking the starting point of developing an internal programme that delivers savings is the first step to linking up with external organizations to contribute in a similar vein. It is also common sense that the way you manage external organizations can have a valuable impact on a sustainable strategy to drive profitability instead of just reputation risk management. Improved external quality and performance contributes to minimizing internal efficiency, which in turn will have cost impacts.

For larger organizations creating an eco-efficiency platform of development will then enable them to mentor and support suppliers' networks that can benefit equally. One hears the cynic suggesting that we should not help others without cost benefit. It may be, however, that that benefits can be achieved in a number of different ways; making suppliers more efficient may not necessarily automatically make their prices cheaper, but it could strengthen their performance in the longer term.

So whilst organizations are internally efficient as a result of years of pressure to cut costs, few, however, have looked beyond their boundaries to understand the value that could be extracted from the overlaps and processes that link suppliers, providers and customers in the value chain. Addressing energy costs, packaging, transport and waste clearly has both a cost benefit and contributes to environmental targets. Sharing knowledge can help to optimize business processes and remove duplication. Eco-efficiency should be the ethos that threads through future business development programmes.

CHAPTER 20

Off-shoring and outsourcing

The trend in recent years has been for companies to reduce their established resources profiles by outsourcing (and, more recently, off-shoring) many previously internal activities. This evolution is part of the growing globalization of the business community. The focus to reduce cost has driven many organizations towards low-cost labour markets for manufacturing and is now a growing trend in business process operations and service provision from external providers. This trend has clearly brought shareholder benefits but perhaps has been less beneficial to the communities that have lost employment and created new pressures in the communities that are (in the short term) winning employment opportunities.

It has already been suggested that these transfers of activity are moving on to more competitive regions. Once the process of transfer is understood then continuous cycling is likely. It must also be recognized that in some cases the consumer market has not reacted well to off-shoring and some organizations make not transferring work overseas into a marketing ploy. On the other side of the equation it must also be recognized that once external service providers become part of the delivery process then exposure through their performance can be more damaging than the potential benefits. Thus, as shown in Figure 20.1, integrating organizations is the real challenge.

This quest for greater competitiveness and optimization of investment in operating costs has opened up the panorama of risk and a wide range of sustainability issues. This has been focused on establishing external and overseas relationships to provide both manufacturing and backroom support services, such as data processing, and customer-facing services, such as call centres.

In many cases this approach has brought varied reactions from the consumer and related bodies, along with a wide range of challenges that emerge when trading across national and cultural boundaries and seeking to capitalize on the potential of transferring internal activities and resources to third-party organizations. Transferring internal support services, developing

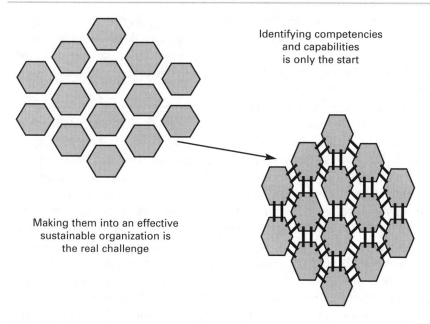

Identifying competencies
and capabilities
is only the start

Making them into an effective
sustainable organization is
the real challenge

Figure 20.1 Integrating organizations

external manufacturing or creating extended enterprise business models produces a whole new spectrum of opportunities and risks. The integration of external organizations into a cohesive business process places increased demands on the trading relationships and those charged with managing these relationships. At the same time, the structure of CSR programmes and the wider sustainability agenda now have to be overlaid across a more complex business network.

Globalization and the pressures from stakeholders to recognize the implications of sustainability and corporate responsibility demand careful consideration in the development of business strategies. The move from a command and control structure to one of interdependence highlights the need to develop a collaborative approach to underpin effective strategies, allowing organizations to capitalize on the opportunities and aid the risk management.

For any business venture to be successful it must first understand its own requirements before trying to develop those of an external organization. It is therefore imperative that organizations take the time to work through their sustainability values and consolidate these into a structured appraisal that can form the foundation for developing an external assessment.

Most organizations undertake performance analysis of their supply chains but often make decisions based on anecdotal evidence which frequently, whilst justified, may be only a symptom of the potential problems ahead. The impacts of off-shoring go beyond these traditional assessments.

The traditional trading relationship supporting vertical business structures is known as the supply chain, which assumes linear relationships. What is now evolving is the concept of 'value chains', linking participants through the delivery process. Each link delimits risks and costs between itself and each of its neighbours on the buy-and-sell sides in a hierarchical structure. The hierarchy can breed internal divisions between functions at the micro level, such as production and sales, and organizations at the macro level. Boundaries are stressed, weakening the connectivity by masking inefficiencies and risks, significant among which will be the policies and processes behind sustainable development. There are many examples where outsourcing has shown significant benefit to operations, but these have also identified many potential pitfalls that arise from moving towards greater interdependence with more complex communications networks. These challenges may reflect performance or reputation issues which need to be addressed as part of any overall strategy. The growth in off-shoring as a means of extending capabilities is seen as an effective tool in reducing costs; however, it quickly identifies gaps in the existing business processes that may not have been visible previously.

The failures can often be attributed to unrealistic expectations which govern the assessment of satisfactory transfer of roles between companies. The potential benefits are diluted by efforts to impose service level agreements and performance that exceed past benchmarks, whilst integrating a less experienced workforce or operation. The implications of poor performance and the potential vulnerability that may result from failing to meet acceptable corporate responsibility profiles necessitate the development of structured programmes that are integrated into the overall business strategy and ethos.

Collaboration methodologies can provide an approach that allows organizations to develop a more open structure in the trading relationship in order to maintain the visibility and flexibility necessary to meet these challenges and exploit the potential of off-shoring more effectively. Effective value chain performance is created through integration of both internal and external providers. Awareness of the holistic impacts of value chain management must extend beyond the functional boundaries of organizations in order to ensure that opportunities are fully exploited.

Innovative approaches, however, must be balanced against a background of risk management. Often what is needed are best practice approaches coupled with the ability to spot and exploit the strategic opportunities within an approach that meets market profiles. Whichever relationship model is adopted it must be recognized that the provider will become an integral partner in the business process. The relationships vertically and horizontally in the value chain are a key factor in exploiting the value creation process, which includes joint responsibility for business activities.

Organizations need to ensure that the providers' operations are based on a compatible ethos and culture. The nature of a service arrangement should be developed based on the objectives and goals from each side of the relationship. How each expects they will be working together will help to define the nature of the contracting relationship and the style of integration and level of interfaces. The key to effective off-shoring is in ensuring a clear definition of scope and services to be provided.

All business relationships are based on the traditional premise that the buyer wants the most for the least and the seller wants to offer the least for the most. The balance of power in any relationship shifts over the period of the association and in an outsourcing context this shift may be critical to overall service performance. Exploitation may seem attractive during negotiations over short-duration contracts but long-term arrangements require that both parties maintain an effective working relationship focused on delivering a seamless service to customers.

The final step in the development process is to address the exit strategy, ensuring that the obligations have met the initial expectations, along with providing a platform for future business. This must include provider performance assessments and recognition of the social and economic impacts that may result.

Off-shoring will raise many questions concerning existing resources and approaches, intellectual property and, most important of all, the retention of skills within the organization. This is where the crunch comes for most organizations within the context of integrating corporate strategy, sustainable programmes and organizational development. Creating an off-shoring programme must be approached in a holistic manner. The implications of the effects of failing to recognize the potential reactions to performance and sustainability issues that can flow through the relationship could be extremely serious. This may be driven by regulatory pressures or the impact of ethically-focused customers and consumers. Either factor will place pressures on the organization and its ultimate success.

It must also be recognized that whilst outsourcing and off-shoring may improve the bottom line, the regulators may be less happy with companies divesting control. This pressure, on top of changes to tighten the financial responsibility of companies, means that regulators retain the right to validate the transfer of financial management systems and processes as outsourcing activities have moved up the value chain from background to core services in the financial sector, for example. Regulators may be able stop transfers where they consider these to be detrimental to appropriate control, and organizations need to understand that they cannot divest themselves of control or responsibility by off-shoring. The UK's FSA, the USA's Office of the Comptroller of Currency (OCC), Germany's Bundesanstalt für Finanzdienstleistungsaufsicht (BaFin) and the Hong Kong Monetary Authority (HKMA) (amongst others) have all introduced requirements to monitor and control outsourced transactions. These controls also reflect to what extent these BPO arrangements encroach on the overall company risk profile.

Developing an effective programme should blend the attributes of diverse organizations, each with significantly different cultures, approaches, standards and levels of customer commitment. Organizations often ignore the fact that their customers' perceptions and the assignment of responsibility bears no relation to the rules of contract. Thus even the tightest of contract rules cannot always offer protection on issues that are more emotive.

The investment profile of any business needs to exploit the longest possible optimum return that will provide the highest return on investment. Short-term exploitation of any low-cost resource not only limits the robustness of the business proposition, but it will also expose the operation to a multiplicity of new challenges, starting with internal resistance, organizational structure and existing operating practice.

Partnering and collaborative business models allow organizations to evaluate all aspects of the business delivery process and incorporate the needs and drivers for each whilst finding opportunities to reduce costs and waste through continuous improvement. There can be few business operations today that are not directly influenced by the spread of globalization. The multi-dimensional nature of the global landscape creates an environment that inherently generates an ever-increasing profile of risk along with opportunities.

The quest to exploit these opportunities and the volatility of the many factors that can change the platform of a business relationship engender a need to focus on managing the risk. This, together with the growing spectre of new competition, means there is a dynamic culture against which to develop a flexible strategy. Technology has provided this business environment with faster communications, raising the expectations of customers to anticipate the benefits of global pricing, whilst still focusing on traditional quality and performance.

The pressures of regulation, sustainability and environmental issues, together with the wider and more indirect ramifications of global trading, are factors that every organization must recognize. The political and cultural challenges of working outside the comfort zone of traditional business networks are complex, and developing a structured approach is critical. The implications for organizations are far reaching and necessitate increasing the focus on risk mitigation and management to ensure success. The attraction of low-cost providers is certainly a potential opportunity for organizations but the implications and risks should not be under-estimated.

The challenge, then, is for organizations to adopt a more flexible perspective that enables the maximization of the potential whilst retaining effective management of performance delivery. Off-shoring captures competitive advantage but this extended enterprise approach brings its own challenges through interdependence and reputation risk. It is easy to recognize someone from another region by their appearance and language, but it is not so easy to appreciate their attitude and approach to business.

Cultural diversity is the result of a homogenized blend of many factors and traits. We often tend to view the world from our own perspective and culture, the assumption often being that what is right for us must be the correct way to behave, but this is seldom the case. Every country is at a different stage of development and following paths that may be widely different from our own. Understanding these and the many other differences that will be encountered around the world is crucial to being ready to develop effective operations outside the comfort zone.

It may seem obvious to suggest that different nationalities require different approaches but sadly very often relationships and operations fail not because of the issues but because we do not recognize the alternative cultural aspects of the business environment and the impacts on sustainable objectives. For those starting out on the road or having to change direction in order to meet the growing international dimensions of business, cultural awareness is a crucial factor. It is important to recognize that every organization is unique and thus assess the areas that should be addressed before venturing out in search of potential partners.

The common failing when developing any programme is that the focus is largely concentrated on the external provider and does not recognize the potential pitfalls that may be resting just below the surface of the internal organization or the customer. This aspect of developing an off-shoring approach is likely to be the most difficult since it requires organizations to think 'out of the box' and realistically evaluate their own capabilities and approaches.

The key to creating sustainable value in the relationship is to fully understand the role of provider and the resources they utilize. The more diverse these organizations are across cultural boundaries, the higher the likelihood of differing approaches to performance, business approaches and priorities, which results in higher possibilities of organizations creating risk by integrating activities. The implications for any organization in terms of linking business ventures through extended enterprise relationships can be far reaching. In the context of reputation and performance the risk is that each party is exposed to the market through the actions of others.

In building alternative business models it is important to establish the roles and practices of the partners to ensure that a focused approach is taken towards the commercial benefits, and also that a programme is in place to address the wider sustainability issues. For many in the business environment the issue of risk management is a natural part of their corporate and management operations. What is not perhaps given as much consideration in this regard are the implications of integrated relationships or the exposure that may develop from less of a command and control model, which may also be customer-facing. The traditional relationship between customer and provider takes on a new perspective in the context of off-shoring.

There are many views of what sustainable development is and often this complexity creates conflicts and challenges in the business arena. What is often lost within this debate is that in most cases, if not all long-term ones, the end-game objectives are the same.

The difficulty for the off-shoring approach is the short-term demand to maximize profitability and return on investment (ROI) for the shareholders. Whilst the customer (whether individual or corporate) is focused on best value for money, which generally translates into lowest price, with a sustainability perspective the subject is related to maintaining business positioning and growth. This environment is often categorized as three dimensions – financial, social and environmental – within which businesses have to operate.

These conflicts and challenges create for business in the short term many risks to offset the opportunities of exploiting the competitive advantage. Off-shoring can and should be developed through mutual exploitation of opportunities and with the aim of creating common sustainability objectives and frameworks.

Changing the rules of the game requires alternative thinking that may be currently suppressed within the confines of current contracting practice. To deliver customer satisfaction the sustainability value creation process must be re-engineered or the concept of value reinvented. This transition can seldom be achieved purely based on internal actions, and so the whole value chain must be addressed.

Selecting service providers needs to take into consideration the type of relationship that will be most effective. The development of a programme should be reviewed from a strategic perspective and with a sustainability evaluation plan set in place.

Understanding what are the clear focuses for moving forward sets the benchmark for establishing the opportunities, capabilities and knowledge that will be necessary to deliver success. Success will be measured against expectations and, in this regard, realistic objectives set an agenda to build on for the future. Whilst there may be an overall outsourcing strategy in place, each prospect for off-shoring will demand a strategy that cascades from the top level.

Outsourcing often fails due to the contracting organizations setting internal expectations that they don't fully understand themselves, or because they have not considered how to measure and manage these goals. These same challenges affect the development of off-shoring programmes. It is important to develop an assessment profile that captures both needs and expectations.

The development of outsourcing programmes has to be created with an eye to challenging past practice. The implementation of off-shoring introduces additional factors to the whole process of supplier selection based on the degree of interdependence and the extent to which this provider may be facing the customer in the delivery process. In this environment the provider is being integrated into the overall process, and therefore, the selection criteria must be extended to evaluate the strengths and weaknesses, as well as the risk this relationship may create. In the case of off-shoring, the provider must not only meet the performance criteria, but must also be able to adapt to suit the demands and stresses of being an integral part of the business process.

More subjective evaluation rests on trying to identify the attitude of the provider and this does not mean the corporate image that is portrayed; it means understanding the internal business culture and the approach of those that will actually be charged with delivering. It is also important to recognize that as skills and knowledge are transferred off-shore, so the traditional pool is depleted. Future transfers or shifts in strategy may become impractical when the knowledge base has vanished.

Despite creating a realistic profile for potential outsourcing partners it should be expected that training and knowledge transfer will be required. The ideal partner may be out there but experience has shown that even the most suitable candidate will fall short in some way of the optimum profile.

This transfer of knowledge should also be considered as a key part of overall sustainable development. Investing in building up the skills levels of regional communities provides both commercial and sustainable benefits.

Training programmes can initially be focused on those areas of an assessment that clearly show room for improvement to underpin the arrangement. As the relationship progresses there will be opportunities to expand the scope to concentrate on aspects that will move the value proposition to the next level. Clearly the basic provisions and objectives that promoted the off-shoring approach must be maintained, but external challenges may introduce alternative thinking that will add even more value to the programme.

All monitoring and measurement should ideally flow directly from the activity. Many key performance indicators (KPIs) are fashionable, but they are often established without considering the effort required to collect the data and the value they deliver. A word of warning attributed to Albert Einstein regarding issues and initiatives related to relationships: 'Sometimes what can be counted doesn't count and what can't be counted does count.'

Relationships between organizations are perhaps the major contributor in the failure to address many aspects of service provision due to the failure to integrate business operations towards common goals and objectives within a mutual ethos and culture.

The traditional command and control management programmes are inappropriate in the exploitation of virtually integrated organizations; therefore, a principal factor in developing a sustainable strategy is the use of integrated programmes to ensure that the right skills and processes are in place to direct and support the programme.

It is also important to recognize that, as in any campaign, the commitment of resources to execute the programme is commensurate with the task. This is particularly important in the early days of any programme since benefits will grow, but those benefits will only be developed when the respective organizations meet the objectives under their control and perform effectively. The strategic approach should therefore ensure that sufficient resources are incorporated in the initial stages to give a boost to set the process in place and ground it. There must also be consideration for the long-term changes that may arise.

Off-shoring may be currently in vogue for many industry sectors, and with a growing integrated global market place it is likely to be a factor for future business models. Sustainability will thus be a constant factor and one which must be developed in an integrated way to ensure that the goals of individual organizations are not diluted or perhaps compromised through the actions of others. Programmes must also consider the wider implications for the communities affected. We should stop seeing outsourcing and off-shoring as a threat, and instead see it as a much broader opportunity to influence and raise the game generally. Unions and NGOs may see these programmes as exploitation but, in the longer term, they provide an opportunity to create inward investment through growth.

From personal experience, the principle of Murphy's Law is certain to arise in outsourcing programmes (i.e., if it can go wrong it will). A frequently asked question in relation to successful outsourcing is 'How do I decide what to retain and what to outsource?' Selecting or retaining service delivery capabilities poses considerable challenges on a number of fronts: planning, operational, financial, management and political. Today these are also intertwined with the implications of sustainable objectives and pressures.

Supply chain architecture (both opportunities and threats) becomes a key factor in establishing risk management propositions within a business and sustainability-focused strategy, particularly in what is becoming a progressively more integrated, innovative and complex market place. Considering functional needs and innovative developments together with efficient and responsive operational resources means accounting for (and developing) organizational tasks, process architecture linking multiple organizations, demographics, investment and overseas interactions and the underlying implications of outsourcing on sustainability.

Let us take as an example the Tong Yang Indonesian (TYI) shoe factory with 8,500 workers, which was improved from a sweatshop as part of the pressure applied by Reebok, one of many high-profile organizations that base their business model on outsourcing. Investment by the TYI and supervision by Reebok improved working conditions, which in turn increased output. Whether the actions of Reebok and its outsourcing partner came from external pressure or not is perhaps less important than the fact that benefits came from a combination of skills, knowledge and needs.

Defining an outsourcing or off-shoring relationship then becomes a crucial part of the optimization and risk management process. Organizations cannot operate on blind trust in a relationship that may seriously affect operational performance but could implicate the parties in regulatory and market pressure across a spectrum of sustainable issues. On the other hand, this increasing practice of networked delivery processes may also provide the catalyst for developing sustainable ambitions through multi-national business operations.

Like many other aspects of the business tool box, outsourcing (and, more recently, off-shoring) can be adopted on the assumption that it is an established approach that simply bolts onto the current operation or replaces part of it. The fact that the words are well established does not necessarily imply that the business models are equally familiar or best practice. The changing business environment, and growing pressures to reflect social responsibility within corporate operations, means that the opportunities and threats have increased. Relationships demand more thoughtful and comprehensive approaches to consider their unique circumstances, and that will promote long-term sustainable objectives.

CHAPTER 21

Future focus

All business ventures should establish their strategy based on a projection of the potential market place and the economic and political environment within which they operate. Many major corporations invest substantial amounts developing scenario-planning approaches that provide the background to their business plans, investments and development profiles; similarly, governments focus programmes on political and demographic changes that may influence their policies and national and international investment projects.

There is plenty of hype around the sustainability agenda and even more channelled specifically towards CSR. The latter is perhaps a question of focusing on how to encourage organizations to take it seriously and how consultants could profit in the process. What perhaps should be a greater consideration for business leaders is to try to understand how this growing pressure will or could affect their business plans. In a similar vein, the wider profile of sustainability must or should also take into account a more practical perspective of the realities rather than delivering utopia. The fact is that we cannot change everyone overnight and neither can we influence a consistent strategic plan for each country given their varying stages of development.

Frequently, what pressure groups promote, although valid, is often more detrimental or painful in the short term to the local evolution than the exploitation they see as being unacceptable. Clearly every nation has its own internal challenges and frequently the help that is offered is diverted. Even worse, some of the help is perhaps not really beneficial in the long term. Witness how religious or political prejudice, that stands between external aid and those in need, often taints the perspective as opposed to those seeing only the dramatic news broadcasts. Development must be practical; as they say, give a man a fish and you feed him for a day, but teach him to fish and you feed him for life.

Business organizations can benefit from effectively planned programmes but, at the same time, they must consider how the wider community will view and respond to these. Thus looking at the realities of sustainability opportunities and threats, together with what these realities may bring to the business agenda, is clearly a factor for business leaders and their organizations. Sustainability, as we have outlined, touches every aspect of the business environment. Thus what happens in the world at local, regional, national and international levels will certainly influence the prospects of success: for example, those organizations that consider sustainability as a corporate objective, as opposed to those that seek only compliance with regulations, will look to build proactive strategies that reflect the trends and challenges of the future. Those that seek only to focus on compliance will continue to be reactive to regulation and pressure in the short term. The strategist, then, is likely to suggest that those with a proactive and integrated approach will gain greater long-term success.

As reflected by Professor Gary Hamel in an article for UK Excellence, 'Strategic resilience is not about responding to one time crisis . . . it's about continuously anticipating and adjusting to deep, secular trends that can permanently impair the earning power of a core business. It's about the capacity to change before the case for change becomes desperately obvious.'

Creating the future is better than predicting it but, in real terms, in order to create a sustainable future and sustainable business, the most that we can hope to do is to measure the trends and reflect this against our best judgement. Clearly, as outlined in Figure 21.1, what we know provides an advantage, while unknowns are a risk to development plans. These trends may not be directly influencing markets but they will over time impact the economic and political environment. At the same, many projected developments are likely to highlight influences that need to be guarded against.

One can look at the future from many different aspects but frequently in the business world the focus is directed towards very narrow and specific targets. However, when one considers the sustainable future there are multiple overlapping layers of developments and considerations. These may not in the narrow arena be seen as significant but the pressures on business planning should not be ignored.

It is perhaps simplistic to consider the world divided into four population groups but, whilst clearly global demographics are more complex, consider how these four foundation groups helps to rationalize the business dynamic:

- knowledge;
- resources;
- processors;
- consumers.

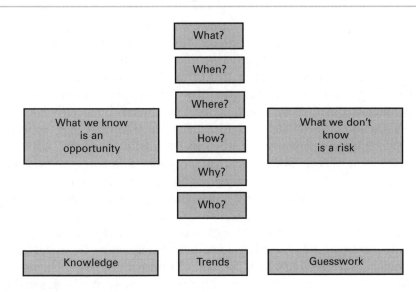

Figure 21.1 Projecting forward

Knowledge frequently gives rise to wealth and power. Resources are a key ingredient for development but often one is dependent on those with the knowledge and power to exploit those resources. The key constituent for any business is the transformation process, whether this stems from growing, farming or production; each depends on appropriate labour skills. The fourth element is the consumer which clearly across the globe represents a very diverse market place, from the glamour of Fifth Avenue to the scratch markets of central Africa. There are those that can buy and then those who survive. The interdependence of the four areas of focus will be clear to all but, in the process of building a business proposition, one should understand the sustainable implications of interactions and pressures.

There can be little doubt, looking to the future, that globalization will continue unabated, fuelled by even greater proliferation of communications technology. We may still consider ourselves under nationalistic divisions but certainly in the business world the homogenization of knowledge, resources, processes and customers has already breached most (if not all) national boundaries. It is in this environment of opportunity and risk that future business strategy has to be developed and where the implications of establishing a sustainable agenda must be integrated with a future focus.

The general consensus, based on NIC research, is that the international community is significantly changing and this will continue for the next decade or so. The year 2020 may be well beyond the radar of most CEOs but the trends and traits that will shape that future are factors for today. Amongst these is a growing concern for the environment and wider sustainable issues. The challenge then will be to blend today's pressures and accommodate the trends and demands of the future market place.

Together with the speed of change that stems from globalization, which may ultimately evolve in many ways, there are some key concerns that flow alongside and influence the globalization thrust. These include the many contradictions that globalization produces from cultural difference, and the rising new powers (both economic and political). These in turn are introducing significant pressures to corporate governance, whilst security remains a concern. Behind these issues there are a number of trends that clearly emerge.

An expanding global economy is assured and with it the challenges of trading across cultural boundaries and business cultures. Technology has made huge advances in the past 50 years but the pace of development will continue unabated. This will increase the pervasiveness of communication but may also bring solutions for shortages of key resources such as water and energy. This globalization will probably further expose the social inequalities that are already apparent and provide a focus for those who consider the business community is exploiting this inequality for competitive advantage.

There are new powers emerging on the global scene and much of their impact comes from economic influence as well as ethnic diversification and religious reach. Increased mobility and regional unrest will continue to promote economic migration, which in turn will increase the growth of ethnic and religious groups and influence across national boundaries. The population globally is facing an aging phenomenon, placing pressures on the developed world to provide the labour resources to support current (let alone future) needs. Thus again we see a trend that may constrain the rapid economic growth in places like China and India but which also increases the need for more flexible labour movement. This demand provides significant security concerns as regional, political and religious links blend across boundaries.

The implications for all of these trends are that international institutions will come under pressure to maintain stability and regulate developments in conflict, security and humanitarianism, while promoting economic sustainable growth. It is not hard then to identify the trends and pressures that business must accommodate in terms of building an effective strategy. At the same time it is not difficult to see where demands for responsible corporate behaviour will spark from gaps between business and the communities globally.

Thus what we do know is that globalization is not likely to abate. What is perhaps less predictable is whether the current growth in the Asian economies will create new trading rules or whether the general economic growth will drag lagging economies up. It is certain that what we now have is a global economy with growth becoming less dependent on individual national influences. This may in turn expand the gaps between the 'haves' and the 'have nots', providing competitive advantage for many business ventures but significant challenge for those driven by responsible customers and consumers.

The growth and development of China, India and others in Asia seems certain to change the dynamics of the trading market place. China already promotes the Pearl River Delta as the manufacturing centre of the world. Such aspirations of course depend on either collapsing or undermining existing or emerging alternatives and remaining competitive. This situation is already being seen as transient and thus in the future those that many have been trying to protect may themselves be at the forefront of exploitation. One only has to look at the moves from India into Eastern Europe, and from China into Africa.

Resources such as minerals, energy and water will continue to be governing factors for economic development and stability. This factor (perhaps more than any other) will permeate the evolution of any sustainable future, alongside the influence of non-government organizations that seek to promote their brand of culture and politics, whether democratically or through conflict and terrorism. A demand-led economic model will then face the challenge of protecting both the environment and supply security in order to continue any progress towards a more balanced sustainable future, with the added complexity that technology may create solutions or aggravate the ethical dilemmas already being debated.

The NIC believes that at no time since the middle of the twentieth century has the international mix been in a greater state of flux. Thus the business community must face growing demand for competitive products, increased service and value, and more responsible corporate practice against a background of diversity, flexibility and, for many, to some extent greater insecurity.

In this rapidly more integrated business environment we also see the emergence of significant new players in the global economic mix. China and India, based on pure population growth, are seen as major elements of a new order. Coming closely behind them are an emerging Russian commercial influence and ever-increasing power base from the South American countries, which (unlike the first pair), combine both natural and labour resources. Africa remains largely fragmented and is likely to remain that way, but as a resource centre it is becoming the political and economic supermarket for resources beyond the exploitation of the nineteenth and twentieth centuries. The only constraining factors for these new players are the impact of HIV/AIDS and the political ability to take over the shaping of their own futures. In time Africa has all the ingredients to be a significant global player since it has both natural treasures and low-cost labour. Education, health support, knowledge transfer and political stability will eventually enable them to overcome short-term resource management and natural disasters.

New powers, such as China, India, Brazil and perhaps Indonesia, have the potential to change the old global structures of east and west, north and south, and to shake up political alliances. The move from the fields to the urban community is also a clear trend and we are perhaps on the verge of seeing the birth of mega-cities becoming power influences in their own right outside traditional national boundaries and affiliations.

In the industrialized countries there is another trend that is emerging in terms of the traditional employer–employee relationship. Knowledge and skills are declining, while centralized business operations are giving way to networks of specialized functions and independent individuals. Technology has provided the platform for individuals to work outside the traditional corporate structure more effectively and more competitively for both parties.

The growth of portfolio careers (mainly, it must be said, as a result of rationalization and global diversification) offers the prospect that as emerging economies move towards urban centralization the developed world will progressively move away from the concept. This adds another complexity for the business leaders of tomorrow who must manage and deliver through a more fragmented network process and be more reliant on maintaining an ethos and vision through acceptance rather than command and control.

The impact of globalization going forward reflects a trend towards connectivity rather than control. Expanding flows of information, technology, knowledge, resources, goods and services will, without doubt, frame the future trading environment. In this diverse mix the influence of consumers spurred on by multiple NGOs will demand more accountability, whilst craving greater choice and competitiveness.

It is unlikely that industrial communities will retain the robust shape that we have enjoyed in the developed world for some 200 years; the process of globalization could perhaps only be stopped by some catastrophic environmental event or major conflict. So the prospect is for continued economic growth although the likelihood is that this will remain unevenly distributed but with new players joining the 'haves' club. There is always the fear that today's so-called exploited markets will become the exploiters of tomorrow.

In this scenario, then, more and more businesses will have to become global to survive and grow. This is unlikely to happen through acquisition and investment but more through outsourcing, off-shoring and alliances. This future model brings benefits but also opens up greater exposure to the interdependence of companies in maintaining their individual standards, ethos and culture. Thus sustainable agendas must either be embedded in these arrangements or left to fate and good fortune.

Clearly this emerging vision of the future also creates pressures on governments. Nation states may continue to address their aspirations but these will become ever more difficult to administer against a business environment that will become more fluid and diverse internationally. Thus we can expect to see more attempts to bring together global regulation, such as Kyoto, but cynically one has to wonder if nation states won't simply negotiate for local economic advantage. Irrespective of these global agreements the business world must recognize that regulation will increase at local, national and international levels. Many will be in conflict and some will pull directly against a commercial core of globalized business operations.

This reinforces the need for (particularly) brand-based enterprises to consider how to protect their reputations and foster their vision of corporate responsibility, not simply in terms of governance but also the deeper considerations of stakeholder values. Some may suggest that global stability and economic development will eventually be the domain of the corporate markets and perhaps the ethos of stock market governors will carry more weight than elected governments, if it does not already, particularly where differing models of democracy may emerge from new economies such as China.

In their 2004 publication *Mapping the Global Future*, the NIC offered up four scenarios for 2020. These provide interesting visions of the future, starting with the state of the political arena based on China and India's economic growth reshaping the global market and providing a non-western face on the political scene. They also considered the Pax Americana concept of a new world order. A third approach is the emergence of a strong religious power coming from Islam that would challenge the foundation of the global system. Beyond this they suggest one scenario where global fear produces an environment that reduces freedom in order to provide protection, much as George Orwell predicted in his book, *1984*. Each of these is perhaps an extreme but is based on the evaluation of the trends and influences visible today. What they do offer, however, is a chance to think outside the box about the world we may be heading for and to consider the world we want.

There are, of course, many views of, and contradictions in, the globalization vision and the more localized market places that businesses have to work within. What is perhaps more important is to look at how one sees these trends within the context of a specific business strategy and, in the terms of this book, how these trends may influence corporate integration of stakeholders' influences as regards sustainability.

At every level of business, from the family company to the megacorporation, the considerations remain the same; only the magnitude of the impact changes. Once one has established that a sustainability policy makes sense in consideration of the multiple influences and stakeholders, then assessing the potential minefields in the future helps to embed this policy into the business strategy.

The population comprises not only the workforce, but also the customer and consumer base. We will probably see another billion people on Earth in 2020 and in many parts of the world there will be an increasingly aging community needing support but no longer productive. In poorer parts of the world food, health, education and stability will remain a challenge where business can facilitate development whilst employing the resources to support demand. These developing environments may be the farming and industrial engines of the future, so utilizing resources will involve balancing benefit and growth against potential exploitation.

Resources are being used up and demand will eventually outstrip availability. In the process of exploitation we create more pollution which further damages future prospects. Thus new technology needs to be deployed and processes re-evaluated to optimize current usage. The exploitation of natural resources in developing countries must be jointly managed to ensure that local exploitation is not driven by demands from the developed markets and short-term opportunism by either local government or the business community.

Technology will be the catalyst of future development for both good and ill. Health and food remain the most important factor for most of the world's population. Trading the benefits for commercial return should replace the historical political demands that followed aid and support. Technology can bridge some of these gaps but it must not over-ride the natural balance: business and the support agencies should be working together with local leaders to integrate solutions. It should also not be assumed that pure charity would provide a robust solution.

Economic development underpins the ability of communities to grow and develop. The power of the economic engines of today and tomorrow could provide the wealth that will allow developing regions to move forward. It will not, however, happen with the speed that many would like to see. Economics is a complex area and the obvious current imbalance provides the competitive edge that will plant the seeds of future regional growth. The challenge for the business community, supported by consumer awareness and choice, will be to draw on the competitive opportunity but establish approaches that are sustainable and constructive for today and tomorrow.

Within this complex and often imbalanced global business environment there are the added pressures of people movements. The developed world needs skills and people resources, and in many ways this demand is being filled by economic migrants. Service operations are being moved overseas to reduce costs, thus creating a gulf between the skill base and the available service functions. This migration and globalization is creating ethnic and cultural groupings whose connectivity may form a conduit for bad practice that puts corporate governance at risk. Thus business leaders have to grasp the opportunities of global business whilst protecting their own standards and operating within the regulatory boundaries.

As ethnic communities become more established they will naturally also create trading channels attuned to their background. This diversity is both an opportunity and a challenge for the business community as trading may be in part driven by ethnic branding as opposed to product brands. It may also challenge many regulations as ethnic choice, work practice, culture and business approach may conflict with established regulations and practice.

Looking to the future, then, is not simply about where the next big market opportunity will come from or where the exploitable resources may be. Globalization as the catchall environment for business brings potential benefits and major challenges to those that will have to navigate the contradictions and conflicts of cultural, religious and political diversity. It will certainly not go away, and whilst competition will become more prolific so will the risks of not being aware of the implications of ignoring a sustainable profile, not just in terms of regulatory and reputation pressure but in real terms of gaining real benefit whilst helping to ensure viable development within the communities involved.

The business leadership of today and their protégés for tomorrow will need to have a strong vision and corporate culture that is not driven simply by local compliance. The nature of business today in the global market is already complex and based on trends certain to become even more complex and interdependent. It will not be enough to base an operation on local regulation and practice.

To maximize the potential benefits and remain legitimate across a global supply network and consumer market will demand that companies embed sound and transparent sustainable programmes within their operating practice. It is unlikely, if not impossible, that governments will ever reach a common platform of regulation and, whilst they debate, business is out there creating wealth and becoming intimately involved with ventures that touch every aspect of the sustainability agenda. Without internal benchmarks there is little doubt that sooner or later organizations will fall foul of themselves and their potential markets.

We should also not ignore the NGOs who are trying to maintain their challenge to current custom and practice against the same cultural diversity. They position themselves as the only protectors of the environment and the under-developed world. They certainly may be the loudest voice at present but perhaps due to the impacts of a changing global club they too will face increased resistance to the cause rather than greater acceptance of their values. Given that the next 20 years will probably be the most significant influence on the next millennium it is time to look for sharing of knowledge and influence rather than conflict positioning. If they can appreciate the need for compromise then much of industry would perhaps be more inclined to seek their advice and support.

The emerging trends, identified by a cross-sectional group of business colleagues in a think tank, followed the broader ideas of the NIC. At the top of the business agenda was global competitiveness where successful organizations would be reliant on an agile and dynamic alliance of eco-systems in order to manage skills, resources, technology, innovation and the supply chain across geographical and cultural boundaries.

In this environment outsourcing would increase whilst companies focused on core competencies. Looking forward the customer experience would probably become the key differentiator, and traditional outsourcing will be replaced by more transformational outsourcing which will be more in demand to maintain the capacity to innovate in response to market conditions and demands.

Sustainability was high on the focus list with increased integration of moral, social and economic objectives. With the emphasis leading to more differentiation between clean and dirty shareholders, it was easy to see that business relationships and alliances would be increasingly sensitive to moral and regulatory issues.

Most felt strongly that the prevalence of global trading would lead to greater flexibility of investment and freer movement of capital, which will clearly challenge the regulatory powers, particularly in respect of money laundering and criminal transactions.

Global cluster developments, both sector-driven and complementary operations, were seen to be one of the emerging business models forced into existence by the increased cost of market entry. These groupings could be a serious challenge to larger global corporations through these extended enterprises. The facilitator is technology, which on the other side would provide the medium for more remote working, though many suggest there will be a greater recognition that traditional relationship skills need to be re-learnt.

The major global trends for the future are not hard to recognize, and the implications for the business community are easy to identify. The more subtle impacts from some of these developments are perhaps less obvious, but what is certain is that globally business operations will increasingly be part of wider supply or service delivery networks. This structure carries with it inherent dangers for corporate responsibility and opportunities for effective sustainable thinking and application.

CHAPTER 22

Profit from corporate social responsibility

There are some who are already benefiting from the focus on CSR but perhaps at present, in the main, they are the consultants. They sit on the edges of the business community providing advice and publications. These promote the virtues of organizations which, through their sustainability profile, have built up a major business opportunity. A few, including the Body Shop, Traidcraft and the Eden Project, have a business which is based on delivering a sustainability-focused business model.

If we are to see a sea change in thinking then the whole sustainability debating ground must be moved towards developing strategies that can both deliver value to the stakeholders and support socially and environmentally sound programmes. It is not enough to simply publish what organizations are doing right, which frequently draws criticism against anything they fall down on; the business leadership must look at how to integrate a profit from bringing CSR into the mainstream business strategy, as shown in Figure 22.1. Much of this entails harnessing customer and consumer focus and engaging them in the overall proposition.

The more the concepts of CSR are fostered and integrated into the business process, the easier it will be to benefit from alternative thinking and perhaps handle the occasional problems that for certain will occur. The more integrated the business process within the value chain, the more opportunity there will be for organizations to influence the approaches of others on whom they depend, thus building collaboration which may even in time blend across competitive boundaries, if there is sufficient customer power. Industry codes of practice have for some time been a mechanism for adopting better working practices, and perhaps we can drive sustainability down the same route.

One has to start, however, from the premise that the business community must create profit in order to survive. Thus CSR should be focused on adding value, not regulatory compliance and public relations. So why do companies publish sustainability reports: is it simply to salve the conscience or to rebuff the rampant protester? Interestingly enough, an article by Sir

Figure 22.1 Benefits of CSR

Peter Mason, CEO of AMEC, highlighted the reaction they got from asking customers, employees and investors for their views on sustainability.

Top of the list was that meeting sustainability criteria is now an important part of how organizations win work, so stakeholders want to check performance. Second, many of their customers were also trying to define and monitor their own sustainability programmes, which then inherently involves their contractors and suppliers. This interdependent dilemma is facing many companies, particularly those involved in environmentally impacting programmes and outsourcing propositions. This leads us on to the third level of interest, which is what experience, knowledge and services can customers share in that would help their own sustainability objectives? Clearly there is growing interest in the business community, which is being driven more by customer and peer pressure than it is by NGOs and regulation, particularly since regulation tends to be years behind the technology and accommodated by compliance rather than by commitment.

It was interesting to find that a survey by the management consultants, McKinsey, found that 80 per cent of investors questioned would be prepared to pay a premium for shares in well-governed companies. Again, after the spectacular losses of Enron and WorldCom investor confidence was severely damaged so this is not that surprising. This corporate governance and financial focus for CSR is clear, but what about the wider implications of sustainable objectives?

Many people still see CSR and sustainability as a governance or environmental issue, though perhaps a few include the local corporate impact on the community. Clearly sustainability is a much more far-reaching concept which is focused on the long-term implications of our actions, and as such it runs through every aspect of business operations and does not rest solely with the environmental officer, if there is one. A sustainable manager seeks not only to support current profitability but also to consider the implications going forward. This would include retaining the best people, supporting customers' programmes and thus retaining customers in the longer-term. This brings stability to the business, so a sustainable strategy is already adding value to the bottom line.

The closer business operations are to the environment the more focus there is on the validity of the approaches, methods and responsibility exercised by its people. Wherever there is a programme that seeks environmental permits and planning permission, there will be both valid and inappropriate protest. A company that has a responsible approach should be better placed to win development permission and execute effective programmes. Thus again the sustainable ethos is not only nice to have, but it is essential for many industries to be able to operate effectively.

Construction organizations, such as AMEC, and personal experience across a range of similar industries provide classic examples in the particular area of industry working across most of the environmentally sensitive mineral-based industries. Irresponsible companies stand little chance of winning contracts where public pressure will be in conflict with the development aims. Having lived and worked in these industries, experience has shown that cowboy organizations do not last.

Consequently, for most companies a sustainable approach can be a value in itself. It also provides the franchise for future business. It will help to build long-term relationships with customers, employees, investors, and suppliers and foster a risk management culture, all of which are essential to a strong investment profile and strong earnings potential to the benefit of all stakeholders. This makes sense and is simply good business.

To change the culture of CSR compliance to business development, companies need to consider within their own environment the potential benefits that can be derived from a robust sustainability programme. We have already seen the importance of customer and investor acceptance, so top of the benefits we see improved financial performance. The stability and confidence that is transferred into a sustainable business strategy will almost certainly reduce operating costs, as outlined under eco-efficiency.

There is no doubt that brand management and reputation can be enhanced rather than simply defended, with considerably lower costs or effect on sales. Improved productivity and quality have been shown to flow directly from improved, safe working conditions. A robust sustainable profile will help to both retain and attract good staff, reducing training and recruitment costs.

There is always the risk of regulatory over-sight that creates impacts across the organization and frequently down to the bottom line. An organization that embraces a sustainable ethos is likely to be always ahead of regulation. Improved access to capital stems from both the reputation of the company but also the increasing focus of financial institutions and government programmes towards reinforcing sustainable objectives. Whole life design and a safety-driven programme will reduce liabilities and enhance product reputation.

Thus for the company sustainability offers benefits which both reduce costs and improve market position, so directly enhancing profitability. There is also an indirect value that comes from the benefits to the communities which companies operate within. Involvement in local programmes improves the local environment, which in turn complements the approach of the workforce and enhances its own satisfaction. Unfortunately, many organizations seem to be promoting only their community involvement whilst ignoring the bigger impacts of their business operations.

The third area of benefit comes from the impact on the environment, and we have already looked at the potential bottom-line benefits of energy conservation and waste reduction amongst other elements of an eco-efficient approach.

Sustainability clearly goes beyond the local community and embraces the global supply chain or, in modern parlance, the value chain. Working with suppliers to improve their economy and community helps to develop a wider integration of sustainable programmes. The mutual development programme will from experience improve performance, quality and reliability, which in itself will underpin a sales proposition. Exploitation may bring a short-term benefit but will seldom provide a sound platform for future development and consistent growth. Each time you have to train a new supplier you lose performance and revenue; thus effective investment and commitment will eventually produce a pay-back.

Community projects are often the more visible aspect of corporate sustainability programmes, which is perhaps reflective of a cynical initial approach that saw more noise than commitment. We should, however, not under-value these programmes for, whatever the motive, many have been very effective in supporting charitable operations, and in some cases they have helped regeneration. Where companies are investing in their local community they are helping to create a more healthy and sustainable environment, validating a licence to operate and where, in turn, improved community value will flow back into the business venture through a more committed workforce.

For many the move to invest in the community was part of a defensive strategy and management of risk, whether this risk was envisaged as coming from local supply chains, NGOs, campaigners of all types or, in some parts of the world, political or terrorist group interference. These are just some of the business drivers, which can also include legislative pressures and the need to merge and recognize the interaction between a business and its employees and perhaps customers. So reputation starts to emerge as a pressure point in the community investment analysis: 'adding values to added value'.

We have already recognized the employment value of a sound corporate approach to sustainability but this is only part of the value proposition. A diverse workforce brings greater innovation and a company's commitment to sustainability can often be seen in the innovative solutions that it delivers to the market. Community programmes that connect the business to the wider world can help to bring in environmental and cost-saving approaches as well as building customer loyalty, market share and enhanced employee skills and morale, all of which ultimately builds the profit profile.

Taking the concept further in terms of building up the local economy, companies should be looking to invest in or support small local companies, the benefit being that as the local community grows, so does the resource base. Many major companies (Shell, Anglo-American, BP and BHP amongst others) have supported small businesses in the proximity which has bolstered the local community, encouraged support, increased stability and provided a reliable cost-effective local support network.

Profit from CSR, then, stems from a realization that sustainability is not simply a defence and risk management mechanism, but an approach that can add value to the business. It is business as usual or business as unusual dependent on your perspective. Certainly for many businesses these are uncharted waters, and whether the challenge comes from globalization or regulation, sustainability does not have to be viewed negatively but should be considered as a real focus for profit.

Sustainable development provides a platform so that CSR can be moved from an investment market gimmick, as it seems to be in many cases, towards integrating the common-sense approaches and realizing the benefits that commitment can deliver. The starting point is the recognition that corporate responsibility is more than financial regulatory compliance and tree-hugging.

The next step is strategic road mapping, enabling companies to align technology to products and business plans with a clear acknowledgement of the sustainability implications. The aim is to develop the linkages between resources and business drivers, identify gaps and challenges in the market, market intelligence and sustainable objectives that are supporting strategy and planning to bring in the essential elements of sustainable impacts.

Organizations will be unlikely to meet every challenge or exploit every opportunity within the sustainability profile. A clearly integrated approach will ensure that it is working *with* the business, not in parallel or conflict. High-profile brands focus on promoting their sustainability face and its links to profitability, but many consider these to be purely cynical presentation. There are, however, serious business operations that have been built specifically to contribute to the sustainable agenda.

We have probably all seen some aspect of the Fairtrade programme which is focused on ensuring that growers, initially, were not exploited and that reasonable profit was reinvested to improve production. This profile has seen an ever-increasing market share across a range of produce. Operating as a charity, its growth in market share demonstrates that customers are prepared to pay a premium for products that they consider are encompassing additional values to added value.

The Traidcraft programme promoting Fairtrade produce and providing a route to market for ethnic products has progressively grown to a multi-million level of turnover. There can be few in the business world that have not witnessed the rise of the Body Shop built on Anita Roddick's dream of delivering beauty products that were free of animal testing and developed from natural products. She further looked to use this umbrella to support the role of women.

The Cadbury chocolate empire was built on very sound principles that today would be considered more than encompassing sustainable principles, and these extended to building a social community to support the production factory with a focus on health care and education. This model is one that demonstrates that committed and focused leadership can create an environment that is productive, profitable and good place to work.

A computer cleansing company that started out by providing a disposal service for organizations' redundant PCs involved a focus on the polluting impacts of the units but progressed towards the issues of security of data. Finding celebrities' personal banking details on a recycled computer is hardly the profile a bank would like to project. Thus cleansing data is a challenge that had to be addressed. The recycled machines were either sold on or exported to overseas charities to provide education and training in the developing world. This business continues to grow, providing a necessary service and goodwill.

There are, of course, many organizations that see themselves in an environmental context: waste management, renewable energy, environmental products, pollution control and recycling to name just a few industries, demonstrate that organizations not only benefit from adopting a sustainable approach, but they can create business ventures that in themselves deliver profit.

Cooperatives have for many years shown how the local community can develop approaches that ensure producers both benefit from their efforts and jointly own the operation. These models particularly successful in Europe, offer an alternative development model for the Third World, where individual exploitation can only be resisted if producing communities are able to take more control of their markets. Of course, these models are not new and reflect the communities of the Middle Ages where artisans traded skills for products.

The whole emphasis, then, should be on seeing sustainability not as a drain on profitability but as the catalyst to protect, grow or create new propositions. Companies may be starting from a position of traditional structures and approaches. Many will clearly be involved in operations that are outside the tree-hugging circle. What is important is to consider whether there is a real sustainable approach that can be adopted or developed which will protect the wealth-creation process but which also recognizes the wider pressures on the community at large.

We should not look to exploit the sustainable agenda since that simply devalues the efforts made by others. At the same time, what should be clear is that many have already adopted approaches on various scales that are making a contribution to the bigger picture without damaging profit; in fact, some are seeing their drive towards sustainable approaches delivering profits.

Profit and sustainability do not have to be contradictions and perhaps if this message could be spread both in the financial fraternity and the NGO community then perhaps we would change to a common drive for the future. Profit is not a bad thing and whilst in protecting their bottom line organizations may not progress quickly to eco-friendly performance, progress should come from collaboration not conflict. Protesting organizations would perhaps have more success with the business community if they focused their attention on demonstrating profitable ways to meet their goals. Some NGOs do collaborate but many still seem to prefer to complain from the side lines.

CHAPTER 23

Change management

There is little doubt that the next decades will bring significant changes to the global community. Cultural and economic change will provide a new and evolving platform from which the business community will need to adapt and evolve itself. At the same time this changing landscape will present more and more challenges to the sustainable agenda and the implications of protecting the balance within global exploitation.

The need to adapt traditional approaches and thinking is already apparent. Conservation is about human change, from desires and aspirations to attitude and commitment. We are already risking many species, we are told. It is suggested that by the middle of this millennium perhaps one-quarter of the world's plants and animals will be facing extinction. If we are to preserve these and eventually assimilate an increase in demand from the developing world then change is not only inevitable; it is crucial. What is certain is that simply telling people about the problem will not change their behaviour. If doing this worked then people would not smoke or over-eat. Instead we must provide them with alternative options that they can relate to and see as beneficial.

Clearly the impacts of the globalized community and the changes to the environment mean we also need to address corporate business behaviours. In the business community this does not mean that organizations should not still be focused on profit and wealth creation, but they will require some alternative thinking and certainly a lateral-looking leadership. Leaders need to focus on a more holistic profile and consider their own contributions to the wider sustainable challenges and then convert these to help customers and the community at large take a wider view.

We must stop looking at globalization as a threat to either our personal space or our business and financial benefits. It is true that as we move operations to other parts there will be a social impact; this, however, is only part of a wider evolution that will not be stopped by artificial barriers for very long. Trading deficits in one industry will eventually lead to increases in others. Jobs that we do not want to do will be transferred or taken over by migrant workforces. Current business models will creak under this changing environment and alternative approaches to business, employment and cultural boundaries will emerge. We could feed the world but it likely won't allow us to today due to political and economic barriers. We cannot level the playing field in a flash so it will continue to provide differentiators that will be exploited for profit. That's the reality.

The global village was a visionary concept of the twentieth century but, through technology, will be a reality of the twenty-first century. Thus what we do today must be balanced against the future implications of our actions. One thing for sure is that doing nothing will only compound the pressures that already are building up, environmentally, socially, economically and culturally. This is not the responsibility of governments, communities, NGOs or the business world: it is an issue for all of us and that means change driven by forward-looking leaders. In the business world this change will be inevitable, both to protect current profiles but also to develop new alternative approaches. It is not an option, but how it is developed will be crucial to its real success.

Transforming the future is not simply about imposing more rules on others: it's about reassessing the current operations and challenging the traditionalist rigidity. The business world is already awash with initiatives and change programmes, but perhaps the CSR catalyst will open the debate for a much more lateral approach. To deliver the benefits there is a need to reach outside the silos of individual organizations. The delivery process and the market demand are factors of the value chain that must be reassessed in order to create parallel benefits of savings in cost and environmental impacts. The more the business leadership creates transparency then the higher the probability that other stakeholders will consider a more balanced approach.

For sustainability programmes to be successful they must inform and support corporate processes and systems and run through the business at every level. Organizations must create development frameworks that reflect the areas where change is practical, and this needs to be incorporated into the business policy and operating ethos. The Agenda 21 blueprint established in 1992 by the United Nations provided the outline for corporate organizations. It created guidelines for tackling challenges such as pollution, over-population, energy consumption and efficiency and biodiversity. But one sees a limited number of organizations adopting their own Agenda 21 programmes.

The key is to listen to the stakeholders and build a sustainability framework that can be used to monitor progress and establish the parameters that those working within the business can use to benchmark their actions. This clearly includes compliance with regulatory demands, although the real impact comes not from rules but from a change of focus at every level. Standards such as those adopted by the World Bank and the Organisation for Economic Co-operation and Development (OECD) are often viewed as the yardstick, but in fact they are only the minimum requirements for organizations. Programmes such as Business in the Community, FTSE4Good and DJSI are merely the outward measures; what makes the difference is how individuals behave and adapt their working approaches.

It is people not rules that deliver success, and across every organization you will find a variety of views and perspectives on the need for change, as reflected in Figure 23.1. These personal styles and attitudes are what influences the adoption of alternative approaches in every aspect of the business culture, from the traditional comfort zone to the visionary who wants action tomorrow. The passive group probably represents the majority of the community, including those in business. Most believe there is a need for change and would like to see it happen. The crunch will come when the changes encroach on their personal dimensions. The more progressive will be looking at how these changes can be made practically. The balance and challenge for business leaders is to harness these wide-ranging styles and traits and focus them on common success. This is not only spurring the emotional support but also looking to the structure of the operations, incentive schemes and recognition processes, each of which influences the way individuals and groups will perform.

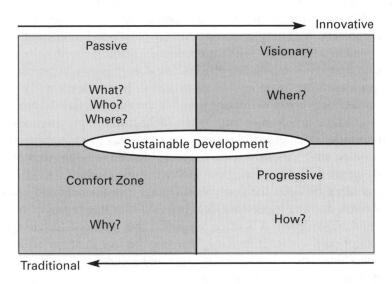

Figure 23.1 Personal styles and attitudes

Sustainability could be the most attractive of backgrounds upon which to address organizational change, since it touches individuals at a number of different levels. If that programme is producing benefits for them personally, the business and the community then it can be accepted more readily than traditional change programmes that are focused solely on business improvement. As we have already explained, each individual is a player in the three pillars of business, the community and the government.

The key is visibility and clarity of purpose, and the seeds of success for any change programme are planted right at the outset. If the goals and objectives are clouded then the commitment and concern that change may bring will constrain progress. It must also be a programme that is connected across the organization. Isolated change initiatives will often deliver locally but create pressures and frictions elsewhere. This is particularly true if the overall impact is only seen in one part of the organization but requires cross-functional input to deliver.

Change programmes are all about leadership. They need a champion with the style and ability to steer the process and provide continuous support. Whether it is a case of investment, research and development, organizational restructuring, codes of practice or cost-saving, these programmes all need to be driven by open leadership and clear commitment. Staying ahead of the game means establishing goals and objective checks and measures that can be openly seen to be delivering effective change. Recycling paper or turning down the heating may focus people's attention but will frequently create more distance than value.

It is also important not only for the organizations but also for the external stakeholders, including investors, that the corporate leadership is seen to be 'walking the talk'. When company cars are reduced to a more economic and environmentally efficient model, it is not appreciated if corporate leaders are travelling in 'gas guzzlers'. But if the company plane is the most effective way to manage time and the business then be prepared to face up to the criticism openly. When rationalization programmes and global operation transfers are a reality then care needs to be focused on the losing community. This may seem obvious, but one only has to read the national press to see many cases that ignore common sense.

The conflict between the concept of change management and change control is one negative aspect that faces individuals within organizations. In the sustainability debate it is often suggested that the need for change is reflective of past wrongs. Obviously this may be true in some cases, but more often than not improved knowledge and technology offers options that previously had not been available.

When influencing the direction of an organization and removing constraints to progress it is important to ensure that management processes apply across every aspect of the business. Control may be focused on error detection, which usually reflects aspects of processes, equipment or training. Sustainability improvements will be most effective when focused on improving the operating processes, tools or resources.

If you look into any organization there is room for improvement in the way it operates and in most cases it would be surprising if the operating efficiency were greater than 80 per cent. This inefficiency must reflect back on many elements of the sustainability agenda (pollution, energy, waste and so on). It is little wonder that sustainability programmes will permeate every aspect of the organization and engender change. Change is inevitable and organizations must establish effective management systems and cultural attitudes.

As the customer becomes more demanding, organizations must stretch their expertise, so looking for innovative approaches that provide competitive edge and sustainability may be the positioning that brings premium consideration. As the business world becomes increasingly global, more opportunities and competitors come into the game. It is also true that temptation to push the envelope of corporate policy may damage sustainability profiles.

The key to managing change is to understand the origins of the particular change and ensure that actions do not cause a worse effect. Many programmes to help organizations brought corrective actions, and many focused on continuous improvement approaches cite the need to keep improving when perhaps a paradigm shift rather than incremental change is what's required. Thus understanding the drivers for change is crucial for driving an effective programme. There is certainly no-one-size-fits-all solution and the pressures of single-focused NGOs seldom reflect the more complex environment that exists. Understanding the influences and drivers provides the basis for innovation whilst creating the right appreciation and ethos.

The more traditional the organization or industry, the more difficult it is steer an alternative route. Finding the core of the issue and establishing the justification for change is crucial to overcoming resistance. Innovation challenges tradition and is the hardest part of mobilizing an organization. The other aspect behind the change comes from the pressures of competition, regulatory demands and third-party influences, such as NGOs. Market pull comes from the customer looking for lower cost or higher performance.

It is also important to consider why change does fail, whether this is due to organizational or production factors, or even both. The biggest obstacle of all is the argument that '*we have always done it this way*'. Some suggest every organization should replace at least 10 per cent of its staff every year to ensure there is no complacency or conservatism within the operation. This is a rather negative concept, suggesting leadership is not able to innovate except through fear. This approach is likely to create protectionism. Fear of failure and a misunderstanding of change create a fundamental block when getting organizations to think outside the box. In the uncharted territory of the sustainability arena, failure brings a heavy price.

Lack of communication and disregard of the knock-on effects of changes will undermine change programmes. People may feel that the problem is someone else's to resolve, so let's leave it for tomorrow. In sustainability terms, clearly tomorrow is the real issue. For the integrated organization, interdependency is often such that it can never be someone else's problem and eventually every challenge must be addressed.

Management by Objectives (MBO) drives most organizations, which is a challenge when change may dilute the short-term focus. The most important part of any change programme is to measure the benefits of change. The quick fix may be necessary but fundamental changes need cost–benefit analysis to lay the foundations for change.

Change is about thinking differently and taking a fresh look at problems, then adapting the approach to meet the challenges, or challenging conventional wisdom, or simply changing the rules of engagement. A situational review should not seek to apportion responsibility but establish the root cause. By focusing blame, or (worse) shifting it to avoid responsibility, the real issues become blurred by self-interest.

An organization which cannot accept that errors will occur will probably be weak in terms of being able to adapt to the market and will fail to harness the full potential of its capabilities. This issue also needs to be taken seriously by those outside the organization trying to impose influence: the more emphasis on blame, the less focus for meaningful change.

Some changes may prove to be uneconomic or out of sync with the overall strategy of the business. It is important that the change process includes evaluation and that change is not implemented without consideration for the implications, both positive and negative.

When organizations are challenged to define value they gravitate towards cash impacts on the bottom line and fail to recognize that value is a wider issue than profit and share dividends. Value can be defined in a multiplicity of ways, dependent on the motivation of that organization and the broader aspects of social responsibility. To harness the operational focus, these must be defined and targeted.

Management of change runs in parallel with a focus on improving quality and productivity. Harnessing people to support sustainable objectives means driving them from being linear thinkers through being reactive, responsive, proactive and finally to recognize their interdependence, which depends on the depth of their participation. The more open and trusting the ethos of the organization, the more likely it will be to react positively to the dynamics of change. The customer's perception of value is a major driver for innovation that takes sustainability to the forefront of change.

Critical success factors (CSF) require people to understand their roles and responsibilities and the need for change, together with how this links to their personal success factors. When incentives are connected to these outputs then the culture for effective and proactive change will be positive. Key performance indicators need to be established to monitor progress and promote performance across the organization. Visibility is important in order to recognize that KPIs can be both positive and negative, triggering the need for change.

Sustainability core issues generally come down to the operation processes; some may not have been changed for years. The change checklist that can be applied to most situations starts with process validation, followed by planning, re-engineer, train, implement, monitor and then revalidate.

A Pareto analysis is often all that is required to identify the high priority issues and can also be equally effective in terms of analysing the potential impacts of change. Frequently organizations use excessive analysis and investigation to avoid taking action. The implementation of costly development programmes focused on environmental impacts often faces review after review when there is no profitable driver behind the development. On the other hand, repeated delays through public inquiries are frequently costly and ineffective in the longer term.

All change requires some investment in people and the more radical the change, the more important it is that people within the organization are prepared for the new dimensions of the business.

Change is inevitable, as the global market will not go away and the impacts of sustainability will continue to be a factor in the market place. Some of the short-term advantages in many cases may prove not to deliver on their promise. Continued customer demand will continue to force changes in culture and, where sustainable, business models will by necessity require greater flexibility and agility. Sustainability-based change will introduce new dynamics to organizations, and within these organizations sustainability will become a critical success factor.

The rapid expansion of the private sector in many emerging countries' markets, together with deregulation and privatization, will spur economic growth by generating pressures to use resources more effectively. The impact of improved efficiencies will be supported by the information technology revolution as companies around the world embrace the ability to adopt best practice approaches, all of which heralds even greater convergence both financially and economically in the world and increased pressure of competition.

Given this forecast, which many suggest underplays the pace of change globally, the business community will face increased customer and regulatory pressure to behave in a socially responsible manner. Integrating these principles into the business processes and culture may be a bigger challenge than adopting technology change. Yet if the sustainability agenda is to heed the warnings of tomorrow, then change must be part of the equation for all responsible business leaders.

CHAPTER 24

Measuring progress not rhetoric

Perhaps the biggest challenge at this stage in the evolution of CSR and sustainability awareness is the scepticism that is created as a result of the prolific outpouring of so-called sustainability reports, many of which simply reflect good works but frequently fail to include a more substantial commitment.

Some of these government-based documents are so full of rhetoric and compromise that they fail to deliver any credibility, particularly when (for example) you see regions and countries alongside each other failing to recognize that measurements are tackled differently and targets are so varied as to be useless. When one considers that the wind knows no borders, why should we give credence to publications that ignore simple principles of nature? Some would say we are at least seeing a focus emerging on sustainability issues. However without effective leadership we are just adding to the sustainability problems by cutting down more trees to produce more publications. Even recycling has its pros and cons.

There are many publications driven by the multiplicity of NGOs on every aspect of environmental issues, including preservation, human rights, equality and so forth. These reports are frequently biased to support their individual perspective. This is not to suggest that their causes are not valid but that bending the rhetoric is not the sole domain of political spin-doctors or corporate PR managers.

On the same basis, there are wide range of sustainability reports being offered up by major organizations as part of the CSR battleground. Many of these are immediately attacked by NGOs based on general or isolated failures by the companies concerned. So if an NGO issues an unbalanced report it is considered focused, but when a corporation endeavours to play it straight they face public challenge. Aren't we *all* responsible for where we are and for the future?

Certainly a number of corporate sustainability reports appear to have simply collected together the voluntary actions of its staff and taken corporate credit. Charitable contributions should be recognized as worthwhile but it is perhaps questionable as to whether these really offset investment strategies that may be seriously damaging, or provide justification for ignoring the big issues. On the other hand, some organizations have made a real effort to embed sustainability, and corporate responsibility, within their business processes by developing internal programmes to ensure these values are supported and promoted.

Being a good company and having a sound policy and sustainable processes in place is viewed as only part of the equation. If nobody knows you're a responsible company, how do you benefit from the investment made? This is one perspective; the other is that in the majority of cases these corporate reporting processes were started to respond to concerns in the market. So now the premise in many places is that they are PR, and if you don't issue one you must have something to hide. We should expect that all organizations and business leaders would operate in a responsible manner, but the world offers a wide variety of cultures and practices where best practice is relative.

The pressure to report, then, is largely not a desire of organizations to promote their responsible approach but to provide the sustainability profile that the market place is demanding, from investors, customers, regulators and NGOs. Once these reports are issued many then start to chip away to find the cracks in the polished front being presented. It does tempt one to ask whether the process is actually delivering value to anyone other than the publishing companies.

The likely answer to this paradox is to some extent hidden within the pages of these sustainability reports. Organizations that have a real commitment clearly demonstrate this through the depth of the content. This in turn also tends to reflect the view that sustainability makes business sense. Those that have limited content clearly have some internal challenges to address.

The problem is that globally and nationally, with industry sector codes, investor initiatives and stakeholder guidelines ranging from the UN Global Compact to Accountability 1000, there is a multitude of directives. These do not include the regulatory controls, which have also increased over the past few years and are all focused on sustainable responsibility. So whatever a company reports, it is likely to miss some aspect that some will consider important. This pressure to be seen to be good is perhaps clouding the issue of whether companies are operating to be good.

The advent of Sarbanes–Oxley (SOX) Act of 2002, in the wake of Enron and WorldCom, has boosted the financial reporting requirements of corporations. It also demands that organizations include provision for potential risks that could influence investor confidence. Clearly there are many aspects of the sustainability agenda that could affect these financial profiles. As such perhaps we are seeing the first formal drive to integrate proactive thinking on sustainability.

The reality is that, as already outlined, the crux of a sustainable programme is not in the regulations and standards but in the ethos of the organization and the conviction of corporate leadership to support this culture. Thus in many ways it does not matter what the sustainability report looks like; the question is whether it reflects a true picture of the organization it represents. Certainly creating a regimented format and precise measurement programme will take years to develop and perhaps decades to ever reach any level of common acceptance. Even then it will provide only minimum rules of engagement and plenty of holes to be exploited.

Given the diversity of industries it is unlikely that there could be a one-size-fits-all structure, and even if that were possible the outputs would probably be so limited as to be next to useless. The International Organization for Standardization (ISO) did propose to develop an international CSR reporting format. This has not yet emerged, but it will be interesting to see the American National Standards Institute (ANSI group) in the USA's views of what could be a common global platform. The cynic might suggest there could be another motive for US-driven standards to ensure it was not commercially respective. The British Quality Foundation did issue its 'Excellence One Tool Box for CSR' to help corporate strategists develop a measurable profile, and Dell, IBM, HP and their leading suppliers all issued an electronics industry code of conduct in 2004 to promote a common approach across their global supply chains.

The starting point, then, should be that each company establishes its own sustainability strategy, which reflects the nature of the business profile. Once this is declared then individual organizations could develop a measurement process that was driven by the business processes, and not by some disconnected report profile. The added benefit of this approach is that sustainability becomes part of the mainstream business processes. Organizations can set out their own sustainability stall and investors can assess for themselves which they wish to support.

Scottish Power, for example, focused their 2004 report on the environment, the market place, the work place and the community, but the most significant issue reported by the CEO was that they were focusing on what CSR meant to them, whereas P&G divided their report into environmental protection, social responsibility and economic development, with a focus on water, health and hygiene. In the same period GE announced the launch of a $20 million humanitarian project to bring improved health care to Ghana. Which of these has the greater impact on the market? Many might suggest that GE's investment is planting future revenue streams.

Other reports issued around the same time included BAe, offering a view on defence and sustainability, which must surely challenge many NGOs; General Motors, which reported its sustainability measurements for the decade along with greater transparency for employees; and Imperial Oil, which announced $9 million in donations and $380 million spent on improved environmental protection. They also claimed to have the best safety record in the industry. These are just a few of the reports that are published each year to tell the world what the organization has done to contribute to the sustainability agenda, and they demonstrate a wide variety of initiatives and perspectives on the issues together with a range of considerations as to their importance to each industry.

Organizations need to have the courage to stand by their declared position, which should already have been validated by the principal stakeholders through structured CSR reporting, as shown in Figure 24.1. If stakeholder expectations are incorporated, then isolated protest will have a limited impact. What is important to gauge the progress of any such strategy

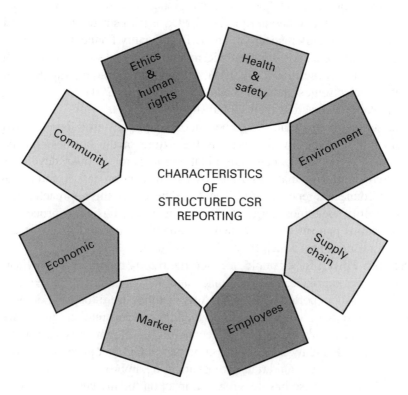

Figure 24.1 Structured CSR reporting

is to ensure that indicators are in place which are relevant, clear, robustly integrated in the business process and comparable in general terms to the competition. It is also important to establish key external indicators that can be used to benchmark results. This ensures that internal profiles are not reflecting external influences that the organization cannot control; to take an extreme example, a pollution control measure when the nearby volcano erupts.

Collecting KPI data from experience has often been a chore because it was not integrated with the business operations, or else there were so many that real value was diluted by volume. Frequently the externally reported measures will be driven from a much broader profile within the organization and the connectivity must be robust.

What will make a difference to the reader is where the organization has a clearly defined policy that matches their business model and environment, where they clearly provide the rationale for this policy and can deliver robust reporting to demonstrate they are on track and performing against the established goals and objectives. The truth will out eventually and organizations that have taken a committed approach (as opposed to simply complying) will deliver more valid and valuable reports to their stakeholders, reflecting both internal and external requirements.

What should not be forgotten in the strategic approach to sustainability and in terms of reporting to stakeholders is the role of the supply chain. Progressive moves towards global sourcing and outsourcing traces organizations with the potential risk of compromising their own efforts towards a sustainable and responsible approach. It would therefore not be logical to ignore this key element of the delivery process. The fact is that in most organizations at least 50 per cent of their operating costs goes on external providers, so the impact on the business is significant. Sadly, from experience too few organizations recognized the full potential value of this resource or the risk that poor management can bring.

The Dow Jones Sustainability Index review came into effect in 2004, covering 300 companies across 24 countries. It is a now a key reference for investors. Alongside this there is the FTSE4Good programme in the UK stock market which also supports other markets. The FTSE group also operates an engagement programme to help organizations to meet the criteria. This focus on the reporting is a worrying aspect of sustainability awareness since it should be the actions of companies producing the reports, not the other way round. It is interesting that a 2004 report by Sustainability, the United Nations Environment Programme, suggested that boards were failing to disclose to investors how environmental and social issues posed strategic risks to their business.

What is starting to come through is the impact of companies playing the responsible sustainability card and then having to rethink their marketing programmes. Consider Cadbury or Walker's Crisps promoting programmes to support schools whilst strongly marketing products that perhaps are not the best ones for developing children. The Nestlé baby food situation certainly caused that company some problems. Indirectly, then, the reporting process can cause internal strategic changes over time, so perhaps the new mantra of responsible reporting is 'competing to be good'.

Such is the profile and potential impact of CSR and sustainability on organizations that many are establishing formal structures to manage the process. This again begs the question of whether sustainability is something that organizations need to manage or a policy and ethos that is embedded in the operation. At least if these structures are established correctly they will have objectives and commitments to report on.

Certainly organizations are appreciating that these reports are progressively getting more attention and, therefore, they need to focus on material matters that reflect the views of stakeholders. Transparent measurements that are independently verified become the core of the report. Many are also finding that the lessons learned in sustainability reporting can be transferred into the broader overall financial reporting; in fact, there are many crossovers of topics. Sustainability and social impacts are indeed financial risk or opportunities so the drive to bring these into the mainstream can only heighten the attention on the issues. The way in which business interacts with the community has an impact on overall performance.

Governments produce numerous reports in support of their progress towards a sustainable agenda and, as with many corporate reports, these too often fail to provide any real information. They are also used to measure one country's progress against those of neighbouring states. The UK, for example, measures 15 target indicators:

- economic growth;
- investment;
- employment;
- poverty;
- education;
- health;
- housing;
- crime;
- GHG;
- air quality;

- transport;
- water quality;
- wildlife;
- land use;
- waste.

These clearly offer a profile of the community and draw their progress from 150 indicators that sit below them. What becomes more difficult is to compare developments against other countries that record similar topics but use alternative measures. So the value of the reporting process may tell you where you are, but will not offer a comparator that is fully validated.

The same challenge faces those who try to compare one company with another. There are so many variables that any comparison can only provide a general perspective. The UK economy, for example, is perhaps more American than its European partners, and thus like-for-like comparisons are weighted by assumptions. Debates will doubtless go on as to the validity of the assumptions derived from the trackers.

Using the AccountAbility model from the Institute of Social and Ethical Accountability, with its five-part materiality test, establishes a framework to create a reporting approach, but does not compensate for a clear corporate declaration of what a company wants to achieve.

- Test 1 – short-term financial impacts from environmental or social impacts;
- Test 2 – policy-based performance;
- Test 3 – business peer-based norms;
- Test 4 – stakeholder behaviour and concerns;
- Test 5 – societal norms.

There are also the BITC (Business in the Community), the London Benchmarking Group (LBG) model for Community Development, and so on. What must, however, be at the core of any reporting programme is the reality of the commitment of the organization. This should also be focused on the business benefits from a sustainable approach because as such it is connecting the drivers of the stakeholders and not isolating the approach from the principal drivers of wealth creation.

In the business arena many have (and still are striving) to establish the direct linkage between CSR and sustainable responsibility and profitability. Those that are convinced of the value proposition will define values and examples of value contributions through reputation. To a large extent this is mostly smoke and mirrors and getting a commitment from corporate leaders to provide support for sustainable approaches must start with a leap of faith. This can be based on the no-negative principle (e.g., if it there is no cost or performance impact by making the change, then start there).

The further developing of sustainable change must then be balanced against economic modelling and corporate aims. The soft issues of internal commitment and customer loyalty clearly add value, but are less easy to validate. Other programmes focused on good practice will (as outlined earlier) potentially deliver improved productivity and quality and reduce wastage, all of which will contribute to profitability.

Shareholder value was the maxim of the late twentieth century and the drive to deliver this fundamentally changed the way corporations worked. The focus was to increase shareholder returns almost without consideration for the effect on the business. Corporate focus on rationalization, outsourcing, globalization and cross-industry migration weakened traditional business values. In the worst cases companies failed or found themselves developing approaches that stepped outside the ethical boundaries that had been the foundation of good performance. Most companies will start the sustainability process based on an intuitive recognition that relationships (both internal and external) can have a positive or negative impact on performance.

The market place has already moved on from corporate valuations being based strictly on assets, turnover and market share. Today the importance of intangibles (such as innovation, management, leadership and knowledge) are taken as part of the valuation process. Brand value and reputation vulnerability are a growing consideration in a market where distributed production and delivery processes can result in customers being at variance with corporate performance.

Sustainability reports, then, are a reflection of the company and of its approach to a wide range of issues that may impact profitability. They are unlikely ever to become fully comparable with a business sector, and never common to the business community as a whole.

It is the differentiation that makes us favour one company or another, and we should expect this to be reflected in their approach to CSR and sustainability. What we should be looking for is a clear picture of the company's aims and objectives. From experience, those with a clearly defined approach will jump off the page as a proactive operation, the implications being that sustainable considerations are in fact embedded in the operation, which in turn will probably mean a better focus on eco-efficiency and less risk of external organizations protesting and raising claims of bad practice. What we should be avoiding are organizations that present a superficial profile which carries little or no commitment to the business end of the operation.

As stated earlier, research involved reviewing a large number of sustainability reports and, to underpin our views about corporate commitment it is worth looking at some of these. However, it would also be wrong to fall into the trap of naming names.

Let us first take a major investment bank based in the USA but operating across the globe, which is heavily involved in corporate investment acquisition and infrastructure development programmes and all that that entails. The major part of its community support programmes is supporting their employees who work on charitable activities or to sponsoring high-profile projects in the arts. It is difficult to find their investment strategy or corporate position that should be reflected in their business activity. We have seen that the Co-operative Bank makes its ethical policy very clear, but others perhaps prefer to be more low key since they only provide funding to clients who carry the responsibility for sustainability issues.

A major mobile phone company in its 2004 report proudly announces its values and key measures, including recycling of phones, CO_2 reductions and use of renewable energy. An employee survey supports the view that the company is doing reasonably well against its sustainability targets. The contributions to community projects are relatively low key but significant. (There of course remains the debate that communication masts may be a significant threat.)

Then take the report from a major infrastructure construction organization. The report reflects the key areas they are focusing on but, more importantly, it clearly links the need for a sustainable approach to their business viability. There is no fluff; merely a structured presentation of the challenges and progress. It displays an honest presentation of a company that has recognized the potential risks of ignoring external and internal stakeholder pressure. An organization that is in the front line of potential protest, often in front of their clients, and whose operational performance can be directly challenged takes the realistic and pragmatic position that sustainability means as much to them as it does to the NGOs.

These are three very different reports which reflect a common recognition of the need to report but perhaps also show a wide-ranging focused perspective or underlying commitment to the benefits of sustainable development. Being a good local charitable giver should not be ignored, but if this is shielding a corporate drive that is funding or delivering potential dangers into the community then perhaps it is a waste of paper. What it does highlight is that as organizations recognize the benefits and risk associated with a strategic development and embed this, so the quality and value of their reporting improves.

Organizations that have faced continued protest over their operating programmes and so-called global exploitation and which still produce reports that declare hide-bound positions relative to corporate and sustainable responsibility, whilst continuously being caught out, run the risk of being viewed as totally unreliable. They may still be able to meet SOX reporting and by delivering high dividends maintain a strong investor base, but the question should still be asked as to how much more effective, profitable and valued they could be with the right strategy in place.

CHAPTER 25

Infrastructure balance

Multiple stakeholders, combined with performance pressures on the business leadership, create a challenging sustainability minefield, especially if one considers that for developed markets to undertake strategies focused on a sustainable future there must be a reassessment of the financial constraints and incentives. It may be easy for governments to establish local, national and even global policy; however, the impact on the business community, unless tempered with realistic support, will conflict with the drivers of profit. This in turn will force avoidance or protective measures rather than real strategic change. It should also be appreciated that whilst some investors and shareholders may have sustainable incentives, many others do not. To influence those with a pure profit motive some alternative incentives will be needed.

Penalties create pressures for avoidance whilst incentives tend to attract proactive interest. Thus balancing policy, investment, taxation and regulation must drive the future delivery of sustainable programmes. Business organizations must be encouraged to establish internal policies that provide the background against which innovation can be stimulated and responses to sustainable challenges promoted to look at the relative values between profit and long-term performance.

At the Johannesburg World Summit, the leaders of the nations who were there made a commitment to accelerate the shift towards sustainable consumption and production. This was focused on delivering continuous economic and social progress whilst respecting the Earth's eco-systems and meeting the needs and aspirations of everyone for a better life and future, by decoupling economic growth from environmental pollution, and then focusing on the most significant environmental impacts, optimizing the use of resources and changing the consumer's perceptions. These well-meaning objectives will evolve (or, more frequently, be diluted) through practical policy application.

Clearly leaders should be setting goals that stretch the global community at every level; however, too often these valuable visions become translated in different ways by separate nations and then are applied through regulation in a fragmented and diffused way, frequently ignoring the dynamics of the business world and thus providing little or no practical support at the coalface to help to bridge the transition from the realities of today to the aspirations of tomorrow, and whilst failing to recognize along the way that wealth created by business is what will actually fuel a more inclusive, sustainable community.

At the core of the challenge are the key ingredients that sit at the heart of the business development strategy and how these influences impact the viable drivers for business and the sustainable agenda. Policy clearly impacts the regulatory developments and pressures that business must contend and comply with. Linking taxation to regulation as a deterrent is perhaps the most negative influence on creating a more focused approach to integrating sustainability. Finding ways of harnessing the investment market through incentives may be the only real catalyst to bring the aspirations of forward-looking business leaders in line with their shareholders and customer demands.

Sustainability is a global issue but the cornerstones can only be established at national or even regional levels. These foundations must not only seek to address the emotional commitment to the future; they should also attempt to remove or dilute some of the constraints that business faces in order to deliver a sustainable strategy through an integrated infrastructure as in Figure 25.1. It may be true that the richest fifth of the world's population consumes nine times more than the poorest, and it is also recognized that people in the developing world want to emulate the benefits of the developed world; however, in reality we cannot support that within current resource usage.

The conflict between the haves and the have-nots will not disappear simply by wishing. The wealth, technology development and innovation needed to achieve these noble goals will only come from the business community, so stimulating sustainable goals should be more effective than enforcing punitive regulations.

Looking at the global market of the future it is not difficult to recognize that many of the challenges of today will increase rather than diminish in the future, not the least of which will be the impacts of the new Asian face of economic development. China and India are already set to be economic heavyweights in the future, raising the prospect of alternative cultural pressures alongside a massive consumer market demand. Asia's economic growth is set to change economic dynamics, and the implications for the business community are that competition and consumerism will become more complex.

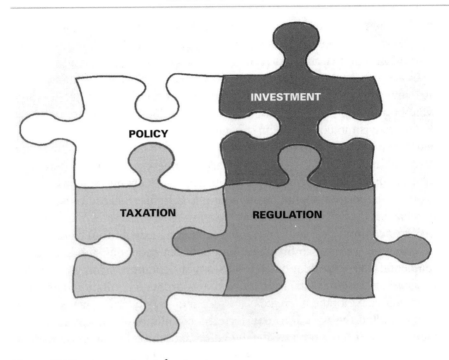

Figure 25.1   Integrating infrastructure

New emerging corporations from Asia will start to make their presence felt in the market place through trade and investment. The implications of conflicting investment standards creates a confusing prospect for the future, requiring regulators not only to look at the impacts of outward investment but also the implications of inward investment. The world's economy is expected in 20 years' time to be almost twice what it was at the start of the millennium, but the gap between the haves and have-nots will almost certainly widen, driven in part by economies which today may be considered developing states, the value of a nation state being largely dictated by how well it can acquire technologies and invest in knowledge and its ability to integrate and apply new technology.

So we face a very variable looking future within a global market place; business leaders are endeavouring to balance investment strategy against the short-term profitability which many stakeholders are demanding. Investment strategy is being measured against the conflict between CEO performance, governments' election cycles and the longer term pay-back of introducing more longer-term sustainable approaches. Already the concepts of outsourcing and off-shoring have been introduced to maintain competitiveness. The growth in overseas alliances and joint ventures shows that the market place is becoming more homogenized, whilst the regulatory controls remain nationally driven.

Given this evolving global commercial battleground it is little wonder that industry and the investment market seek to exploit differentiation, which is after all the foundation of the trading ethos in that those that have resources wish to convert them or want to have a natural flow of business. But when you seek to influence one sector to take a more pragmatic sustainable perspective whilst allowing the emerging regions to build up their demands and aspirations then you artificially distort the market. This is not to suggest we should not try, but it highlights the need to look at all influences.

If, for example, we are to decouple economic growth from environmental pollution we have to break the link between economic good and environmental bad. The relationship is extremely complex since growth puts pressure on the environment in terms of resources and pollution. However, economic development creates new technology to make better use of resources and the wealth to pay for cleaner solutions. There cannot be a paradigm shift but a progressive evolution and, through this process, there is a need for balance on all sides of the stakeholder profile. The rules for business are a crucial ingredient of providing a practical approach.

Policy sets the tone for the implications on investment, regulation and taxation, which are all factors that strongly influence business thinking. The Kyoto agreement and human rights sound impressive, but, with varied degrees of real commitment, how effective are they? Some states sign but don't apply, whilst others stand out against signing something they know will be detrimental to their national objectives. What perhaps all governments should be considering in this global village is the African maxim that it takes a whole village to bring up a child, and that means global focus.

To achieve results, then, policy should be supporting a drive to change the way we produce and consume goods and services. This affects resources, manufacturing, distribution, waste and end-of-life product management. It also influences the way we see competitiveness and consumer demand. These in turn impact investment strategy over the short, medium and long term, in more efficient production and returns on investment. Looking forward, policy needs to encourage innovation technically, socially and within the institutional frameworks, changing the market's perception of sustainability and enhancing demand to support the wealth creation process, not simply constraining it whilst its competition grows.

The implications for the policy development process mean that there needs to be a consistent cascade effect from global aspirations, to national regulation and regional application. Those that look at the EU will appreciate that even the common regulatory approach is then diluted or distorted around national drivers. This becomes even more complex when you integrate the implications of cultural and religious diversity with creating common aims. The indications for the next decade or so clearly suggest that the political order will continue to be in a high state of flux with economic growth being perhaps the catalyst for greater stability of focus.

If the key is economic growth then policy should be providing the stimulus and should be balanced against capability and support to be proactive. Recognizing the realities of business and wealth creation policy involves balancing the passion of the NGOs, the ambitions and ego of politicians, and the vast majority of business and consumers who in general seek to maintain or improve their life without damaging the planet.

Investment is a crucial element in establishing a proactive and progressive application of sustainable strategy. Clearly companies that can harness these values or which can demonstrate that implementing a responsible approach can enhance production and value through eco-efficiency will have a natural advantage. Stimulating innovation in production (not only technology but also business models) means providing a stimulus for investors to accept alternative business profiles. Investment returns will also be influenced by the way the market place responds and supports alternative approaches. Business must remain committed to meeting consumer demand more efficiently, which can bring value and competitive advantage.

Clearly institutions such as the IMF and the World Bank have a significant influence on the global market place. There is certainly a major impact throughout the developing world from the implications of trade and aid for development projects, but at the same time the implications of debt must also be balanced. In consumer societies there are those that suggest promoting debt conflicts with social responsibility. Both nationally and at an individual level there is a responsibility to ensure that debt can be managed and that finance gets spent appropriately.

Banks such as the Co-operative have made their position very clear through a code of conduct and they translate this into their business approach by controlling their activities within clear ethical guidelines. Others would argue that they are not being unethical by funding projects in areas that are environmentally damaging or socially exploitative, or even arms and defence programmes. One hopes they are not breaking any laws, but their investment strategies are clearly more liberal and within their right of choice. Perhaps, however, the more focused sustainable projects could be incentivized differently by governments to make them more attractive.

Corporate responsibility is gaining growing support from individual investors but perhaps less from the corporate investor. Again there is a question of choice, but to locate the advantages of CEOs following a sustainable investment strategy we need to find the appropriate stimulus or tax incentives. The value of investment houses establishing sustainable share rankings that could attract tax incentives could perhaps provide the stimulus for CEOs to seek sustainable endorsement. It would be interesting to see if NGOs find themselves being sought out for advice and endorsement of corporate sustainable strategies.

Certainly there is a case for considering that in terms of corporate reporting and other demands (such as SOX reporting risk) they should incorporate sustainability management including ethical trading and not simply governance. These aspects of sustainable awareness – potential risks to the business community, as well as opportunities in eco-efficient productivity – are risks all of which many organizations fail to manage other than from a reputation perspective.

Government regulators should be looking to create policy-driven frameworks that provide incentives to corporations rather than challenging them simply to comply. This means working with the business community to develop appropriate approaches. The majority of regulation starts from a position that all corporate organizations are looking to exploit the environment and the community. Frequently the regulatory approach fails to recognize the difference between an organization's process discipline and accidental failure as opposed to exploitation. One also expects that organizations have a duty of care to their stakeholders. This challenges the concept of creating single focused regulations, which then becomes diluted through consultation with responsible companies, whilst failing to place robust demands on those that are set on exploitation.

An eminent UK police chief once suggested that 5 per cent of people were basically honest, 5 per cent fundamentally corrupt and the rest just waiting for the opportunity to be corrupt. Many may contest this view but perhaps looking from a sustainable viewpoint, these percentages are a good benchmark. Some 5 per cent of organizations will promote sustainable approaches, 90 per cent would like to be able to adopt appropriate approaches but need support, and the bottom 5 per cent will perhaps never accept responsibility and would always seek to exploit any profit opening.

Regulation, then, should be punitive to those that default and spare no effort to establish real penalties not token insurable fines. This should ensure that organizations do not take the easy route and that responsible companies are not forced to protect themselves unnecessarily. Encouraging those that waver should be the focus, whilst damning those that have no desire to comply.

A focus on common ground to bring in regulation has often been the reason for it not being effective. Because responsible organizations contribute to the debate, they inevitably find themselves being commercially disadvantaged, whilst irresponsible organizations generally do not participate and try to flout the regulations anyway. Steering this conflict towards a positive driver is key to creating a platform of sustainability. Perhaps the best rule would be to focus regulation on intent rather than detailed definition, so fewer words and more commitment should be the maxim.

Perhaps the most effective tool available to government (which is also highly visible to the business community) is the whole area of taxation. Sustainable tax benefits could be the incentive to help business leaders move more towards effective programmes, while at the same time attracting investors to sustainable projects and organizations which are no longer disadvantaged but perhaps even benefiting from relief on their sustainable investments.

Products that are environmentally produced and incorporate whole life considerations may be made more attractive. Investment towards improving production and resource use should be encouraged and will eventually produce a more competitive consumer product. Tax advantages could also be focused on the consumer to progressively change the demand profile and perhaps flatten out the differentials between responsible products that have been produced within ethical parameters and those which simply deliver low cost. Sustainable consumerism will remain the prerogative of those prepared to pay a premium, so inducing a change in thinking must address all sides of the equation.

Corporate investment programme support that delivers sustainable advantages should be able to attract tax concessions. This would provide some balance to the conflicts of being truly responsible and delivering shareholder dividends, which could be earmarked to deliver some advantage for supporting the corporate responsible company.

Value Added Tax (VAT) provides a highly visible, consumer-focused means of supporting a sustainable culture. On the one hand, non-sustainable imports could attract high import duties from regions where sustainable responsible programmes either are not in place or where there is a clear failure to support sustainable or ethical policies. This may damage developing communities in the short term, but would provide a balancing of responsible approaches. This global enforcement works for some endangered species, so why not as an approach for the global community?

Perhaps one aspect of the taxation arena that also needs attention is the issue of clarity and visibility concerning how current taxes are collected and apportioned, e.g., petrol tax is supposedly linked to GHG but the reality is that it is more of a general tax revenue stream. People should be free to spend how they please and to temper their spending against personal aims or aspirations and know where their tax is going. Some have limited options and thus must gravitate towards low-cost choices despite wishing to support a more responsible approach. In these cases a sustainable tax advantage could help to reshape the market place.

Creating sustainable benefits is perhaps part of a much wider recognition that the integration of business and consumer stakeholders' drivers can be progressively adapted. At the same time, levelling the playing field may remove some artificial imbalances that deter responsible organizations from adopting a more proactive approach. What is clear is that these aspects of policy, investment, regulation and taxation cannot be addressed without recognizing the potential impacts and benefits that an integrated approach could provide.

CHAPTER 26

Alternative business models

Technical innovation, market pressures, dynamic changes in the global business community and the goals of sustainability cannot be separated. They are all factors in the volatile business arena but what they all herald is the need to consider the implications of a more adaptable and integrated business model. Globalization is drawing organizations together but at the same time it is no longer acceptable for any major organization to claim immunity from a supplier's or a partner's problem.

In many cases the ability to meet the challenges of the market place means greater interdependency. This creates opportunities to enhance the market competitiveness but also brings with it the risks of interdependence. The impacts and challenges of globalization are realities faced by most business organizations. The volatility and need for flexibility, together with a fast response to change, means that customers want the providers to be more local. These demands and challenges can only be met by a networked community. In real terms the building of multi-cultural organizations offers many benefits, both in terms of exploiting the local connections but also in the wider sense of bringing connectivity to the capability globally.

Taken together these factors point to business sustainability in the future resting more on agility than size. This environment and background opens up the potential for developing the virtual organization as a response to present and future business realities. Through challenging questions in respect of traditional views of the trading environment, virtual integration draws on traditional approaches and relationships adapted to the business landscape of today and the future. The eighteenth-century economist Adam Smith had a vision of perfect competition and perfect knowledge which may be beginning to emerge from the rapid expansion of globalization and technology. This new environment is changing the way that companies compete and share market information, creating an evolution of business models. Throughout history business models have changed to reflect the development of the market place. Innovation in technology provides the platform for even more radical re-positioning and the need to consider organizational development in the fluid environment of outsourcing and alliances.

Changes in the business landscape in terms of consolidation of companies, globalization and technology have added more complexity to the competitive environment. At the same time political and economic change, whilst driving the pressures towards sustainability and environmental responsibility, are adding increasing demands on the strategic development of organizations. The increasing need for flexibility to be able to respond to change effectively has prompted organizations to look at alternative delivery and investment models.

The 2005 publication by Leon Benjamin, *Winning by Sharing*,[8] provides a valuable perspective that reflects how the Internet and global changes have initiated the creation of a new working model. Rationalizations in the Western world have brought about a rethink of the traditional employment model. The advent of the portfolio career and a focus on the work–life balance is changing the shape of the knowledge pool. Wealth creation, then, is founded in sharing competences, relationships and intellectual capital.

Skills and knowledge may in the future lie outside organizations and be drawn in as required. The freedom that this creates for the individual could engender an alternative positioning in terms of which organizations one chooses to work with. Thus in the future organizations could be come more vulnerable because of their image, whilst at the same time corporate responsibility performance becomes more dependent on external individuals or small companies. As we look back at business models and then consider the next evolutions, there is a need to ensure that sustainable values become even more embedded since they will have to bridge organizational and individual responsibility perspectives in the future.

This evolution will be more dynamic and probably more rapid than the transition from farming communities to industrial complexes, which has been relatively fast in historical terms. The changes in the next decades are likely to seem instantaneous by comparison. However, future business models may be more like those of the pre-Industrial Revolution than those of the mass production age. Tomorrow's idea is often an evolved version of an old one, adapted to new conditions.

The Fordist model proved its robustness through several economic cycles and was copied around the globe to meet increasing consumer demand. Its weakness eventually proved to be the rigidity of the formula. Global changes to patterns of production, rapid adoption of new technologies and shifting demand made it harder to keep the vertically integrated operations optimized and more difficult for them to adapt. Exploiting just-in-time (JIT) principles became the new model for mass production.

The potential for organizations now is to develop integrated networks that provide end-to-end delivery processes that are configured to meet current market needs whilst remaining independent companies in their own right. Advances in communications technology and reach have enabled the traditional local complementary trader model to now be effective in the twenty-first century and on a global scale. The potential for more holistic integration provides an even more radical opportunity to exploit the inter-dependence and complementary nature of business relationships.

The development of business clusters has generally been based around geography and to a large extent focused on specific industries, such as Silicon Valley. In other sectors, whilst there have been trade communities, these did not work together other than to address issues of labour rates.

The future of holistic network clusters in the development of alternative business models has significant potential to introduce options, particularly for the smaller business operators (see Figure 26.1), where the pressures of the market have concentrated on consolidating supply through national or global centres. The concept of virtual integration allows smaller organiza-tions producing similar products or complementary products to link into trading bodies that can match the larger competitors.

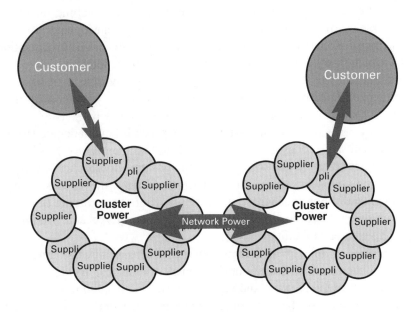

Figure 26.1   Network power through clusters

The globalization of purchasing by big corporations places increased competitive pressure on small/medium-sized local suppliers. Rationalization of the supplier base and consolidation of requirements through single source supply have exacerbated this effect, placing many SMEs outside the trading circle. Traditional local providers may be unable to offer comprehensive supply packages or the logistics to support delivery, and the cost of servicing global markets can be prohibitive.

By linking specialists together a number of virtual enterprises could be created with greatly reduced investment and thus improved value to the customer, with these entities possibly established for limited periods. The widening reach of the Internet has given true connectivity and has shown the promise for the small company or group of companies to come back into the market not only at the local level but also globally. Niche players now have the opportunity to extend their reach.

There is an even greater opportunity, and that is the consolidation of like-minded companies to link their specialist talents, skills and resources in order to match those of big league players. By developing complementary partners they can extend their potential delivery and service capability into the solutions market place, recapturing traditional supply but also now building extended offerings. These configurations can also be adapted by changing, where necessary, certain partners to extend the network geographically and perhaps offer specialist delivery propositions.

Supermarkets providing banking or utility companies selling insurance are examples of potential developments for the extended enterprise. In these cases the objective is to take the specialized skills of one organization and exploit them through the customer base of the other partner. The concept can, however, obviously be deployed in many aspects of business development in terms of creating alternative outlets, linking skills into alternative solutions or combining skills to address new markets.

In many cases the extended enterprise approach is being adopted simply to build delivery processes that are based on complementary capabilities rather than investment and ownership. Collaborative approaches have been used more frequently in the past decade to help manage the process of inter-dependence through outsourcing. The future offers the prospect of organizations being more constrained in terms of investment and needing to maintain greater flexibility.

The concept of virtual integration may seem somewhat unrealistic against a background of traditional business challenges. To highlight the development of the idea and the reality it is worth considering some of the key changes that have been factors in the past decade and the pressures that will continue through the current decade and beyond. These factors are common aspects of business today, from the growth in globalization, which has created a much wider competitive market place to the growing pressure to meet social and environmental responsibility targets. The explosion in communications technology has opened up both opportunity and challenge.

The business world has always adapted to the demands of the market and its customers. The current diversity of opportunity and risk prompts organizations to look at what has been the background to these developments and to consider what may be solutions.

We define a virtual organization as a semi-permanent network or cluster of interdependent product and service providers who deliver supply propositions to customers by creating end-to-end, value-based solutions and configurations utilizing their individual assets without any single party owning the complete process. The creation of virtual entities offers a new focus for business, although it incorporates many concepts that have been part of trading environments for hundreds of years.

The new facilitator is the Internet, a flexible medium that can be used to create greater possibilities, rather than to destroy traditional business. Technology, however, is a small part of the equation, which is only likely to succeed based on robust and stable relationships. The key ingredients of trust, mutual responsibility, clear objectives and value creation will become the platform for innovative approaches and the glue to support virtual integration. The rationalization of industrial sectors, along with the convergence of industries based on alternating economic cycles, has seen an increase in mergers and acquisitions on a global scale. Many organizations have used their relative market value to adopt a more diverse profile, crossing both industrial and cultural boundaries. An additional development has been the increase in outsourcing and relocation of workforces on a global scale to capitalize on low-cost labour markets. Though not an entirely new development, improvements in technology have prompted organizations to consider more readily the idea of 'follow the sun working'.

The expectations and realities of many of these ventures has shown that whilst the opportunity may be there, the challenge of integrating multi-cultural organizations effectively has fewer successes than the media would perhaps suggest.

Virtual integration is far more complex than simply changing the name of a company. Transferring knowledge, even within organizations, can be a difficult task. Looking for commonality or economies of scale across industrial sectors and national cultures adds further challenges. The development of a programme to build effective relationships within a virtual environment may be easy to instigate with a single management directive but is perhaps often more difficult than within a cluster of independent and mutually focused players.

The Internet has become part of our daily vocabulary and for many businesses it is seen as the new marketing territory, ripe for exploitation. The bursting of the dot.com bubble will eventually be seen as little more than a blip in the progress of e-commerce. Electronic data interface (or EDI) showed the way, but the Internet today provides greater connectivity at a fraction of the cost. The web also allows the development of lighter and more flexible control. Advances in security and interfaces have now enabled linking of backroom systems as well as communications and data transmission. The adoption of the Internet has been faster than any previous technology and it continues to grow. The dot.com boom forced us not only to appreciate the potential but also the difficulties, most of which stemmed from weak business propositions and the failure to recognize the importance of business relationships. For suppliers, customer relationships have a trading value and should be the backbone of sustainable business. For customers, trust and accountability are major factors when considering a purchase. Although excellent e-business concepts were created, in many the business fundamentals were lacking.

Every business operation has to recognize that one of the major challenges for the twenty-first century is the effect that growing pressure to meet the goals of sustainability and the increasing focus on social responsibility has on how organizations not only manage and regulate their own performance, but also their interfaces with other organizations.

Sustainability is a triple platform, which addresses economic development within the three perspectives of financial, social and environmental impact. There are multiple standards that have been developed to focus on best practice and each of these adds to certain aspects of the total picture.

The scope of sustainability is wide and should be considered within the context of best practice and business benefits or potential if it is to be addressed in a more proactive manner. The challenge today is that few business operations act in isolation and so the interfaces between organizations produce opportunities and vulnerabilities. Exploiting these interfaces could in the longer term produce both substantial contributions to efficiency and effectiveness at the same time as actively supporting the wider agenda of sustainable development.

Eco-efficiency therefore offers an opportunity to organizations to focus not on the (perhaps sometimes) emotional aspects of sustainability but more on the real returns on investment that can be derived from more effective integrated operations. Most organizations are sensitive to their social and environmental impacts; virtual integration would allow organizations to share information and optimize processes to capitalize on benefits and contribute to the long-term environmental challenges.

Traditionally the balance of power in the supply market has been dominated by the large organizations. Over the past four decades the merging and consolidation of many well-known companies has been driven by the influence of low-cost competition moving into established markets. This same consolidation has also been taking place at the customer end, presenting the market with more focused buying power. The impact has been to create new barriers for the medium and smaller supplier, whether product- or service-based, and social implications at local levels.

Further up the scale one is starting to see many organizations at the top end of the food chain using their customer connections to build new propositions. The common feature of both approaches is that the Internet provides a new option to exploit a foundation that was in place. In a similar vein the development of partner concepts has provided some organizations with the ability to enhance their existing business models with added value to the customer.

The challenge for these new configurations will come from the large competitors' sector where their current business model has been developed to secure market direction. This is not new and these virtual organizations have a very good chance of building highly flexible and competitive models, which will be based on mutual interest and be far more adaptable.

By negotiation and mutual interest, rather than acquisition, these dynamic groupings can utilize partnering models to build and extend their capabilities into virtual organizations, using network power to match capability to customer need and creating virtual market strength

The past four decades have seen the merging and consolidation of many well-known companies and the market has been dominated by the economies of scale controlled by major organizations, partly driven by the globalization of business and the influence of low-cost competition moving into established markets and, on the other side, cross-industry migration based on the relative strength of sector economic cycles.

The advent of the Internet showed the way towards offering an alternative route to market with extended customer reach available to almost any organization, irrespective of size, at the same time as opening the way to more globalization. This vista of the market and the potential melt down that the Internet professed to be able to provide was the driver behind the dot.com boom.

The true potential of the connectivity of the web has provided an opportunity for the small and specialized organizations to strengthen their place in the local markets and move globally. In a similar vein, the development of partnering and the extended enterprise concept has provided organizations with the ability to enhance their existing business offerings in combination with others to provide added value to existing and new customers.

There is an even greater opportunity, and that is the consolidation of like-minded companies to link their specialist talents, skills and resources to match those of the larger competitors. The test for the virtual network is to establish and validate competitive solutions that will encourage broader vision from the customer perspective. The idea of virtual integration may be one that offers many the opportunities to develop alternative business models. It is, however, not a simple solution and may challenge organizations to change their operating methods, training, strategies and overall organizational approach.

Many organizations, particularly those operating from multiple sites nationally or globally, are facing many of the challenges that collaborative ventures need to address. These may vary from a lack of social networking between staff to failure to exploit the benefits of value chain integration. The need to meet the demands of the market for flexibility and competitiveness will probably increase in the next decade and the constraints of fixed operations and rigid organizations will need to be adapted.

Finding new value in the existing processes or creation of new value propositions will remain a focus for all organizations. The potential to enhance these opportunities by linking external organizations may prove more flexible than traditional ownership-based approaches, which could limit innovation and value creation.

Future business models may well open channels to extended, flexible and networked value chains, creating competitive value propositions that expand and contract to meet changing demands and specific customer needs. This virtual enterprise will depend on a social structure that is very different from the traditional boundary-based business culture. Interdependence will be a recognized and exploited feature rather than perhaps a factor that many organizations reluctantly manage.

The challenge for business leadership will be building a team without perhaps bringing all the players together. Many technologists will not see this as a problem since their cyber world is predicated on operating in a wired world. Experience, however, would suggest that for the majority of business trading, the importance of established and stable relationships based on trust is crucial. Thus as we start to see the interdependence of organizations being networked and integrated the social enterprise challenge will also need to be addressed, building at both a personal and organizational level effective relationships that will support the further exploitation of connectivity.

The leadership for these new business models will be faced with development complications which cannot be solved (as they historically were) around the coffee machine. The role of leadership in this virtual environment is far more complex than for traditional organizations; not only do they have to meet the normal demands of team building and motivation, but in a virtual context this has to be achieved against the variable background of time, power, distance and cultural diversity.

The virtual team must meet the everyday demands of the business landscape. It also has to contend with the internal stresses and strains of being divorced from, or out of step with, its many home organizations. Under this umbrella the team leaders have to coach and motivate whilst maintaining focus on the overall objectives.

A regular interaction is necessary if the team members are to harness the true potential of their joint skills and resources. This must be driven through a common structure and discipline to ensure that over distance there is both understanding and acceptance of the integrated solution. Where appropriate, the team leadership must be prepared to address contradictions with local rules and business culture. This is certain to be the case when considering the global context of operations spanning business cultures and ethics. This is a sensitive subject when crossing national boundaries as the values of an organization can be easily challenged by what is accepted locally as normal practice.

Developing a virtual organization is greatly influenced by the nature, style and history of the organizations involved, but organizational structure has a major influence in the operating success of the venture. In many companies the networking capability of individuals often operates at a sub-level behind the formally documented lines of authority. Whilst this allows organizations to function, in reality it means the true strategic focus may be lost. A newly formed virtual team would necessarily have the benefit of this networking structure.

The past six decades have produced alternative organizational initiatives and each of these has brought with it changes in the corporate structures. This perhaps heralds serious consideration for the development of virtual organizations as a practical solution to the dilemmas of corporate structures within a varied global market where each business culture has evolved differently. If the contributors of resources to these virtual entities accept to some extent a degree of control loss, then each grouping can be created for what ever period is necessary in the manner that most suits the market pressures.

The question of why one should go down this route comes in response to a changing market and the need to be more flexible and increase focus on the customer's objectives and goals. To achieve innovative solutions and recognize the short-term interdependence we can form groups that are solely driven by objectives and not by long-term corporate strategy, although these strategies will eventually encompass this virtual concept as mainstream either fully or in part.

Most management expertise has been developed around the idea of collocated teams, where the social integration is something that happens as a matter of normal human interaction. The coffee machine conference provides a platform of personal involvement to recreate the same degree of interdependence and ownership across time and cyber space in new territory.

Capturing the potential value of the virtual model and exploitation of the virtual team or organization is fundamentally dependent on relationships. Technology only represents perhaps 10 per cent of the picture and relationships account for 90 per cent of the key ingredients for success. This issue of relationships is often lost in the technological world in terms of how it sees the developing future business communities. This disconnect is surprising when you consider the networking and cluster communities that have grown up around the development of technology. The crucial impact of trust between customer and provider is, and will remain, the key ingredient for successful business models of the future, whether virtual or not.

The level of trust in a relationship is directly proportional to the effectiveness of the interfaces: the stronger the relationship the more efficient the network. Most indirect costs result from the level of control and information requirements that are driven by a lack of trust, so the more one improves the relationship the lower the cost to ensure compliance and the greater the opportunity to improve the methods of working and the business processes by removing all the duplication that emerges from poor interfaces.

One of the key benefits that comes from integrating organizations is derived from sharing knowledge that combines the attributes and skills of the partners. It is also the main area of concern for those moving towards greater integration. The only real secret is one that is shared with no one, and in a business context that's impossible. Thus exploiting the knowledge effectively in a commercial environment where the partners mutually benefit may in the end be more beneficial than trying to protect it. As long as the relationship delivers value to both sides, dissipating the knowledge further is to no one's benefit.

There is no business venture that does not involve a degree of risk, and the highest returns generally run in parallel with the highest risk. Risk also generally increases in direct proportion to the number of steps in the business process and exponentially increases with the number of people involved. Thus it is easy to see that in developing the virtual organization, which may involve thousands of people, spanning both organizational and geographic boundaries, the potential risk profile can be very complex. The implications of global trading and cultural diversity add even more potential.

The challenge for all business ventures is to continually find ways to meet customer expectations and to satisfy the requirements of stakeholders throughout multi-layered relationships that fill the landscape. The stretch now for many organizations is that innovation must go beyond their individual structures and involve the value chain, driving both commercial benefit and frequently the contributions to a sustainable agenda.

Innovative thinking is often constrained by the awareness of existing limitations, particularly within organizations. Often new ideas are not pursued because of a known lack of resources or a perceived lack of management support. The potential within the wider concept of virtual integration is that for the right idea there are no resource or skill limitations since by linking with the appropriate organization these additional attributes can be adopted or incorporated (providing there is a mutually beneficial commercial deal to be made).

The Midas proposition (see below) explores the integration of businesses into virtual networks, challenging many of today's concepts and considering necessary culture change and risks that may exist against a background of accelerating change. Linking people as well as systems, 'follow the sun' working is now a reality, but social and political obstacles have still to be managed in the new borderless business community. In exploiting the potential of a frontier-free trading environment, existing thinking and relationships will come under pressure. Using business networks is not novel, but the Internet has added new dimensions. Specialist interest networks or communities have burgeoned. Businesses have formed trading communities and driven the creation of online market places and industry or product-based networking platforms, with competitors joining forces in collaborative ventures. Eventually a new breed of networks will emerge, entrepreneurial structures bringing together organizations whose combined skills and resources create new value propositions. Developing virtual companies and groupings, they will focus on particular activities for variable durations.

Multiple, Interdependent, Delivery And Supply

The creation of virtual entities offers a new focus for business, although it incorporates many concepts that have been part of trading environments for hundreds of years. Developing innovative value propositions will require past rules to be re-evaluated and validated, but traditional business skills must be used to ensure a robust and sustainable model. Virtual integration offers the potential to build alternative solutions and business propositions that can provide alternative options and responses for many of the challenges that today's market place can offer.

The implementation of the alternative models introduces a number of additional factors to the whole process of partner selection based on the degree of interdependence and the extent to which this provider may be facing the customer in the delivery process, whereas traditional linear supply programmes allow the prime supplier to control the performance profile to some extent. In this environment the provider is being integrated into the overall process and therefore the selection criteria must be extended to evaluate the strengths and weaknesses, as well as risk, this relationship may create.

The integrated model also provides a unique opportunity to look at many of the eco-efficiency focuses from a more complete position. Since future business models will be less rigid they may be able to accommodate more lateral thinking and innovation in terms of sustainable production.

What perhaps is even less apparent to those heading down this route is that interdependence means selecting partners who share your organization's corporate values and sense of social responsibility, not to mention the need to ensure control and management of corporate governance issues through glass walls. The result is that new business models based on integrated delivery processes are built up not based simply on resources and capability but also on the ethos and style of the management and leadership. To this end there has to be a change in the training we provide to future managers so they are able to work in a virtual infrastructure that no longer relies on command and control.

CHAPTER 27

Competitive balance

With all the hype about sustainability and the protests of those who wish to stop business pursuing its legitimate plans there must be recognition that business has to remain competitive. What governments often seem to ignore (and certainly the puritans of the eco-warriors clearly disregard) is that business has to remain competitive if it is to survive and create wealth. In the global battleground, it is more difficult to maintain a level playing field when organizations start from positions that are not common, either from concern for the environment or the business culture. This is further complicated by political, cultural and religious diversity

There is no panacea for all the ills of the world, whether these be environmental, social or economic. The diversity of cultures and the variable stages of industrial evolution clearly create a landscape that is uneven and in many ways it is this differentiation that provides the energy for competitive edge. It is against this background that the business community has to make judgements, which many will see as exploitation. Commercial exploitation is perhaps a reality that we must accept as being part of the global patchwork. It must be tempered with social consideration that frequently can be promoted and viewed as delivering value. Business leaders must balance these factors with the influences of stakeholders, policies and pressures. Customers and consumers then must be engaged or educated to ensure they do not become the driver for exploitation.

This complex business environment as seen in Figure 27.1, necessitates an even more complex multi-tiered chess game that requires a balancing act between the drivers of the market, the expectations of the stakeholders and the growing regulatory pressures. The essence of competition is the differentiation between one or more products or services. This is nothing new but traditionally price, quality and service would in themselves be the benchmark for selection.

Trading organizations have in the main developed very effective ways of delivering competitive products and services through global sourcing, outsourcing and traditional trading methods. So price is addressed (or, in

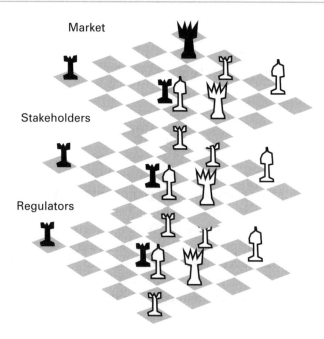

Figure 27.1   Competitive balance

the case of branded products, ignored). Quality has always been the stumbling block to bringing products from the developing regions, but in essence this is only a question of skills and training. Many organizations have found that quality standards can be increased rather than diluted. As outlined earlier, by investing in training and facilities production and quality can be improved. Service in a traditional sense was always a differentiator but today many would see this element being complemented by desire for responsibility. This of course is a two-way street: consumers, for example, cannot expect the lowest price and still maintain a demand for fully sustainable approaches. The NGOs may see this as irrelevant but then they do not make up the majority of the consumer market.

It should be clear to all that delivering a sustainable programme is likely to force compromise in terms of the key marketing ingredients. Until all customers or consumers are ready to pay premiums for sustainability-based products then the business community has a difficult balance to consider. Certainly responsible organizations can achieve bottom line benefits through application of eco-efficient practices and good, common-sense people-management approaches. However, there will always be someone who is ready to ignore good practice and exploit opportunities to reduce cost.

With ever-increasing demands on business from NGOs, media, governments and wider society there is a need for organizations to manage their social responsibility profile. The successful companies will tend to be those that are able to re-engineer their approaches and build sustainability into the delivery processes, thus engaging and contributing to the wider economic, environmental and social stakeholder community.

The key, then, is to raise the bar in terms of corporate reporting with a focus on managing expectations. In a global trading environment it is likely that, despite the best efforts of business leaders, mistakes will happen and problems arise, which carry with them exposure to both regulatory and image pressures. Companies need to be establishing and publicizing their sustainable vision and the specific areas they intend to focus on. This will not satisfy every cause that is out there (which is probably not possible in any event).

A balance is needed and if this is clearly defined then the stakeholder expectation will be better tuned to the business plan. In developing these benchmarks each organization must balance its true needs and engage with the major stakeholders to improve understanding and acceptance. This profiling and visibility will contribute to ensuring that sustainability is not disengaged from the business strategy and in turn it will contribute to (or reduce) the potential competitive negative impacts of unfocused pressure.

For sustainability approaches to be successful they have to be integrated into business operations, at the same time as being made visible externally and responding to the regulatory demands. The benefits of internal focus from sustainable approaches and initiatives can be significant in terms of business performance and risk management. These also include a greater integration of governance and compliance rules, which become an employee-driven application rather than a policed programme, thus making it far more robust.

The impacts on employee performance can also be significant as sustainability awareness brings with it an individual sense of satisfaction and responsibility. Working for a good organization is a stimulus for staff recruitment and retention. Providing a catalyst for collaboration, sustainability and corporate responsibility creates an additional drive to improve and develop. The desire to find solutions increases intellectual capital and can often produce technology and operational innovations that can contribute to greater business effectiveness and competitiveness.

These programmes at the same time do need careful management; overforceful positioning can engender in some organizations a legal compliance culture that will divert proactive innovative development. Highly detailed internal rules restrict the localization and thus ownership of programmes.

Those that are implemented without external stakeholder consideration will inevitably be in conflict and thus counter-productive.

The benefits of engaging with external stakeholders through sustainability are that it provides a common thread to explore and understand these groups. Whether these be customers, shareholders, community groups or investment houses, they all contribute to the business landscape that shapes strategy and growth. Drawing on these influences provides business leaders with the ability to structure product development and marketing as well as establishing the right things to monitor and measure.

All these exchanges help to build a more effective risk management profile whilst at the same time establishing a company's positioning in terms of governance and responsibility which will probably underpin investment thinking. This openness, however, must be balanced against the need to integrate the approaches and be able to deliver on the promise. Thus moving forward with an approach that is either predominantly internal or external will distort the focus and rather than capture benefits, it may generate additional risk.

Given the performance complexity of environmental, social, economic and ethical implications, competitiveness will quickly become challenged by an imbalance between internal initiatives and external positioning. The establishing of corporate values and decision-making must be embraced into the daily management operations, which then flow into the value proposition that is presented to the market. This balancing or blending may be akin to social chemistry or even alchemy. Competitiveness is a blend of what is available versus what people want or think they want. In this complex mix the competitive focus for a sustainability-driven organization is to capture the added value of proactive thinking in delivery processes and capitalize on the market positioning that a responsible approach can present.

The process of competitive balance, then, starts with the definition of corporate mission and values, together with identification of the stakeholders. Defining commitments and responsibilities needs to be communicated and training programmes put in place where appropriate. Assessing and modifying management programmes will probably follow, along with creating meaningful measurements that can be made visible both internally and externally. Setting targets and monitoring them is a traditional part of any management programme, but making sure the appropriate assurance programmes are also activated is essential.

Reporting is thus the visible commitment to delivering the promise, but it must not become an end in itself. Unless it is linked to management programmes it will within a short time become a millstone rather than a promotional differentiator. Sustainable competitiveness needs continuous stakeholder engagement and continuous improvement programmes, but perhaps what is more important is instilling value-based decision-making throughout the organization.

Bridging the performance gap and the communications gap are not isolated activities. The challenge for business leaders is to achieve this bridging by moving organizations from reactive to proactive thinkers so that operationally they always take an informed responsible sustainable perspective.

Within the context of stakeholders it is important to recognize the role and potential impacts of the supply community. As this sector in the majority of business ventures represents a significant cost factor it has to be a consideration in terms of competitiveness. What is frequently less obvious is the vulnerability that complex and diverse supply chains can bring to an organization. The implications of perceived exploitation, ethical trading practices, transport, pollution: the list is extensive and all too often dependent on external operations that are selected without consideration beyond price, quality and delivery. Increasing visibility at the top means that conflict, contradictions or exposure lower down the food chain can have significant impacts.

The balance between low price and quality is one that has been well understood but, as the business community becomes more holistic in its production approaches, so the need to carry corporate values down through the supply chain is crucial. Balancing these values and cost negatives is a challenge that has frequently been an excuse for avoiding commitment to the bigger picture.

In fact, we have already seen that a more integrated view, which combines ethical trading with social responsibility, investment, training and knowledge transfer, can provide long-term competitiveness and make investment sense. The economic pressures are clear to all, but short-term global switching and exploitation may not be the most logical solution if the full implications of investments are taken into account.

The first step is to ensure that organizations know their supply chain and can identify the high-risk areas. Understanding the productivity balance of local working practices is a key step in appreciating the short-term value and the potential for a constructive change programme going forward. Relating corporate values to suppliers should be part of any evaluation process to ensure that key elements of internal programmes are not compromised by external organizations. Audits and benchmarking are only an initial part of the development process; what is more important is to engage in a real dialogue around objectives and understanding, which should also try to identify the potential for education, integration, innovation and a proactive mutual approach to good practice.

Supply chain architecture is an important consideration in the development of exploiting the global market place. Measuring the functional capabilities of traditional structures includes predictable, stable and consistent approaches, whilst on the innovative side it becomes volatile, unstable and variable. Given this type of change the implication for sustainable programmes is that unless they are embedded in the operation they will be lost in this more volatile environment. This creates a pressure on operations to move from stable and efficient to variable and responsive.

Organization of the process from customer demand through design, acquisition, production, delivery and recycling requires a focus on the resources necessary to operate these functions. These activities may more and more in the future not be owned by a single company. The decoupling of tangible resources (such as buildings, materials, people and so on) and intangible resources (such as knowledge, capabilities, attitude and reputation) provides an environment where corporate visions are not delivered through command and control infrastructures. An operation where processes span organizational boundaries clearly opens up the risk of mutual performance and thus requires the development of some commonality of internal and external emphasis in terms of corporate direction.

The challenge is to become better customers and suppliers by doing things differently rather than establishing value-based objectives but failing to change the day-to-day activities and by motivating others to become more proactive in problem-solving to develop sustainable solutions within a framework of risk, investment and return.

In this competitive environment there are those who would argue against the whole concept of corporate responsibility and sustainability. Some would suggest that as shareholders own businesses, any money spent on sustainable programmes is theft since sustainability is a charitable approach and therefore shareholders should make their own charity decisions. Some, as Elaine Sternberg reported, argue that there is a human rights case against CSR because it is depriving people of choice. This of course assumes there is no dialogue between the shareholders and the business leaders and that sustainability is a charitable approach rather than an effective development and risk management strategy. If a company's market capitalization exceeds its property value then brand image and intangibles represent the difference, many of which can be directly linked to corporate responsibility.

Some suggestions have been made that companies who report on their social responsibility are crazy, given that some of the most respected market leaders (for example, Jack Welch, then CEO of GE, and Bill Gates of Microsoft) did not succeed by being Mr Nice Guy. It is true that when restructuring GE Jack Welch was pretty brutal and that Bill Gates has been very aggressive in dominating the market. The reality, of course, is that we do not live in a fairy-tale world and business sometimes has to do things that others see as bad practice. Once again, it must be recognized that the role of business is to create wealth by satisfying the needs and demands of the market, and companies should not be judged only on their failings.

Often one hears that organizations are too busy surviving to worry about the more global implications of their actions. Taking their eye off the ball to address corporate responsibility is of course no longer an option given the growth in legislation, but benefiting from effective implementation is unlikely with a negative perspective. It would be better to recognize that if sustainability means taking your eye off the ball it is not embedded in the operation, and will probably never deliver either value or risk management.

When times are hard it is easy to drop nice initiatives in favour of core drivers but pollution, social interfaces, staff retention, local growth, ethical practice, exploitation, segregation, heath and safety, customer preference and regulation are not optional. It is this perceived lack of linkage between good business and good practice that stops organizations moving forward and integrating sustainability within a competitively balanced approach. It's not an issue for others and neither does it need to deflect from the drive to make more profit; often it should be considered as a way of securing profits.

Frequently we hear the cynical voice coming through that all business is corrupt and corporate leaders are only there to milk the poor globally. In many parts of the world this perspective is compounded by a business culture that tolerates (or even, by default, promotes) corruption; we have heard the expression the 'the world is built on bribes', which experience from working in many parts of the world suggests might be true. Bribery costs money and in some parts of the world is seen as the only way to win business. Transparency International, in their 2005 report on corruption in construction,[9] suggest that bribery bankrupts countries, costs lives, prevents development and perpetuates poverty. They calculate that corruption costs $2,300 billion per year and they monitor countries and report on their assessment of those which are most corrupt.

Some high-profile cases, such as the LHWD project, Cologne's incinerator programme, Yacreta's hydropower project and the Bakun Dam, all show that not only were these damaging to the environment, but being found guilty was bad for the companies involved. It has again to be part of the corporate vision and policies that address these issues around the world.

The World Bank, IMF and governments are starting to get balance into trade and aid programmes to stop corruption. It does not take a brain surgeon to work out what happens when companies and individuals get caught, and what it may cost any organization both directly and indirectly.

Clearly there is a long way to go and there will continue to be conflicting views across the spectrum of business communities. The bigger the name, the more consideration that needs to be given to the balanced approach. Take, for example, reports on Tesco, a major UK-based retail company and expanding globally, announcing billions in profits and being the darling of the investment market, whilst at the same time being attacked over its purchasing approach and pressure on small producers and suppliers. Pressure to maintain competitive edge in the high street has prompted supermarkets generally to adopt a very aggressive approach to their supply chains, leaving many small companies devastated or bankrupt. Is this simply following market pressure, or is it simply ignoring ethical practice and long-term common sense for short-term profit?

Profit is good, but we also have to balance our views in that respect. When major corporations such as banks and oil companies announce major profits the protests are growing alarmingly loud. We love to hate banks and frequently ignore the tax associated with our petrol bills, but these organizations are a crucial part of the economic infrastructure and we would not be happier if they made losses and closed down. It's all about competitive balance, responsibility and consumer drivers in the market.

We can look at new business models as part of the evolving market place, where smaller companies are losing ground and strength in the face of the major players. Take the example of Areoalliance Inc, which developed the cluster concept to bring together component suppliers to produce and sell major components to the aircraft industry, building both strength and value. Collaborative clusters could provide the competitive balance and opportunities for many smaller companies to create added value that reinforces their value to customers. Larger organizations, however, offer little encouragement for initiatives of this type as they fly in the face of the traditional application of market power. As customers look for more responsible leadership, initiatives such as these could be supported as differentiators.

Advancing technology is also changing the nature of business structures from the traditional head office with spokes to branches to what is now being called multi-localizing. This means that organizations as diverse as HSBC and Astra Zeneca operate with distributed functionality that in effect makes everyone part of the head office. This should facilitate a common approach to the market and good practice in terms of sustainability programmes. However, this homogenization is likely to come into direct conflict with local custom and practice.

This prompts the questions about where is the centre of that world, and how do we balance sustainability concerns and competitiveness relative to that position? If you look at a map of the world China is in the middle. This means that Manhattan is in the Far East in relative terms. In the seventeenth century China was the biggest economy in world, and perhaps it will be again. Thus when we consider any programme of corporate responsibility or sustainable concern it is worth adjusting one's perspective. Competitive balance needs to be evaluated against the market pressures and environments that are being addressed.

In this context one should also consider the stateless multi-national. It is estimated that 60 per cent of GDP is held by corporations outside the boundaries of their country of origin. For example, Nokia is perhaps only 10 per cent in Finnish ownership. Thus the originating cultural background may initially drive the design of corporate value but over time shareholder influence can change that perspective. The current pressures on China because of concerns over human rights may influence the strategies of some organizations in dealing with Chinese companies, either as customers or suppliers. If Chinese external investment continues to grow as it has in the past ten years then China may eventually own the companies that have reservations based on a human rights agenda.

It is also useful to consider in the competitive world the next developments in the electronic business environment. The dot.com boom saw many mega-investments fail because they did not consider the fundamentals of good business practice. Some, however, did survive and blossom to become extremely wealthy. The futurists would now suggest that we are looking towards intelligent e-commerce with particular focus on individual customer propositions. These exponential developments in technology and electronics are likely to bring even greater global trading implications and risks, whilst at the same time the speed of adoption will certainly continue to divide the wired from the non-wired world (the digital divide).

Customer loyalty is a crucial part of the competitive evaluation and thus balance that should engage those customers to drive sustainable agendas. Forward-thinking corporate leaders have recognized that customer loyalty is driven by the company's loyalty to the customer. McKinsey researchers reported that customers did not want a relationship with their suppliers; they wanted decent service. It is debatable that the quality of service is part of the relationship-building process. The key is to link the corporate mission to the customer's agenda as one of the key stakeholders. Building sustainability into that mission is clearly adding to the customer's feel-good factor and personal commitments.

As part of evaluating competitive balance one should also be looking to the wider aspects of the sustainability profile, such as fighting poverty through trade. Take the model of Traidcraft: helping small business to access markets and develop is at an extreme of the corporate spectrum but both ends have similar drivers in terms of delivering customer value without resorting to exploitation and corruption.

Developing competitive balance in terms of a sustainable programme means stimulating sustainable innovation. In many cases, such as Traidcraft, these business propositions are isolated cases but progressively these initiatives are increasing, alongside greater consumer recognition that a more responsible approach is better for all, from creating more eco-friendly products with recyclability designed in to adapting the production approaches and capabilities of developing markets to optimize output and provide a more sustainable growth profile.

Competitiveness can be simply seen as lowest cost but, as most business leaders appreciate, the mix is far more complex. Driven by total cost of ownership or customer preference, competitiveness can be evaluated in many ways dependent on the drivers. Modelling any competitive approach must consider the broader picture and requires a more proactive approach to integrate sustainable approaches. Frequently, these may be viewed as fair play rather than fair price but, with a constructive approach, these values can both be addressed within a competitive profile.

CHAPTER 28

Collaborating for the future

There is clearly a challenge for the business community to rationalize its traditional activities against a wider sustainable agenda. It should also be apparent to most that delivering a more sustainable profile requires collaboration across all stakeholders to balance the benefits and competitive edge. Moving further into areas such as eco-efficiency means collaborating across organizational boundaries. From the reverse approach, future business models which are more holistic than hierarchical mean that the relationships between organizations will become a crucial part of delivering sustainable objectives and protecting corporate missions and visions.

The vista of partnering and collaboration has been on the businesses agenda for the past two decades, though perhaps its practice dates back to the first artisans. What becomes clear from the challenges of stakeholder drivers is that only through collaboration can the alternative business models be developed and exploited (see Figure 28.1). The Johannesburg Summit on sustainable development in 2002 charged the business world to meet the challenges of sustainable development through partnership and informal networks.

It is the gaps between organizations that offer the greatest opportunity to find and eliminate waste, whilst removing duplication in the process. Passing knowledge across these boundaries provides the scope for updating traditional approaches. In exploiting these gaps organizations can jointly deliver sustainable benefits and simultaneously enjoy cost-saving opportunities.

Bridging the value chain supports and accelerates the complex flow of ideas, ingenuity, resources and expertise that inter-connect designers, producers and consumers. This network of interdependence forms the foundation of an overall approach to social responsibility performance.

The key to exploiting relationships is the development of trust and openness which allows the parties to evaluate their joint capabilities and resources focused on building business programmes that provide a robust platform of commercial competitiveness and long-term development. What

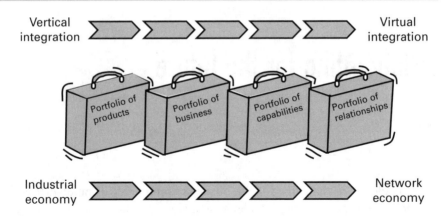

Figure 28.1   Moving towards virtual integration

must be part of the thinking is to establish a process for building effective relationships.

Each stage of a relationship journey has very distinct processes and these in turn give rise to an evaluation of the risk that may be encountered or exploited along the road. The first stage is *awareness* of the landscape of risk and reward. This is supported by the need to draw on the wider *knowledge* base of potential partners and benchmarking across the industrial spectrum.

Many risks are self-inflicted and a process of *self-assessment* helps to recognize issues that may create challenges and risk from delivery processes. Clearly the process of getting the right partner means that *partner selection* is primary in the risk management programme. Once this has been achieved the risks that can emerge may be managed by effectively *working together*.

Value creation is crucial to a relationship since if it does not add value then it is failing. In this regard the exploitation of risk as well as its management becomes a major factor. Moving the process on, the real essence of risk management comes from how organizations address *staying together* and working proactively to address risk and implement mitigation strategies. Finally, in any relationship there comes a time when the partners will decide that the arrangement has reached its maximum potential and then the risks associated with how one formulates an *exit strategy* are vital to ensure that all parties protect their future in terms of the knowledge gained.

Today the paramount challenge for any business is to create value for its shareholders, whilst meeting the demands of an increasingly competitive market place. The complexity and volatility of this business environment creates a landscape that requires constant flexibility of approach and resource investment. Integration in the supply and delivery network, both locally and globally, can be optimized by opening the boundaries between organizations to focus on what each does best in a complementary business process.

Exploiting the interfaces between companies is not an aspect of the traditional business culture. To enhance competitive edge many organizations are now looking both vertically and horizontally in order to develop a collaborative approach to release potential value and innovation, which has not been recognized historically.

The rush for gold in terms of exploiting off-shoring is commonly focused on the promise of significant cost savings. Whilst this is clearly possible, the ability of organizations to capitalize on the opportunities depends very much on how the programme is evaluated. Defining clear objectives provides the framework, which will help to assess aspects of knowledge transfer and the wider implications of meeting customers' expectations and demands.

Environmental responsibility has been a major consideration for the business community for many years, but with the increasing impacts of globalization and increased awareness through improvements in communication, the implications are far reaching. The wider implications of these external pressures on business strategy run in parallel with developing sustainable business models within the context of extended value chains.

Long-term strategic initiatives for organizations must consider the integration of supply chains and outsourcing operations within this arena of global change, not simply in order to react to public opinion on issues of Third World exploitation but also in the development of sustainable business propositions. There is a difficult balance between the corporate drivers of competitiveness, shareholder value, and the implications of ignoring sustainability implications when investing in overseas operations, either directly of indirectly, on top of which business leaders have the pressures of balancing government and NGO drivers.

Building effective business relationships is a crucial factor in exploiting the potential of extended value chains and also in evolving solid development programmes that support the long-term sustainable objectives, jointly addressing the sustainability agenda (to their longer-term benefit) and the wider social implications.

As the business landscape becomes more complex and challenging the relationships between organizations also take on new and varied configurations. The pressure to improve competitive edge and develop alternative value-based solutions has introduced the need to ensure that organizations can work in an integrated way to maximize potential benefits. The application of partnering concepts and approaches across the value chain can help in the integration of both horizontal and vertical relationships to create value.

For the business leaders of today and certainly tomorrow, the considerations go beyond simple market-sector competitiveness. The impacts of an expanding range of competitors from across the globe means a constant focus on the many factors outside the traditional product/customer relationship. Every change in direction or demand places even greater pressure on the business planning process both to meet the conflicting demands of the shareholders' quest for return on investment and the customers' increasing demands for greater innovation against a background of lower prices reflective of a global market place.

The challenge, then, is to reach out into new markets either for sales or supply, and in doing so to consider the implications these opportunities may also create, often with the same shareholders and customers, since within these alternative business cultures the pressures and standards that are accepted traditionally may be in direct conflict with those more industrialized markets. The sustainability agenda may be viewed as restrictive in the short term, but the integration of business aims and objectives can provide opportunities for long-term value creation.

There are many views of what sustainable development is and this is generally because there are many different sectors of the global community addressing elements of the whole picture. It is often this complexity that creates the conflicts and challenges in the business arena. What is often lost within this debate is that in most cases, if not all, the end-game objectives are the same.

From a business perspective the subject of sustainability is related to maintaining business positioning and growth. This environment is often categorized as three dimensions, financial, social and environmental, within which businesses have to operate. In a wider context it is the integrated process which aids people to improve their quality of life, whilst protecting the environment.

The difficulty is that these multiple agendas are developing on different levels and at different speeds, often failing to recognize the rights and wrongs of each other's priorities. These conflicts and challenges create for business in the short term many risks to offset the opportunities of global sourcing and the exploitation of competitive advantage. It is not realistic simply to place the responsibility on business through regulation or, at the other extreme, to try to maintain the status quo in the face of change.

Often the impacts on business are not given the full consideration that they deserve, or are lost in the pressures of day-to-day activity. However, the inter-relationship between business and the ramifications of the sustainability agenda are very closely intertwined. All business operations seek a plan that underpins the long-term business objectives. The pressure may be in the short term driving organizations to seek relief from the regulatory demands and the depth of public opinion that can be invoked when the issues are not fully appreciated, or are exploited for initial gains.

The profile of sustainability and environmental aspects of business operations can be included and linked into both marketing and shareholder value. The development of sustainable programmes requires the integration of multiple business relationships focused on building long-term operations that recognize the global implications. The furthering of local agendas that support growing economies adds value to an organization's business profile.

Whilst the business environment comes under continuous and growing competitive pressure, the manner in which business conducts itself may have significant impacts on the ultimate perceptions of the market place, which is seldom a level playing field.

It is often easy for those outside the active business arena to demand standards of practice that are in direct conflict with the realities of the local cultures and diversity. These varied considerations must be part of the business planning profile and need to be addressed when considering integrated partnerships.

The sharing of knowledge can help to build more robust commercial structures and create investment profiles that address many of the potential risk implications of cross-border trading. Sustainability should be seen as a focus to create more effective and efficient business operations that can adapt to the market as platforms for robust commercial sustainability to benefit the wider society.

The sustainability agenda offers many challenges to the business community but, at the same time, if developed effectively it also has the capacity to open up many opportunities. Building a business strategy that addresses these issues in an environment where many diverse organizations may be involved in the value chain demands a high level of focus on the relationships that bridge the organizational boundaries.

The challenge for business leaders is to develop the ethos within their respective operations so as to consider the competitive opportunities and build into the processes a chance to share the responsibility for the sustainable objectives that may be both cost-saving opportunities and long-term developments for the various parties involved.

The growth of global trading and the increasing drive for competitiveness at every level of business is a fact of life. This pressure may be tending to subjugate the individual desires of business people and organizations to recognize the long-term impacts of short-term commercial actions, as opposed to considering innovative approaches that may satisfy these objectives whilst improving the efficiency of the business operations. Building collaborative relationships across geographic boundaries can be deployed as a platform to create long-term sustainable commercial ventures which can also support the wider global sustainability objectives.

The sustainability agenda must recognize the need to support the short-term business communities' challenges. There is also a role for governments to support business in the development of long-term programmes that can eventually merge with a consolidated programme. The approach for the business sector is to focus on the sustainability issues, not from a defensive or compliance position, but to exploit the opportunities that can emerge from integrating their business operations (both horizontally and vertically) in the value chain.

The principal benefits that can be derived from collaborative relationships are focused on streamlining the business delivery process and eliminating unnecessary activities through improved knowledge. The by-product of this improved approach to commercial enterprises is that it reduces waste, power consumption, packaging, transport needs and resource consumption. In general there is a natural contribution to the sustainability environmental agenda.

When considering the challenges of integrating overseas partners and the potential for benefits from low-cost labour, the development of long-term training or support programmes will underpin immediate production needs, whilst creating a longer-term platform for future development. Better conditions improve output and a stronger, more educated workforce provides the catalyst for further innovative and competitive propositions. Programmes that focus on worker improvements also have the benefit of creating an answer to those who see simple exploitation.

Starting the process of developing an effective programme that blends the attributes of diverse organizations must begin with recognition that people may have significantly different approaches and demands. This may be more clearly apparent in the context of global trading, but should not be ignored even in the more localized and traditional market.

Alliances and collaborative business models allow the parties to evaluate all aspects of the business delivery process and incorporate the needs and drivers for each whilst finding opportunities to reduce costs and waste as a by-product of continuous improvement.

The goals of the shareholders and the regulatory demands must be uppermost in the profile of the corporate direction, and these must be reflected externally as well as down through the whole organization, empowering the front-line operations to recognize the principal objectives of the organization. The effective implementation of collaborative ventures must be based on the establishment of a robust mandate from board level. In order to take a robust position down through the value chain in respect of the organization's sustainable issues this imperative increases. Partnering offers the opportunity to draw the organization together and to exploit the savings that can be made, releasing duplication within the business process. Cross-training builds stronger long-term foundations that meet the commercial and environmental objectives, whilst underpinning the whole concept of corporate social responsibility, creating a sustainable business that adds to long-term shareholder value.

The essence of a collaborative relationship is that the independent parts function through an integrated business process. Thus the leadership may be devolved across several organization boundaries. Effectively delivering a common agenda to satisfy both commercial and social parameters may involve the leadership in effectively confronting traditional contracting edges within each individual organization.

Relationships have always been the foundation of business activities but, in more recent times, the stresses of more complex trading have in many ways diluted the traditional values of performance and trust. In the context of developing a programme of corporate social responsibility and building towards sustainable objectives, the strengthening of relationships is crucial. These relationships will be across internal factions of a single organization or between partners, suppliers or service providers. Each level of interaction has an impact on the overall outcomes and the success of each linkage, both horizontally and vertically, in the value chain; it provides a common strategy to support the sustainability profile.

In terms of the sustainability agenda, the integration of relationships allows the parties not only to address the key pressures from sustainability but also to work proactively on developing approaches that benefit the commercial outcomes as well as the social implications. The development of a sustainability strategy can focus on many differing levels of innovation and, whilst supporting the drive to greater competitiveness, these may also provide contributions towards social responsibility.

Best practice is something that can be shared at any level across the business process, and improving the processes brings efficiencies and thus savings that can be shared whilst supporting the sustainable agenda. The longer-term strategy may involve the transfer of knowledge and training that help to create new skills across the value chain.

The more diverse these organizations are across cultural boundaries, the higher the likelihood of differing approaches to resource management and, as a result, the higher the possibility of organizations creating exposure by incorporating social issues. The implications for any organization in terms of linking business ventures through extended enterprise relationships can be far-reaching. In the context of sustainability and social responsibility, the risk is that every partner is exposed to the market through the actions of others.

Sustainability is a subject that at an individual level either inspires people to be very proactive, or engenders apathy in terms of it being someone else's problem. In a collaborative culture the key ingredients to success come from the joint commitment to a set of common goals and objectives. The structuring of incentive programmes can often be diametrically opposed to the idea of building a sustainable future, focusing simply on short-term exploitation.

In the wider aspects of social responsibility and sustainability, the objectives may not be separate and can be integrated, but it is important that the partnering team fully appreciates the big picture and does not undermine the programme with localized improvements. People are the most important resource in the business environment, and their ownership of the agenda is paramount if the whole programme is to be driven towards success.

There are many that view the issues of sustainability as being mainly negative for the business community and thus they create the idea that compliance and public image are the only factors to be considered. The reality is that many of the factors that are raised as issues of sustainability are also key facets of business process improvement.

Eco-efficiency is focused on exploiting the potential benefits from capturing cost savings and passing these to the bottom line, whilst simultaneously contributing to the long-term sustainable returns. The spin-off from these partnering activities has a direct impact in areas of efficiency improvement, which include subjects such as waste, energy and so on.

By integrating business ventures, companies seek to improve competitiveness through collaboration in design, manufacture, transport and distribution. These and other aspects of business each contribute to the overall framework of CSR both in terms of business process development and also the market perception of organizations through badly-managed exploitation.

Many of the traditional contracting and management approaches have been built up over time reflecting historical experiences rather than specifically focused on need and practicality. Whilst many of these processes may have a sound basis, there are always opportunities to find potential savings and cost improvements. In particular the cross-border interfaces are generally where the biggest opportunities can be found. Often these improvements result from re-addressing existing demands, but under an umbrella of trust and cooperation that enables both parties to take a more pragmatic perspective.

Business-to-business focus on joint objectives is a fundamental part of the collaborative approach deployed to incorporate sustainable issues. The prime drive of a business relationship is to improve competitiveness and deliver more effective customer value and thus satisfaction. There is often the assumption that sustainability and profitability are different issues. In fact sustainability, social responsibility and profitability are all linked but also complementary. In terms of sustainability the definition of value may be viewed as being less commercial, but in reality, if business is to prosper itself and help developing areas, then commercial concerns, market demands and profitability have to be viewed as interdependent.

The development of integrated business processes poses the problem of how you measure the impacts and performance within the arena of sustainability. The reality is that whilst profitability is clearly an important aspect it is generally a symptom of how a business performs rather than a driver. In today's market place the ethical investor is becoming more focused on the investment approach and management culture that underpins its results.

Measuring the business, therefore, means, apart from the results, addressing issues of sustainability and social responsibility as part of the overall performance. Many organizations have already adopted structures such as the business model to gauge traits for successful operations as well as building the measuring and monitoring process into daily operations.

Deploying these models on the wider trading front can also provide a sound basis for integrating overseas business operations into the social structure that supports the business development and the sustainable drivers. Finding a common measuring platform for partnering relationships can prove to be difficult, and thus adopting a standard model framework that already addresses most of the key aspects enables partnerships to get quickly to the essential business.

Beyond the commercial benefits that are usually the prime focus for pursuing partnering in terms of finding or improving competitive edge, partnering offers a robust platform on which to support and develop sustainability targets.

Relationships between organizations are perhaps the major contributor to the failure to address many aspects of the sustainability agenda. Partnering by its very nature looks to integrate business operations towards common goals and objectives. Trust develops through mutual performance, and it is through this trust that greater in-depth evaluation can take place. This development in turn can identify opportunities for cost and time efficiencies, while at the same time creating contributions to a wider social and sustainable profile.

The relationship between customers, suppliers and sub-suppliers is a significantly complex environment. As the market place becomes even more complex globally, these inter-relationships will come under increasing pressure to perform, whilst meeting ever more restrictive regulation and demands from socio-economic groups.

The future holds increasing challenges and, as a result, organizations must consider in their longer-term strategies how to meet the changes, maintain the business profiles and profitability, and help build sustainable strategies within that wider business concept. Within this environment the implications for optimizing the sustainable agenda are far reaching, and establishing joint targets for improvement provides common and mutually beneficial objectives.

Sustainability is not simply about ethical development or environmental considerations and pressures; it also has a significant impact on profitability and growth. Business ventures are seldom established for short-term targets, and as such the long-term perspective is an important factor. Within this context the sustainable agenda also has a role to play in that short-term exploitation may in its own way create risks to the longer-term standing of the business. Sustainability issues are key factors in this competitive agenda since not only do they help the process of reducing the cost base, but they also address the aspects of continuous improvement and product development.

The prospect of developing alternative business models, which are focused not on traditional contracting relationships but formulated around collaborative concepts, offers a further challenge to the business community. The proposition that a number of independent organizations form themselves into a virtual operation has many benefits but is likely to meet the barrier of traditional institutional thinking. These integrated relationships can offer significant opportunities in respect of the sustainability agenda.

The long-term objectives of sustainable development need to extend the relationships beyond the direct commercial interfaces to incorporate a wider agenda. Clearly the prime partners can benefit from localized integration but, over time, the community at large also needs to adopt the principles of exploiting a more comprehensive perspective on the key areas. Customer- or consumer-driven initiatives will help to focus the business community. A stronger influence, however, will be the recognition that sustainability and social issues are in fact commercially sound strategies in the longer term.

The integration of business processes and a joint approach to long-term strategic planning will enable organizations to identify the training and development needs of partners that will be necessary to fulfil those plans. Reducing waste, duplication and energy helps to reduce costs, and thus improve competitiveness. The creation of a sustainable value chain underpins a business operation.

Eco-efficiency highlights the potential to move the integration process beyond an initial one-on-one partnership and seeks to move the profile into a customer-focused approach, even incorporating the customer in the delivery process. True sustainability can only be achieved within a holistic trading environment, which will probably take time to develop. In the meantime, the benefits of closer working relationships can be exploited to commercial advantage whilst supporting the wider principles.

Sustainability is in fact itself a valid catalyst through which to build on the common objectives and benefit from the implementation of an effective collaborative approach. Business relationships are founded on trust, and the longer organizations work together, the greater the probability that additional value will be identified and exploited to the benefit of partners. In the case of sustainability issues, sensitivity to the many factors involved will increase and place more pressure on organizations and their value chains to find alternative solutions.

The growing need to work in a global business environment to maintain competitiveness and find new market opportunities will bring more focus on the ethics and approaches of the business community. The increasing emphasis from investors and consumers to seek to influence business investment strategy will lead to a demand for greater visibility, which is already a factor of many Internet sites. In terms of regulatory demands the playing field as yet is far from level, but major development projects and the financial institutions seeking assurances of best practice and local industrial enhancements are governing infrastructure investments.

The future is likely to demand even greater attention to the whole spectrum of sustainability issues and focus on corporate social responsibility. Organizations may see this as intrusive, but in real terms the potential benefits that can be delivered through a structured approach can satisfy many of the challenges within a programme that is focused primarily on the commercial advantages.

CHAPTER 29

Creating sustainable value

Corporate social responsibility has become the watchword for ethical governance but to explore its roots involves a much deeper understanding of sustainability, encompassing social responsibility alongside environmental and economic drivers. Socially responsible business leadership and enterprises are not new. Victorian visionaries, including the Lever brothers, the Cadbury brothers and Titus Salt, through the Co-operative movement to modern innovators, such as the Body Shop or Ben & Jerry's ice cream have all tried to build up a business model that did not exploit people and contribute to the community.

The vision was not simply to realize short-term gain by improving the lot of the workers or integrating the ethos and values of the owners; it was focused on creating long-term sustainable businesses that reflected and benefited from a more socially aware management approach. There was, of course, a clear recognition that improving the working environment and contributing to the wider social community brought greater commitment from the workforce, which in turn complemented and enhanced productivity. Sustainable value, then, is not just about compliance or common-sense workplace management: it is about developing approaches that provide benefits and one must expect more sustainable business models in the future.

Many may not know that Ben & Jerry contracted with Greystone Bakery in Yonkers, NY, to provide brownies for their ice cream. Greystone is a company that uses its profits to provide housing for the homeless and train them to be bakers. The value proposition for Ben & Jerry's contract thus went beyond the traditional parameters of business evaluation. Whether the aim is to build links with community groups, eliminate waste, improve employee relations, establish ethical trading or build environmentally sound supply networks, CSR formalizes traditional philanthropy.

Whilst the pressures of cases such as Enron and the introduction of regulation to prevent further abuse have become the primary face for business, the wider implications of meeting sustainability agendas are starting to influence business strategy. Business is beginning to consider not only the potential financial penalties or risks to reputation, but also the broad interactions and influences of stakeholders on the operational performance. These influences create a kaleidoscope of considerations that impact every aspect of the business agenda for today as well as tomorrow.

The more traditional business perspective is now giving way to a realization that corporate responsibility touches not only the economic issues but also the social community, including employees and customers. The adoption of sustainability programmes and approaches has also been seen to deliver practical benefits. If companies only adopt CSR and sustainability to provide good public relations, then they will never derive any significant long-term benefits. To add value to the business, it must be based on values that are relevant to the business and its stakeholders, otherwise it simply becomes expenditure aimed at being able to get a tick in the box on investment portfolios. What is certain is that the reporting gloss and PR value will be progressively eroded, and one significant incident or challenge could completely unravel even the most professional of spin.

Sustainability in the business environment is also driving technology development and business opportunities. Creating solutions for today's problems and tomorrow's challenges stimulates alternative business approaches, models and processes. These can in themselves deliver new wealth creation and revenue streams. Social responsibility has even, in a number of cases, become an alternative competitive edge, particularly for smaller niche companies. The high-profile development of the Body Shop captured a large section of the market place, satisfying concerns over traditional product development practices and at the same time supporting a drive towards Third World equality.

CSR is becoming an investment differentiator, benefiting companies that have clear ethical and sustainable missions complemented by tangible and transparent reporting. Investors may be viewed as purely interested in profit, but unethical operations eventually fail, to the cost of investors. Therefore, corporate responsibility must also be seen as a benchmark in terms of sound risk management. Customers and investors provide business with a licence to operate, so failing to meet their behaviour expectations prompts withdrawal of their support. One only has to see how Anderson failed to recover after their involvement with Enron, despite being eventually cleared of malpractice.

The concept of value is as diverse as the stakeholders that look to benefit from that value. Sustainable revenue was always the aim of business, which traditionally meant that profits could be returned over the long term. This has been extended in more recent times, driven by CSR, to focus on

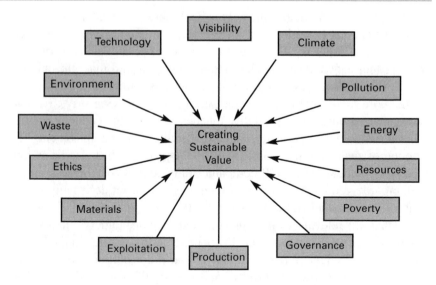

Figure 29.1   Creating sustainable value

the assessment of a business operation and how it influences or contributes to environmental and social community by creating sustainable value (see Figure 29.1). Frequently this is initiated by regulation or media pressure supported by a myriad of NGOs. Each party in this complex environment has a different measure of value and this leads to differing levels of tolerance. It is certain that despite effective management and processes there will always be incidents or accidents and it will be a measure of companies as to whether they find themselves publicly attacked or acknowledged for their corrective actions.

This of course should not detract from those organizations that flout the market place and in many cases resort to criminal or unethical practice. There will always be some and it is right that they should be given no quarter. The balance, however, should be in favour of the majority that endeavours to do the right thing. Thus one would hope that all stakeholders would take a measured view of their value aspirations against a broader perspective.

To create a more sustainable future that recognizes the many diverse groups that make up the community it is essential to raise the profile of value within a sustainable environment. This does not and is unlikely to ever, result in a global acceptance of a common set of values. What is more important is to create a dialogue where the values of others, are recognized, along with their right to hold those values. Defining value for any organization is the first step in developing a strategy to deliver it. For the business community today there is perhaps a much wider consideration than the traditional pure profit standpoint.

Organizations need to understand their relationship with the multiple stakeholders and external organizations that may influence performance and the success of the business proposition. Taking these many issues and building them into a dynamic strategy that will deliver has moved traditional business pressures to new levels of complexity. It is too easy for those outside the business environment to demand black and white solutions and instant implementation with a complete disregard for the cost and market impacts.

It is also unlikely that every business will be able to satisfy the range of requirements that groups and individuals may press upon it. Compromise is a factor in the business world where negotiations are focused on finding a way forward. If business is to seek the support of its main stakeholders and avoid attack from the minorities then it must be prepared to declare openly what is and is not practical in its business context. Those that have specialist objectives, must accept that, unless they can provide practical solutions or alternatives for the traditional business, they are unlikely to find a willing voice.

This matrix of stakeholders provides a limitless number of connections and interconnected issues for business leaders to address and endeavour to satisfy, both internally and externally. CSR and ethical trading are firmly on the agenda for many high-profile companies but those that are smaller or slightly out of the direct public glare have an equal responsibility to contribute. Long-term profitability is driven, as we have seen, by harnessing and engaging with the stakeholder communities being served.

The risk in the exploitation of resources, whether materials or people, is that it is unlikely to provide a stable long-term business platform. Success requires a long-term strategic vision that looks to capitalize on, and sustain, stakeholder support. Sustainable production approaches in every aspect of the process, materials and resources have to provide a more substantial future profile, which in turn should provide a more focused workforce and medium to long-term investors.

Governments clearly have a significant role to play as the voice of the community, but this must be tempered with a realistic appreciation for the implications of politically expedient regulation. Wealth has to be created before it can be cascaded, and the imposition of constraints on the wealth creators without consideration for the implications must dilute the value creation potential. Promoting the commercial benefits and encouraging innovative approaches, particularly with small companies, would be more productive than legislation and regulation which turns CSR into a mill-stone. As we have seen, good practice and common sense can bring additional value to companies and support sustainable objectives; these just need to be encouraged. Creating imbalance in the commercial sector in order to follow, for example, Third World challenges simply diffuses the drive and is ultimately unsustainable.

Social enterprise offers another model, which could contribute to the wider agenda, though it has to be said again that some would like to see progress so fast in this direction that government policy and NGO pressure may force mandatory quotas. This may ensure a quick take-up but it is unlikely to create sustainable value. If commercial rules are ignored then ultimately these businesses will not survive. This does not mean that companies and business ventures could not be run for the purpose of distributing profits in the community: what is dangerous is the fact, that efforts to force-feed the development simply create short-term wins that have no substance in an economic sense.

Many corporations and business ventures are of course taking a much more proactive approach. Forward-looking organizations have recognized that there is significant commercial sense in leading the charge towards a much broader sustainability agenda both internally and in the wider market place. The Co-operative Bank's programme, which has been running since 1994, started with a linkage between customer activity and charitable donations. More publicly the Bank has defined a robust vision for its business activities and actively campaigned on many social responsibility issues. It would seem that its customers support this position and, whilst they may not be growing to the same extent as others with less defined approaches, they are growing nevertheless. Time will tell if the customer base will maintain the vision.

Companies seeking to raise their game and enhance their investment profile are more and more looking to investment advisers to help polish their persona. The danger in this is that they are not building in the drive, but simply promoting the image. On the other hand, there is a growing trend for companies with robust programmes to seek help to offset the negative value against more short-term focused competitors. Corporate reporting frequently takes little account of the ethos of an organization and thus favours those exploiting rather than building sustainable growth.

The biggest challenge to all stakeholders is the environment, and efforts by forward-thinking companies to address some of these issues have created new value. It is also true that in many cases companies have shifted the problems outside the line of sight. In fact in many cases as discussed earlier, eco-efficiency programmes can add to the bottom line, so contributing to climate safeguards could be beneficial in both the short term and the long term. It may not be considered a suitable trait for managers to focus on green issues, but there is little doubt that cost savings and performance improvements would not attract similar negativity from either with the organization or its investors.

Human rights and animal welfare invoke equal amounts of media space and occupy the minds of many in the stakeholder community, as do health and equality, but all of these are only elements of a much wider and complex community within which we all have to coexist. For the business leader, there is always going to be some sector or special interest group whose vision and concept of value differs from the major stakeholders. Whilst researching aspects of this book, the Internet provided a huge amount of information but it also promoted a quick survey of sites related to various aspects of what people value.

For example, the largest number of sites related to music, health and sport whilst pollution totalled only 10 per cent of these. In fact it is sad to say pornography raised 600 per cent more sites than sustainable development hits. This snapshot carries no scientific value as a survey but perhaps does prompt the question as to what stakeholders do value. The answer perhaps lies back with Maslow's hierarchy of needs and the realization that creating sustainable value may often be a long way from the current needs of many stakeholders.

As we have seen, much of the exploitation of natural resources has been by developing countries capitalizing on the demands from the developing world whilst trying to improve the local economy. It then becomes apparent that value concepts will also change over time as one progresses up Maslow's pyramid. Clearly of course one can argue that it is the responsibility of those that have and understand to manage the future for those coming behind, but this also means superimposing values on others at different stages of their development. This in itself must be questionable in some respects.

It would be easy for many in the business world to use this dilemma as a defence for doing nothing and raise a hue and cry from those who follow various specialized and valid causes. The truth is that the business landscape is changing both in terms of the players and the demands, so standing still is unlikely to be an option. In his book *Leading the Revolution*,[10] Gary Hamel presented the view that the basis of innovation lies in the sensitivity to radical changes in the business environment. What we are perhaps now seeing is a reflection of the nineteenth-century social entrepreneurs and philanthropists in the creation of new business models, through which we will see technical innovation together with new processes and networks for delivery focused on meeting the challenges of critical global problems.

Integrating these new forward-looking ideas and harnessing enlightened business leaders will inevitably result in corporate values changing to reflect their vision of the future and the demands of more active stakeholders.

The difficulty is that defining sustainable value is an almost impossible task for whilst the generic concerns and drivers may be clear, the complex cocktail that results from any given business or stakeholder mix will be very different. It thus becomes even more important that companies (and, more importantly, business leaders) develop and make visible their individual sustainable value focus.

It requires, as was highlighted by a number of CEOs, the confidence to seek input from stakeholder communities. This has been shown to be a valuable resource for strategic thinking and planning. They must then take this background material and integrate it into the business operations such that it becomes the ethos of the organization and thus is more likely to be delivered and sustained. They also need the courage to defend their approach, as there will almost certainly be some sectors that will protest.

For organizations that have recognized the common-sense value of developing a sustainable approach, much of this will simply be establishing the linkages across what should be established good practice. For others the challenge is to take a step back and perhaps appreciate that short-term policies and practices will seldom (if ever) create a sustainable business model in traditional terms. Exploitation is not sustainable and, when fully financially modelled over time, is not likely to be economically sound either.

Shareholders' and investors' vision of value may also need to be re-tuned to the more sustainable investment profile that incorporates social responsibility since this is likely to reflect a more robust investment over time. Customers and consumers have to take a similar look at their spending power and influence to support those organizations that share their individual visions and values.

CHAPTER 30

Common-sense leadership

Responsibility rests with the organization's leaders and this means that they cannot blame their subordinates when things go wrong. The senior management of any organization sets the ethos and culture; by walking the talk, they provide an example, and through personal commitment they energize their people to respond to identified objectives.

Businesses need to adapt to change and competition by effectively deploying their resources. Leaders drive the process by establishing visible strategies for the organization to execute. Perhaps the most important thing is to engage their people in the front line to support these strategies and objectives. Frequently the temptation as organizations strive for growth is to seek opinion and manage by committee. In the context of corporate social responsibility, leaders have to balance stakeholder inertia through management by committee with their responsibility to create wealth.

The future of the business community will always be driven (or at least certainly influenced) by the market landscape within which they have to operate. There is clearly a growing interest to ensure that creating wealth incorporates recognition for the communities that they trade with. Much of the underlying ethos and practical application behind CSR programmes is common sense and the more complexity we build into our business operations, the more remote it becomes from practical experience.

The better you treat people and the more complementary the working environment, the more they will be likely to deliver. The culture and positive objectives of organizations contribute to this ethos of sustainable value. Customers' demands have to be balanced against the ethos of the organizations serving them and the regulatory barriers that are in place. Creating new business models that can both adapt to the market place and provide the structure against which to find cost benefits that also conserve resources will challenge the business leaders and entrepreneurs of the future.

Sustainability can be a business opportunity and market differentiator that can be exploited. The business managers of tomorrow must be developed to look beyond traditional structures and equations, and focus on the newly emerging influences and challenges that globalization is creating. Meeting stakeholder demands for corporate responsibility should not be considered simply as another burden but viewed as an opportunity to develop alternative, sustainability-based business models. Taking the practical application of good sense into the operational processes can provide direct commercial benefits and establish a platform for more innovative thinking.

A report from John Whybrow, Chairman of Wolseley, offered the view that managers talk a lot about change management but invariably assume that it is for others, not them. What drives the issue of change is the changing world and, as the environment changes, so we must adapt our business processes to meet our objectives. The world outside will do what it wants to do and we must respond today, not tomorrow. He was looking mainly at operational change but, as we all share the same space, we cannot isolate our business from the community. Gary Hamel, in his book *Competing for the Future*, captured this, saying: 'a company's blindness is due to an unwillingness or inability to look outside its current experiences'.[11]

Reading a report on a leadership review suggested that most managers were frustrated by not having the authority to manage, whilst senior managers were equally frustrated by not having managers that could operate without day-to-day decision-making. This mismatch is the danger area for implementation of sustainable strategies. In contradiction, Christopher Browning's book *The Origin of the Final Solution*[12] suggests that central orders were never issued; extreme measures were implemented by local commanders who saw this as a way to curry favour from above. A clear message and focus, then, is absolutely crucial to avoid localized functional approaches driving isolated targets and compromising corporate strategy. Incentives and financial targets can be used to divert focus from the more ethical goals of corporate leaders.

Sustainable profiles must therefore be integrated into the overall operation if they are to be effectively combined with the ethos of the business objectives. There may be cost considerations or cost benefits that are being ignored for the sake of narrow targets. It is never going to be possible to define and regulate every situation, so the leadership must embed a commitment and awareness that influences decision-making and ensures checks and balances are cultural.

The high-level issues for leaders start with examining how the business processes operate to match the values of the business. There is a clear requirement to reduce the impact on the environment and operate within resource constraints whilst enhancing the quality of life against society's expectations. Maximizing knowledge and networks helps to provide the background to develop innovation. Leaders in the twenty-first century face an ever-increasing complexity and one has to consider the profile of these supermen. John C. Maxwell offers some characteristics in his book, *The 21 Indispensable Qualities of a Leader.*[13] In the context of developing and implementing a robust sustainability programme each of these has clear links, and the 21 qualities are given below:

Character	Charisma	Commitment
Communication	Competence	Courage
Discernment	Focus	Generosity
Initiative	Listening	Passion
Positive attitude	Problem solving	Relationships
Responsibility	Security	Self-discipline
Servanthood	Teachability	Vision

A Manager's Guide to Leadership[14] by Pedler, Burgoyne and Boydell claims that leadership is concerned with finding direction and purpose in the face of critical challenges, whereas management is about organizing to achieve desired purposes, efficiently, effectively and creatively. Without challenging tasks there is no call for leadership. Certainly, for managers to operate effectively they need to understand the vision and objectives.

Corporate social responsibility may be a relatively new concept but it is increasingly influencing decision-making in business as well as driving best practice. It remains a new road for most business leaders. Accountability beyond the traditional financial profile is focusing attention on so-called 'good' businesses as well as on more controversial industries. Take, for example, the actions of British American Tobacco where one might say that any form of social responsibility can hardly be appropriate for a business that is fundamentally viewed as being bad for society.

One would not attempt to comment on their product, but this does raise the question as to whether they too can contribute despite the nature of their business. However, their approach to stakeholder involvement, position on pollution, energy, ethical trading, and exploitation outside the product, visibility and openness must in the long term add to developing a responsible future. Not qualifying for investment measurements, such as FTSE4Good, they had no driver to influence the markets but still their leadership elected to publish reports. Many cynics might put this down to PR but at least they have taken the stage to present their perspective of balance.

The Global Leadership Network was formed in 2004 by nine major global players (including General Electric, FedEx, GM, 3M and IBM) to fund a project to look at how these companies balance the pressures of profitability against society's demands. At the same time The Business Leaders'

Initiative on Human Rights has responded to the UN commissioners' call to establish guidance for trans-national operators in respect of human rights. This highlights the strength of concern for high-profile companies but also begs the question as to whether these actions are founded in a desire to improve or a need to define the boundaries of competitive compliance.

Throughout the research activity for this book a further common question which kept arising was that whilst we are perhaps now taking a more holistic view of the business environment, do we actually have the skills to convert concern into practice? We talk about the sustainable community but in each of the three interlocking influences of society, business and regulation we need the leadership to take it forward; especially given the diversity of the global business arena, this leadership has to energize outside the traditional command and control structures, inspiring others at all levels to contribute and balance their actions within an operating culture that traditionally sees these sustainable concerns as being long term and of limited value to the business targets of today.

The integration of leadership, project management, planning, financial management, production and stakeholder management requires a focused approach to analysing the real benefits and costs of implementation and effective communication is a crucial factor. Developing and implementing a corporate responsibility management system is only part of the process.

The four key tasks, as shown in Figure 30.1, provide an initial framework for continuous development as part of sustainable integration.

Figure 30.1   Four tasks of leadership

Starting by engaging with stakeholders and then developing a gap analysis and risk assessment provides the foundation to identify best practice and translate this into operational approaches. Ensuring that effective measurement is in place to monitor progress and not simply to provide publishable PR will help to underpin internal engagement. It is this internal commitment and understanding that leaders must energize to move thinking from the strategic platform to the hands-on application of ideas.

Stephen R. Covey's recent book, *The 8th Habit*,[15] led back to his original book which focused on seven habits for highly effective people. The eight together make an effective framework for looking at leadership and sustainability, and are shown below. By being proactive Covey means taking responsibility for your life: how we respond to circumstance is a question of choice, so clearly if corporate responsibility is a driver then business leaders have a choice. Perhaps there is no visible long-term final aim but certainly having clear objectives will help to focus the organization. The third step is one that has to be recognized in that it is important to address immediate issues and potential risks before trying to find the perfect solution. Progress is better than inertia.

1. Be proactive
2. Begin with the end in mind
3. Put first things first
4. Think win-win
5. Seek first to understand – then to be understood
6. Synergize
7. Sharpen the saw
8. Take action

The background to eco-efficiency is that it provides a focus for looking at commercial benefits and contributions with sustainable objectives being the spin-off, not the prime goal. At the same time, the whole subject of social responsibility entails focusing on where the approaches benefit both the business and the community. Take the issue of labour exploitation, which in general will perpetuate low performance; targeted investment and training can improve the outcome for all.

There is a clear need when considering any sustainable strategy to engage with the variety of stakeholders that either directly or indirectly influence the business. Understanding where their aspirations and concerns are in relation to the future is the key to linking and harnessing their support throughout the development of programmes and future business. Taking this knowledge and integrating it into the business, then monitoring and reporting, provides a robust platform for further development.

We have already outlined the need for less prescriptive regulation (either internally or in the legislature) and more individual commitment to the ethos that will shape actions. The more synergy there is within an organization the less conflict there will be towards compromise, which ultimately will lead to more effective implementation of integrated actions. Sharpening the saw is Covey's way of ensuring that continuous development and improvement are part of any development programme. The world changes, market drivers change, and so organizations must adapt and change to stay on track. Keeping the saw sharp means that cutting down the tree will take less time. This is perhaps not the best analogy for the tree-huggers, but one hopes they will appreciate the aim.

The latest addition is Covey's eighth habit, take action, since action is the father of thought. It may be useful to talk and publish reports on how organizations should behave, but if this is not translated into action then it will be of limited value. One of the observations on CSR reporting is that in many cases it is window dressing and not a reflection of a committed organization. The result for some organizations is that as it provides no real progress it is soon devalued and in fact could have a detrimental effect. Making progress, however limited but with measurable benchmarks provides a proactive perspective.

There is a crisis of trust in big business. Employees, suppliers and customers want to be associated with an organization they can trust and whose values they respect. Take the profile of Anita Roddick and the Body Shop, which is rated as one of the 30 most respected companies in the world. Under Anita's leadership the company recognized the value of bringing the human spirit into the workplace alongside responsibility, focusing on equality for feminine values, creating a focus of being different and building passion into the workplace with the impact of creating credibility and trust. It may not be the model for every business but it does demonstrate how passionate leadership can deliver value.

Corporate leadership has to appreciate that the buck stops with them. Many organizations have already found themselves the target of aggressive investigation by the media, shareholders and NGOs. Companies that ignore these pressures will come unstuck but this should not be the only driver for action. Companies may be heading down the route of appointing CSR officers but it must be remembered that the corporate board must be convinced and committed to programmes. It is also important to recognize that appointment of internal champions will not replace the need to instill this commitment at the coalface where the day-to-day decisions will be made.

For sustainable initiatives to succeed they must have executive support. Champions may help to spread the message but the leadership must be seen to be openly following the programmes and ensure that every employee has a clear view of their responsibilities. Effective programmes must be embedded in the operational processes. The integration of risk management, corporate governance and the implications of broader relationship management with stakeholders must be evaluated to ensure the elimination of duplication and bureaucracy.

This process management becomes an even greater challenge to leadership when looked at through the evolving aspects of tomorrow's worker and the growth of outsourcing as a core strategic tool. Recent studies have looked at the growing challenge of managing the flexible worker in the future where remote working and networker programmes offer the view that the obstacles are more related to managers being comfortable than the workers operating at a distance. This compounds the problems of integrating outsourcing approaches that connect with sustainable programmes.

The appreciation of leadership in business is at last perhaps being distinguished from the traditional operational management of activities and delivering results towards strategic leadership that is focused on challenges and changes in the current operational paradigm. Individual management performance has traditionally been the dominant or only focus with some consideration for not screwing up the activities of colleagues. The strategic leader should stand to one side and view the operation, seeing where it ought to develop. Management may develop into more integrated approaches but the leadership will be looking to focus more on the external stakeholders. Management systems need to be reviewed to ensure they support leadership goals, whilst the leadership focuses on empowerment and challenging the workforce and energizing partners.

It is wonderful when the people believe in their leaders; but it is more wonderful when the leader believes in the people.

Looking to this brave new world the next question one must ask is, do we have the leaders capable of taking us there? Leadership is the capacity to translate vision into reality. Despite those high-profile business leaders who stand head and shoulders above the rest, one sees little investment on the wider front to train those who should be taking up the banner. The results of a survey carried out a couple of years ago which addressed over 400 companies across Europe showed that only 16 per cent had any effective training plan and 30 per cent had no plans, although 86 per cent said management training should be part of an organization's goals. One must ask whether management is disconnected from business needs.

Why does business need more leadership skills? We have already identified the impacts of globalization on sustainability. This has moved most if not all business operations outside the traditional local comfort zone. Growing global disintermediation is placing greater pressure on organizations to operate in new spheres of activity and this in turn opens up the impacts of cultural diversity. This presents an environment where the pace of change is accelerating whilst the complexity of trading is increasing.

Since the days of the cavemen leadership has been based primarily on strength or hereditary position. Through the Industrial Revolution the power and direction came from ownership, which often was almost as absolute in real terms as feudalism. In the later part of the twentieth century the power shifted toward the professional manager but still lay within traditional structures. Now the key to leadership is perhaps inspirational as it seeks to motivate and direct across corporate boundaries and exploit the relationship rather than the direct control.

The current younger generation see the computer and its connectivity as being the new business environment. Computers can take out the drudgery but we doubt we will see one in our lifetime with an artificial imagination. Certainly the younger generation has an advantage in that they have never known a time without being part of a wired world. Now we should also focus on how to give them the capacity to build the new virtual environments that harness both the technology and the futurist thinking that can exploit the technology and support sustainability.

As we have already suggested the financial market place is starting to recognize the potential for different business models and shareholders already place greater store by the charisma and profile of business leaders. It is therefore reasonable to assume that if the virtual organization is to be accepted then the standing of business leaders must also reflect confidence to the market. Leadership skills, starting with vision and strategic thinking, will need to be merged with inspiration and communication as never before, since much of the future virtual team may need to function without daily or hourly direction but must share and support the corporate goals from afar.

An old adage was that he who wants to lead the orchestra must sometimes turn his back on the crowd or, to put it another way, a good leader can step on your toes without messing up the shine. Taking an organization from a traditionally-based transactional approach and transforming it into an integrated delivery networked process will require much more than the rule of authority. In this new era of virtual integration, the leadership needs to focus on maintaining a balance between control and innovation.

It is difficult to measure leadership except through results. The connection between leadership and performance is an indirect one but intuitively we believe that leadership is a major contributing factor. Management development does not directly impact on behaviour: it is seen through a sequence of changes from theory to awareness, skill enhancement and then on to behaviour. Leadership training will influence management capability, which will affect implementation skills and thus performance. In this virtual world we are looking to stretch the envelope of business relationships so the leadership has to be futurist. The challenge for most organizations is to find these hybrid beings, or can they be developed from existing management pools?

Effective leadership is about more than applying checklists of tactics; it goes beyond pure theory and being straightforward in one's dealings with the team. Good leaders believe in what they are doing and constantly cross-check events against these ideas and involve their teams on a regular basis. This may be more difficult as we progress more towards 'follow the sun' working.

Best practice organizations		
Leaders	**Employees**	**Performance**
· Enthusiastic	· Focus on customers	· Effective measurement
· A vision which is known	· Encourage ownership	· Systematic approach
· Meaningful mission	· Employee consultation	· Continuous improvement
· Strategy understood	· Employee participation	· Key performance indicators
· Set realistic targets	· Employee development	(KPIs)
· Lead by example	· Promote new skills	· Internal benchmarking
· Communicative	· Effective communication	· External benchmarking
· Champions learning	· Update knowledge	· Learning from others
· Culture of continuous	· Recognize effort	· Action results
improvement	· Reward contribution	
· Clear leadership	· Equal opportunities	
responsibilities		
· Authority and resources		
· Training programme		

Figure 30.2 Best practice organizations

Ultimately the challenge for leaders is to clearly define the sustainable objectives for their organization and bring together the best practices they can find to ensure effective implementation. Driving these complex agendas within the traditional concepts of wealth creation and profit generation and building a programme that looks to integrate best practice (as in Figure 30.2) and harnessing the value of sustainability as opposed to imposing a structure of compliance has to provide a more robust future.

The changing business environment is likely to become more complex in the future and thus so will the challenges for its leadership. Sustainability and CSR in the main is not about complex theories but about translating practical common sense into the corporate machine. We have made the corporate world very complicated and yet the basic principles have existed since trade, production and manufacture first started. The following simple benchmarks are perhaps the starting point for business leaders when addressing sustainability for their organization:

- markets are driven by customers and investors;
- resources are not infinite;
- healthy workers make healthy products;
- ethical performance protects reputation and brand.

These may seem trite but, if one seeks to look beyond the rhetoric of CSR and address sustainability proactively, then starting from the basics clears the line of sight. Developing a clear vision and the values to support it is the first step in defining a leadership approach that has the conviction to embed sustainable objectives and maintain a commercial perspective. Recognizing that these two can operate within an integrated strategy is a crucial part of delivering long-term sustainability.

CHAPTER 31

Conclusions

At the outset of this book the objective was to take an impartial but commercial view of the sustainability battlefield and to test my perceptions of both CSR public relations and the conflicting worlds of business, government and society. I use the term 'battlefield' because that was my perception of the high-profile missiles being hurled between the various participants. As one would expect, in the course of this journey of investigation and deliberation I learned much about the challenges, contradictions and passions that exist at every level of society. The issue is whether the journey has changed my views and perceptions; in my case fundamentally it has not, though it has perhaps encouraged me to be a little more tolerant of the tree-huggers, and I wonder if it will stimulate readers to challenge their own thinking. We are after all part of the same global community.

In the first place there is clearly a need to encourage effective dialogue between the three main communities of society, business and regulators to ensure that in the process of doing good we don't create a complexity that dilutes or diverts our efforts. From a business perspective the focus must remain on creating wealth, but this does not have to be at the expense of implementing sustainable approaches.

For customers, consumers and investors there must be a recognition that some aspirations cannot be assimilated apart from a desire for more availability of choice and competitiveness. Whilst this may in some cases stimulate innovation, in others it will simply be a recipe for exploitation.

For NGOs the observation is that they have undoubted commitment and a wealth of knowledge. They should first outlaw those who will not follow protest legally and who prohibit business going about its legitimate purpose. Second, they should examine their motivation regarding attacks on companies because of the media value of the name. Third, perhaps they could consider contributing their knowledge to business to help innovative ideas, recognizing a joint need to manage the future and the progress that has been made by many corporations.

Regulators and governments need to consider the implications of what may be considered green strategies for the community at large, which reflects both society and business. Greater regulation does not necessarily mean better governance or commitment; in fact, it could engender more effort towards avoidance. There also has to be a balance between humanitarian aid and the desire to speed the evolution of developing nations towards equalizing the global consumer society; focusing regulation on obvious offenders rather than, piling requirements on legitimate business would promote dialogue and direct innovation, thus utilizing incentives to invest for the future rather than taxing for the present.

Business leaders must understand that they serve, and are supported by, the community, which includes a broad spectrum of stakeholders either directly or indirectly. Failure to take a measured position may in the end be detrimental to long-term business and profitability. In many cases sustainable approaches may stimulate cost savings or more profit if considered within a wider vision and, even more simply, just by considering total cost.

In the end we must all take a balanced, sustainable view of today and tomorrow

DAVID E. HAWKINS

References

1. Tom Peters, *Liberation Management* (Fawcett, 1994).
2. Arctic Council, *Arctic Climate Impact Assessment* (2004) www.acia.uaf.edu.
3. World Business Council, *Making Good Business Sense* (2002) www.wbcsd.org.
4. National Intelligence Council, *Global Trends 2015* (2002) www.cia.gov.
5. World Bank, *Environmental Matters* (2004) www.worldbank.org.
6. Article 13, *Business Unusual* (2004) www.article13.com.
7. National Intelligence Council, *Mapping the Global Future* (2004) www.cia.gov.
8. Leon Benjamin, *Winning by Sharing* (Cognac, 2005).
9. Transparency International, *Global Corruption* (2005) www.globalcorruption report.gov.
10. Gary Hamel, *Leading the Revolution* (New American Library, 2002).
11. Gary Hamel, *Competing for the Future* (Harvard Business School, 1996).
12. Christopher Browning, *The Origin of the Final Solution* (Heinemann, 2004).
13. John C. Maxwell, *The 21 Indispensable Qualities of a Leader* (STL, 2002).
14. Mike Pedler, John Burgoyne and Tom Boydell, *A Manager's Guide to Leadership* (McGraw-Hill, 2003).
15. Stephen R. Covey, *The 8th Habit* (Simon & Schuster, 2004).

Index